GUIDANCE, COUNSELING, AND STUDENT
PERSONNEL IN EDUCATION
WALTER F. JOHNSON, Consulting Editor

BAILARD and STRANG   *Parent-Teacher Conference*

BENNETT   *Guidance and Counseling in Groups*

BERDIE   *Testing in Guidance and Counseling*

BERNHARDT   *Discipline and Child Guidance*

DETJEN and DETJEN   *Elementary School Guidance*

HOPPOCK   *Occupational Information*

JOHNSON, STEFFLRE, and EDELFELT   *Pupil Personnel and Guidance Services*

JONES   *Principles of Guidance*

WARTERS   *Techniques of Counseling*

PRINCIPLES
OF GUIDANCE

ARTHUR J. JONES

Fifth Edition

McGRAW-HILL BOOK COMPANY, INC.

New York   San Francisco   Toronto   London

PREFACE TO THE FIFTH EDITION

When I reread the Preface to the first edition of this book, published in 1930, I found myself in a world nearly as strange and primitive as that which saw the founding of the National Vocational Guidance Association in 1913. It seems almost impossible that so many changes have been made in these last thirty years. The tests used then would now be called unreliable and their validity questioned. Such terms as "counselor-centered" and "client-centered" were not in our professional vocabularies. Even the term "counseling" itself had but one brief mention, and then there was no discussion of training and certification. In spite of the differences between that time and this it is comforting to remember that the basic concept of guidance has not changed. Then, as now, guidance implied a concern for *all* personal problems, not just those involved in the selection of a vocation.

It is always inspiring to recall my old friends and coworkers, few of whom are now left. I remember especially Meyer Broomfield, John Brewer, Jesse Davis, Fred Smith, W. Carson Ryan, William Proctor, Edward Rynearson, F. J. Allen, Harry Kitson, George Myers, along with scores of others. Often we agreed, but sometimes we disagreed violently, although we always remained friends in spite of this.

My only hope is that this edition will receive the same warm welcome that has been given to its predecessors.

It will be noted that the title of this edition is *Principles of Guidance*. The term "personnel work," which appeared in the title of the fourth edition, was considered for inclusion in the title of this one, but "guidance" was used instead for a number of reasons. "Guidance" implies a service to be given; "personnel work" connotes the machinery and method involved in the offering of guidance and related services. Personnel work has come to be associated with higher education and business and industry, whereas guidance pertains to services in elementary and secondary schools. Because this edition is concerned largely with services at the elementary- and secondary-school level, the term "guidance" seems more appropriate than "personnel work."

I am much pleased that Anna R. Meeks consented to write the chapter "Guidance in the Elementary School." She is considered to be one of the leaders in this field, and her excellent treatment of the topic enhances materially the value of the book.

I wish to express my thanks to many persons who have given sympathy and help to me in "time of trouble," especially to my son Donald P. Jones and his wife Ethel for their sympathy and for the trouble I have made them. My deep gratitude is also given to the U.S. Office of Education and the Office of Vocational Rehabilitation for furnishing up-to-date, reliable information in matters relating to their services. I wish also to thank Eleanor L. Liddell for doing such a good job in deciphering my none-too-clear writing and for transforming it into clear and neat copy.

Arthur J. Jones

CONTENTS

ix

PART I

A POINT OF VIEW
ON GUIDANCE

CHAPTER 1

THE MEANING AND FUNCTION OF GUIDANCE

Guidance is the assistance given to individuals in making intelligent choices and adjustments. It is based on the democratic principle that it is the duty and the right of every individual to choose his own way in life in so far as his choice does not interfere with the rights of others. The ability to make such choices is not innate but, like other abilities, must be developed. One of the functions of education is to provide opportunities for the development of such abilities. Guidance is an integral part of education and is centered directly upon this function. Guidance does not make choices for individuals; it helps them make their own choices in such a way as to promote or stimulate the gradual development of the ability to make decisions independently without assistance from others.

THE MEANING OF GUIDANCE

In its beginnings guidance was centered on problems related to vocations. It was largely concerned with getting jobs for young people. One of the reasons for this was to reduce juvenile delinquency. Teen-age boys and girls, many of them not in school, had nothing to do; they had time on their hands. Such a situation breeds delinquency.

Even in its beginning, however, the purpose of guidance was more than just finding jobs for youth. Much attention was given

3

to a "wise" choice, that is, one that was suited to the abilities and needs of the individual. Although the vocational aspect has always been stressed, guidance has gone far beyond this; it is now concerned with the entire individual, in all aspects of his life, and with the interrelation between the individual and society. It helps youth to attain a life that is individually satisfying and socially effective.

THE GUIDANCE NEEDS OF YOUTH

Some individuals need guidance throughout their entire lives; others need help only during their youth or in unusually critical situations. The chief guidance responsibility of society is toward children and youth and those who, because of congenital defects, disease, accident, or political-social handicaps, do not have equal opportunities for activities that will satisfy their individual and social needs. Situations that call for guidance are varied and numerous. Guidance functions whenever choices are to be made and where help is needed in making intelligent decisions. Even when there is no choice possible, guidance may help the individual understand and accept the situation; that is, it may enable him to "cooperate with the inevitable." Guidance may also operate when the individual is not conscious that a choice is possible by pointing out the avenues that are open to him. In still other circumstances the time may not be favorable for making a choice because of fatigue, emotional strain, or influences that will make an intelligent decision unlikely. In such situations the best help may well be to suggest that only those decisions be made which are mandatory, leaving open as many as possible until a later, more favorable, time.

Experience As a Source of Guidance

Choices are often made on the basis of a person's own past experience or that of others. A person may call to mind some choice that he or one of his friends made in a situation that seems similar to the present one. If what was done before was satisfactory, he might choose to make the same choice again; if the result was unsatisfactory, he might decide to do something else. Such a decision may result in a good choice or in a poor one. The two situations, although similar in some respects, may be very different in others. The choice may have been a good one once, but with the passage of time and with changed conditions, it may be quite unsatisfactory now. Guidance may help here by assisting the individual to examine the two situations carefully to see in what ways they are alike and in what ways they are different and by helping him to get a broader view of the possible choices.

It is often possible, even while still in high school, to get some preliminary experience in an occupation that is being considered. Jobs held after school, on Saturdays, holidays, and especially in the long summer vacations, provide helpful experience. Such jobs may be available in stores, in offices, on the farm, or elsewhere. The guidance value of such experience varies greatly and is dependent upon the attitude of the youth, the supervision given, and the physical and social environment of the job.

When youth attempt to use their own experiences as a basis for choice, they are handicapped by the fact that their experiences are neither extensive nor of great scope or variety. Choices made on such a basis are not likely to be good ones, but very often they do not see this danger. With youthful enthusiasm and undue confidence in their ability, they often make hasty and unwise decisions. Other avenues of life work may begin to make a strong appeal to them in later years. They may realize too late that these avenues might well have offered success and satisfaction. The necessary training cannot now be secured without great financial sacrifice that would jeopardize the comfort and welfare of the family. Although they may realize that their early choices were unfortunate, they can do nothing about it now. Wise guidance could have been of great value by making them realize that their experience was too limited to give them proper perspective. It could have helped them review carefully the entire range of occupations within their interest and capabilities.

Advice As Guidance

Another very valuable source of help which is frequently used is the experience of others expressed through advice. The value of this source of guidance is clearly seen in the history of mankind. Man's superiority over the lower animals is due, in large measure, to his ability to profit not only from his own experience but from that of others; without this ability there would have been little progress. Such experience may be utilized either directly, through advice given by others, or indirectly, through a knowledge and understanding of history.

Although advice is an old and widely used method of guidance, some guidance authorities condemn it in any form, maintaining that it is harmful. They even go so far as to say that the only time it is safe to give advice to others is when you know they will not use it. This statement grossly exaggerates the dangers of advice and is plainly untrue. Industrial firms spend millions every year on advice, and it pays. Older men who have had years of experience either in the industry that employs them or in similar industries are used as consultants or advisers. The value of their services is evident in the large salaries given to such men. Throughout history sages have been singled out for great honor and reverence. The advice given by a person who has traveled the same way before may be very valuable; however, it can neither be rejected merely because it is old nor accepted just because it is old. The old Chinese dynasties stagnated because of the national credo "Walk in the trodden way," but some of the most valuable sources of help are found in the recorded thoughts and experiences of men and women of the past.

All aspects of the past—social, industrial, economic, scientific, artistic, and religious—have much to teach us. Such sources of understanding are too little used in our present programs of guidance. To be of any use the lessons of history must be read and interpreted not only in terms of the past but also in terms of the present. Teachers of English, history, science, art, and music can open up these sources of help and interpret them as well. The lessons of the past that are of the greatest value are those that state fundamental values of life and general principles of conduct. These lessons will help in many different situations because they usually do not indicate exactly what one should do but leave it to the individual to determine what definite action will be best. This is in accord with the principle that the purpose of guidance is the development in the individual of the ability to solve problems without the help of others. Conditions may have changed so much that the present problem is quite unlike the old one, and what was once a desirable solution may no longer be satisfactory.

Such changed conditions are especially likely to appear in affairs involving youth. The changed attitude of parents and teachers toward youth, the greater freedom given to youth, the new emphasis on self-determination, and the relaxing of discipline have profoundly altered the nature of the problems of young people. Today youth are far better informed on scientific, economic, and social conditions and developments than their parents were when they were of the same age. This development greatly increases the complexity and difficulty of the problems of youth and those of their parents who are trying to help them. In boy-girl relations the restrictions that were once thought desirable have in large part been removed, and some conduct which was once frowned upon is now considered acceptable. When the problem relates to the use by teen-agers of our modern high-powered and complex cars, advice based on the days of the horse and buggy or the Model T is entirely inappropriate. These changed conditions make skillful and well-organized guidance imperative. Guidance now calls for wide experience, deep wisdom, and infinite patience on the part of the one who counsels.

Advice is usually received best and carries more weight when the one who seeks it comes voluntarily to the counselor because he feels the need for help. Gratuitous advice is usually of little value because most people regard such proffered help as an intrusion on what they consider to be their own affair. Such advice is also often given without knowledge or consideration of the needs of the person advised.

In summary, one's own experience as well as that of others may be very valuable in guidance, but it may not be a safe guide in itself. To be of real value, experience must be interpreted in relation to the particular problem that is at hand. Is this problem the same as the one previously faced? Is the solution that was made in the past as satisfactory now as it was then? There may be differences, even though slight ones, in the present situation that may be very significant, thus making the solution that was once satisfactory quite unsatisfactory now. For example, action taken fifty years ago based on a certain religious belief may have been useful then, but it may be quite useless or even undesirable now. Even now two persons may have the same beliefs regarding the worth of the individual and his relation to God and yet be on opposite sides of such a social problem as segregation. One may honestly believe that the best interests of the Negro can be secured by segregation; the other may believe just as sincerely that they can be attained only by desegregation. The previous family and social experience and the background of each person have a powerful influence on the belief which is held. Guidance must help young people to develop techniques of utilizing their own past experience and that of others for the solution of the problems facing them in making their adjustments in life.

Definition of Guidance

Guidance is the help given by one person to another in making choices and adjustments and in solving problems. Guidance aims at aiding the recipient to grow in his independence and ability to be responsible for himself. It is a service that is universal—not confined to the school or the family. It is found in all phases of life— in the home, in business and industry, in government, in social life, in hospitals, and in prisons; indeed it is present wherever there are people who *need* help and wherever there are people who *can* help.

GUIDANCE: ITS RELATION TO EDUCATION

Very early in the guidance movement Brewer,[1] a consistent advocate of vocational guidance, recognized the close relationship between guidance and education. Throughout the years the nature of this relationship has been a source of much concern and controversy. The different points of view are largely owing to differences in the meaning of the term "education." "Education" may be used to mean (1) the process of changes that take place within the individual, (2) instruction, or (3) the conscious effort of society to guide and direct the physical, mental, emotional, and moral growth of the individual so that he will be able to live a life that will be socially effective and individually satisfying. To make clear the relationship between guidance and education each of these meanings needs to be examined more closely.

[1] John M. Brewer, *Education as Guidance,* The Macmillan Company, New York, 1955.

Education Is the Process of Changes That Take Place within the Individual

From this point of view education is essentially a process; it is something that takes place *in individuals;* it is the process by which changes are made in the individual[2] or, better, by which the individual makes changes in himself. At birth human beings are the most helpless of all animals. They are absolutely dependent upon others for their very existence. For long years they must be fed, cared for, and protected in order to preserve life and to ensure normal growth and development. Man is much less adjusted by nature to his physical environment than any other animal. He must learn to walk, to eat, to make those adjustments that are necessary to cope with physical nature. Habits must be formed, skills developed, and facts learned before it is safe for him to go out into the world alone. Since he is not naturally suited to his physical environment, changes must be made in him before he can be adjusted.

If this is true of his physical environment, it is much more so of his social environment. Very few adjustments to the social environment are because of nature. Man's physical nature and equipment have remained practically unchanged for centuries. His stature, his features, his brain are essentially the same now as they were when the great pyramids were built. Although man essentially has not changed, the structure of society has become tremendously complex. Social demands have so far outstripped man's physical nature that the gap between the social plane of the infant and that of the adult is very wide—impossible to cross, in fact, without assistance. As civilization advances, the gap is ever widening. The method by which the infant is enabled to bridge this gap, to raise himself from the social plane of childhood to that of manhood, is education. This is accomplished by certain changes that are made by the individual so that he acts in appropriate and desirable ways to situations that confront him. The number of changes and their quality are such as to require long years and special techniques for their development. Education is, then, the process by which the individual makes these necessary changes.

[2] For a more complete treatment, see Arthur J. Jones, *Education and the Individual,* Appleton-Century-Crofts, Inc., New York, 1926.

From this point of view education is essentially and wholly an *individual* process. It is some change that takes place in the individual as a result of something that *he* does. It is "the upbuilding of a world in feeling or consciousness."

Each individual builds for himself the world in which he lives. His images, his memories, his thoughts and feelings, his ideals are formed from his own experience—what he himself does. They are his own, and no one can share them; nor can anyone take them away against his will. When we view education from this standpoint, there can be no guidance, for guidance implies assistance given by someone to the one who is educating himself. In so far as the individual is really self-educated, there is no guidance; however, if we think of education as resulting only from what the individual himself does—if he is the active agent—what is the relation of instruction to this process?

Education Is Instruction

The teacher knows the ends to be accomplished; in this he is merely the agent of society. He also knows the best ways by which these ends may be attained, that is, by which effective learning may be achieved by the pupil. His role in the older conception of teaching was comparatively clear and simple.

1. He had to have definitely in mind what was to be learned, but it was relatively unimportant for the pupil to know this.

2. He had to have, in the form of textbooks, materials, outlines, problems, etc., stimuli that were calculated to result in the desired responses by the pupil.

3. He had to see that the pupil made the responses desired. If he made responses other than the desirable ones, he was compelled by punishment or other means to make the "correct" ones.

4. He had to test for product, skill, habit, attitude, etc., and see that the end had actually been attained.

All this made the teacher the active and to a large extent the determining factor in learning. Much teaching is still of this kind; it is directed mainly at forcing the child to learn. Still too frequently the learner is considered inert or even stubborn and not actively interested in or concerned with learning.

But even this more or less mechanical teacher-controlled process is not so simple as it may seem. The child is, even here, a very

important and an extremely variable factor. Situations in the classroom are not simple. They are composed of many different stimuli;
some of these are the selected stimuli provided by the teacher, but
others are supplied by many factors in the immediate environment
of the pupil, including the pupil himself. The child can and often
does choose from among the stimuli that make up the situation the
one to which he responds. He may single out the teacher's prominent nose, her gaudy dress, the wasp in the window, or any one of
a dozen things to which he gives attention and to which he responds,
rather than the words of the teacher or the material in his textbook.

Efficient education requires not only that a person respond to
a stimulus but that he select the desirable groups of stimuli to which
he responds—desirable, that is, from the standpoint of education.
Again, even though he singles out the desired stimulus, he may
respond to it in many different ways. Suppose the topic he is studying is the products of South America. He reads the words in his
book describing them; these words are the stimuli. What responses
does he make? He may go off into a daydream of voyaging on the
high seas, of pirates and Spanish galleons; or he may plan a hiking
trip when he will take along some of the products mentioned. There
are many ways of responding that may seem much more desirable
to him than the responses that the teacher wishes and that are demanded if he is to learn what the products of South America are.

To the teacher trained in the older method these variable conditions are extremely annoying; they must be eliminated if possible.
The methods used in eliminating them constitute what some regard
as guidance, since, in a sense, these rewards and punishments direct
the learner. But they are in fact entirely teacher-directed and teacher-controlled; the individual himself has no part in the planning; he
is passive; there is no choice. It is, therefore, not guidance as we
here consider the process.

Happily, this method is rapidly giving way to one that is not
only fundamentally more sound but more effective as well. In the
new method, teaching is thought of as helping the child to learn.
The child is the active agent in the process. As before, the teacher
still determines for the most part the ends to be achieved, although
even here there may be pupil cooperation; but he also assists the
pupil to understand the ends and to accept them as his own. Assistance, so directed, is guidance. If the pupil is able to select his

aims, if, after understanding and accepting the ends, the pupil is able to see by himself what he must do to accomplish the ends, the teacher steps aside; no teaching and no guidance are necessary. Whenever, in the learning process, the teacher *assists the learner to choose,* guidance is present.

There is also another way in which guidance enters into the process of education. The teacher, as an agent of society, sets up ends to be accomplished by the pupil, but the method by which different pupils reach the ends may vary. Reaching the ends is important; the method by which the ends are reached is relatively unimportant, except that it should be the method best suited to the individual pupil. Choices in method are often, if not always, possible. The efficient teacher is continually trying to help the pupil find the one that is best suited to him. When the teacher selects the method, there is teaching but no guidance; when he assists the learner to choose a method, guidance is present.

Whenever, in the process of accomplishing the ends (that is, in learning), the pupil needs help, it is the teacher's function to give it. This help is usually stimuli in the form of outlines, references, suggestions, leading questions, expressions of approval and disapproval, incentives, and anything else that may help the pupil to learn. This is teaching or instruction; it may or may not be guidance. Teaching conceived of as assisting the learner to choose ends or methods is guidance.

Education Is a Function of Society

It is a conscious effort on the part of society to guide and direct the physical, mental, emotional, and moral growth of the individual so that he will be able to live a life that will be socially effective and individually satisfying. In this broader concept of education, guidance and education are closely related.

This statement does not satisfy the ultraprogressive educator who reacts strongly against any form of control of individual development by society and who contends that the only object of education is the development of the individual. This development is to be determined not by what society wants but by some inward force or law or principle which, if followed, will result in the maximum or optimum development of each individual. Nor will it satisfy the ultraconservative who emphasizes the need for social efficiency as opposed to mere individual development. Each of these elements must, of course, be present, but they should be complementary, not antagonistic. This concept of education might seem to make guidance and education synonymous both when we stress the development of the individual for himself as an end and when we emphasize the needs of society, for education is thought of as the conscious effort of society to assist the individual.

It should be noted, however, that the important words in this sentence are not "the conscious effort of society," but "assist the individual," and the role of society in the education of individuals may not be "assistance" in the real sense. When society merely determines what shall be taught and does nothing to assist the individual—when the individual is thought of as passive—guidance is not present except in a very indirect and remote way. In a sense the entire conscious effort of society to see that the individual reaches certain goals set up by society is assistance. The physical and social environment which is selected and organized by society for the purpose of making sure that the child will develop properly, the curriculum, the textbooks, library, and laboratories, the organized life of the school, all are instrumental in making sure that the pupil develops in certain ways. The habits and skills developed, the interests and attitudes formed, all are powerful factors. This is, at best, a very mechanical and deterministic kind of assistance. In one sense it is not really assistance at all, for assistance implies more or less independent action on the part of the individual, that is, the enlistment of the individual in the enterprise. In the same sense we could say that we assist the plant to grow by watering it; we assist the post to stand upright by digging a hole and placing the post in it; we assist the boy to be clean by washing his face. This is a misinterpretation of the term "assistance." This mechanical assistance, even though it helps to determine the development of the individual and may materially affect his choices, can hardly be guidance, for it leaves out the all-important part that the individual himself plays in the process.

This broader concept of education includes guidance only when the modern, progressive viewpoint of the place and function of the individual is accepted. When only the goals of society are considered, we may have education but not guidance, for guidance implies assistance in making choices. These choices are individual

ones and imply a compromise between, or a synthesis of, the needs
of society and the needs of the individual. There are certain situations in education where the element of choice by the individual
is prominent, and there are others in which it is not.

Guidance and Purposive Living

If one views the life of the individual as a whole, guidance may
be said to have as its purpose helping the individual to discover his
needs, to assess his potentialities, gradually to develop life goals
that are individually satisfying and socially desirable, to formulate
plans of action in the service of these goals, and to proceed to their
realization.[3]

This statement clearly identifies the purpose of guidance with
that of education. It places major emphasis upon the development
of the whole individual who is now functioning and who will function in the future in a social environment. It is a useful concept
because it stresses the unity of one's life and shows the impossibility of separating one aspect of life from another. It is based upon
the belief that each of us builds up, step by step, a life purpose or
goal which serves or should serve as a center of integration for our
desires and ambitions and as a guide for our plans. One of the most
vital elements in our efforts to educate individuals is the assistance
we give in connection with choosing and developing these life
purposes or goals. From this point of view guidance and education
are seen to share the same purpose and sometimes the same methods.

Education Is Distinguished from Guidance

There are still a few people who regard education and guidance as separate and distinct, but their number is rapidly diminishing. Such a complete separation is impossible; it violates the essential nature of both elements. The differences of opinion now are
chiefly between those who would make guidance and education
synonymous terms and those who regard guidance as an aspect
and an essential element in education. The reason for this contro-

---

[3] A more complete discussion of this concept will be found in Arthur
J. Jones and Harold C. Hand, "Guidance and Purposive Living," chap. 1
in *Guidance in Educational Institutions*, Thirty-seventh Yearbook, National
Society for the Study of Education, part 1, Public School Publishing Company, Bloomington, Ill., 1938.

versy is found partly in the different meanings attached to the term "education" and partly in the failure to distinguish between the parts played by the teacher and by the learner in the process of education.

The position taken by the author is that guidance is found in that area of educational endeavor which involves assistance given by agencies or persons to the individual in making choices and in helping him choose a line of action, a method of procedure, a goal. It is not choosing *for* him or directing his choice; it is helping him to make the choice.

Education deals with the entire scope of human development. From one standpoint it is the conscious effort of society to change and develop the individual so that he may conform to society, take his place in it, improve it, and in doing this secure his own optimum development. From another standpoint it is the conscious effort of the individual to adjust himself to his physical and social environment, to improve it, and so to secure his own highest development.

Here are two forces, the individual and society, working for the same ends. When society merely determines what will be learned and how it will be learned and does nothing to secure the cooperation of the individual in the choice of things to be learned or methods to be used, guidance is not present, for there is no choice by the individual. Society in general and the teacher in particular may need to influence or direct the growth of the individual since wise choices in later life are dependent to a large extent upon habits and attitudes formed in early years. This might be considered good education, but it is not guidance. On the other hand the individual may consciously attempt to establish a goal without help. When he does this, guidance is not present. Although education may, and often does, take place through the effort and initiation of the individual alone, the same thing is true as above: this is education but not guidance. It is only when the cooperation of the individual is secured and assistance given him in choosing his goals or his methods that guidance is present. All guidance is education, but some aspects of education are not guidance; their objectives are the same—the development of the individual—but the methods used in education are by no means the same as those used in guidance.

GUIDANCE: ITS RELATION TO DISCIPLINE

A peculiar phobia appears in some guidance leaders when they consider the relation of guidance to discipline. Apparently they fear that any contact with discipline will interfere with the success of guidance workers. This fear is quite unwarranted and arises largely from misunderstandings. Guidance functions in all sorts of problem situations, past, present, or future. It is help given or received by all personnel in the school system—superintendent, supervisor, specialist, teacher, custodial worker, student. It is found wherever there are problems to be solved in teaching, in supervision, in discipline. In fact discipline offers one of the most useful and rewarding areas for guidance.

The confusion of these leaders is best resolved by examining the meanings which may be attached to the term "discipline." Discipline has two different but related meanings. First, discipline is a planned series of activities or exercises considered necessary for the attainment of a certain goal. An example is the training of an athlete for a race or for some other athletic contest. This meaning would include the development of regular exercise, eating, and sleeping habits as well as certain restrictions. Another example of this meaning is the college curriculum leading to a degree. In this first sense discipline also means a set of rules or laws affecting conduct such as the discipline of the church, the law, or medicine. This meaning may be called "positive" discipline.

Second, discipline means punishment for conduct that is considered undesirable. Failure to achieve a required standard in school, for example, may result in punishment or "discipline." The punishment may also be the natural result of undesirable conduct such as the "morning after" a "binge" or failure in a contest because of breaking training. This meaning may be called "negative" discipline. Its purpose is to prevent conduct that is undesirable. It is intended to help the individual understand what is necessary to attain the goal and to motivate him to keep to the exercises and the rules that have been set up.

It will be seen that the two meanings of discipline are closely related and that guidance has a unique function in both of them. Guidance helps set the goal and develop a program of activities leading to it. It also encourages and motivates the individual to keep at the activities and exercises that are essential in attaining the desired end.

Guidance As Punishment

When discipline means punishment by some authority for unacceptable behavior, guidance may help the student to understand why the behavior is unacceptable. High school is not too early to help students to understand the function of punishment as seen in the history of human society and to comprehend what their community would be without laws leading to the punishment of offenders.

The responsibility for assistance to students in cases of discipline, in both its positive and its negative meanings, may rest upon any school personnel. Teachers have responsibility in this area because they deal directly with that part of the curriculum which is allotted to them. They are responsible for helping the pupils in their classes or subject areas to understand the educational content, to do the exercises required, to attain the desired goals. They must provide the motivation necessary for the attainment of the objectives and administer such punishments as may be necessary for failure to study or to achieve academically. In addition each teacher is responsible for the behavior of the children in his class and to a large extent for their attendance and health. Without a doubt the chief responsibility for all these guidance services rests upon the teacher.

Preventive Guidance

By far the most effective discipline is that which operates before the crisis occurs and helps the student to understand and accept the type of behavior that is demanded by the school. In most cases discipline of this kind helps the student to realize what is required and therefore makes punishment unnecessary. Here the teacher is the most important factor, but the counselor may also be of real assistance. This type of discipline is not always possible, however, because one cannot always foresee the approaching crisis. Furthermore, not every crisis can be prevented. When a crisis does come, the student is in dire need of help, and the counselor has a clear responsibility to give him help.

Role of the Counselor in Discipline

Authorities in the field of guidance agree that counselors should not be charged with the responsibility for the administration of punishment. The reason for this is that, by so doing, it is difficult or sometimes impossible for the counselor to establish and maintain the rapport that is so essential for counseling and guidance. Experience amply confirms this opinion, but this does not mean that the counselor never has any responsibility in the field of discipline. In fact, discipline offers one of the richest and most rewarding areas for guidance.

Just as the counselor should not be involved in the actual punishment of the student, neither should he be the "lawyer for the defense" and seek to free him from punishment. If he has established rapport with the student, however, he may be able to find out why the misdemeanor was committed. He may discover what the student wished to accomplish by the act and help him to understand why his purpose was undesirable and what the effect of such behavior would be on other students and on the school.

The counselor can often help the guilty student to realize and frankly confess that his act was undesirable and to accept his punishment as well deserved. Thus it can be seen that the counselor may have a definite responsibility in cases of discipline and may be able to make a real contribution to the student and to the school by helping the student to understand and modify his antisocial behavior. In summary, guidance and discipline are closely related, and the counselor's role, even though it does not involve the administering of punishment, is both clear and unique.

GUIDANCE: ITS RELATION TO OTHER EDUCATIONAL SPECIALTIES

One of the most important developments in the field of education during the past century has been the increased specialization in educational services. Among the first specialties to emerge were the four large areas of teaching, counseling, administration, and supervision. More recently the specialized services of the physician, the psychologist, the psychiatrist, the dentist, the social worker, and the health educator have been recognized as important to education.

Additionally, we now see the subject-matter supervisor, the curriculum coordinator, and the remedial expert coming into our schools and performing useful functions needed in a complex educational setting. Each specialty has a distinct title and often requires a definite course of training leading to a certificate issued by the state or by some professional organization of high standing; each one also has a fairly definite core of work and responsibility. Each employs some techniques that are especially characteristic of the specialty. These characteristics and requirements have given a clear and definite professional status to the many educational specialties. Such specialization has some disadvantages and dangers, but there can be no doubt that it has greatly increased the effectiveness of the entire educational system.

Although each of these areas has a definite responsibility for certain services and uses characteristic techniques and thus makes its own contribution to the overall program of education, the lines separating one area of service from another are not entirely clear and distinct. There is considerable overlapping in objectives, in content, and in the techniques used.

The interrelation and overlapping in objectives and techniques may be seen by a brief discussion of the four large areas of service previously mentioned. Teaching is concerned with helping students to learn. Counseling deals with helping students to develop the ability to solve their own problems. Supervision is responsible for providing leadership in improving instruction. Administration is concerned with the control, direction, and management of the school, that is, the provision of conditions favorable for learning.

Common Objectives

It is clear that the basic services of the school are found in teaching and counseling since both deal directly with the individual student, his problems, and his needs. The function of administration and supervision is to promote the effectiveness of teaching and counseling. All four areas are bound together by the same objectives. Each should supplement, assist, and increase the effectiveness of the other areas in helping students to develop those habits, skills, attitudes, and ideals that will enable them to adjust to modern democratic society and attain a life that will be worthwhile.

Common Techniques

Although there are techniques that are characteristic of each area, they may be used in other areas as well. For example, each of the four areas is concerned with help in learning, and the techniques of teaching are available to all educational specialists and are used by them. Every member of the school staff faces situations that involve face-to-face counseling, and therefore all should use the special techniques of counseling. Many principals and superintendents fail in their dealings with teachers and parents because they do not know the techniques of counseling, and many teachers fail in their relations with students for the same reason.

The close relationship between guidance and instruction is clearly brought out in the 1955 yearbook of the Association for Supervision and Curriculum Development.[4] The authors of this yearbook define teaching or instruction as helping the child to learn and say that it is fundamentally guidance, since guidance is assistance to individuals in meeting new situations, in solving problems, and in making adjustments. Some of these problems are related to occupations, others to social relations, and still others to the mastery of school subjects. Some of the most important problems of children are connected with learning to read and write, to understand arithmetic skills, to comprehend and appreciate literature. A paraphrase of the standard definition of vocational guidance might be as follows: "Instructional guidance is the assistance given to individuals in understanding and accepting responsibility for the development of skills, in providing situations favorable for learning, in developing the desire to learn, and in making progress in learning."

Some of the best guidance and the most effective counseling is given by skilled teachers to pupils in their classes. This matter will be discussed in detail in a later chapter, but we can agree in any event that guidance techniques are needed by teachers in dealing with both parents and students. At one time or another every teacher has pupils come to him with problems relating to out-of-

[4] Association for Supervision and Curriculum Development, *Guidance in the Curriculum*, National Educational Association, New York, 1955.

school, family, or religious difficulties. It is quite natural for students to seek help on such problems; the teacher has, or should have, close contact with students, for he meets them much more frequently than the counselor. He knows, or should know, about previous difficulties, home conditions, financial problems, and other matters that have troubled them. Whether the teacher is able to give the needed help or not, he cannot refuse to confer with a pupil; if he is a real teacher, he must be interested in him and in his problem. Every teacher should know what general methods to employ in finding out what the real problem is, and he should make the pupils feel that he cares. He should be able and willing to recognize his own limitations and, when necessary, to refer the student to the counselor or someone else who may be better qualified to help him. He should know the best ways of making such referrals because they are among the most important elements in guidance. He should prepare the student for the referral conference by pointing out that the counselor is able and willing to help him. At the same time he should retain his own interest in the student and make him feel that he will always be ready to confer with him.

Because even the most skilled teacher is not able to give adequate assistance to all pupils for whom he is responsible or to deal successfully with all types of problems, there is now, and always will be, a definite need for well-trained and competent counselors in the elementary and secondary schools. These counselors should be consultants to teachers and parents, helping them to deal with more difficult cases. They should also be resource personnel, assuming responsibility for more difficult problems and for special cases. In the teamwork method which will be described later, the counselor might well be the chairman or leader of the group.

Necessary Teamwork

There are still some authorities who seem to believe that such overlapping in objectives and techniques is very undesirable. In their efforts to develop and maintain a special professional status for the counselor, they contend that counseling is the sole prerogative of the counselor and that teaching is the sole prerogative of the teacher. They believe that, when a teacher attempts to counsel a student, he steps out of his role as a teacher and becomes a counselor and that, when a counselor teaches, he becomes a teacher and is no longer a counselor. This idea is the result of the unfortunate confusion in the use of the two terms. The word "counseling" is used both for a technique and for an area of service (that of the counselor); "teaching" is also used to indicate a technique and a position (that of the teacher). The counselor often employs the technique of teaching in addition to others, and the teacher uses many techniques, one of which is counseling. But the teacher does not become a counselor because of this. He does not have the training or the assigned role of a counselor. When a mother uses first aid for her child, she uses one of the techniques of a physician; but this does not make her one. Neither teaching techniques nor counseling techniques are the sole property of any one area of educational service.

The fact that every service in the school involves the techniques of teaching, counseling, and other educational skills is of extreme importance. It should serve to emphasize the pressing need for planned cooperation among all school services. It also means that in the preparation of administrators, supervisors, teachers, and counselors there should be sufficient emphasis both on teaching techniques, so that all can teach well, and on counseling techniques, so that all can give effective guidance.

GUIDANCE AS AN ORGANIZED FUNCTION

Guidance Inherent in the Entire School

It is apparent that guidance is inherent in every part of the school which is concerned with assisting the pupil to make choices, adjustments, and interpretations. Any attempt to confine it to a given area of assistance or to restrict its function to a particular group of the school staff is certain to fail. Such an attempt to simplify the situation by an arbitrary division of the complex whole into separate parts inevitably sacrifices the unity of the process and results in greater confusion. Guidance involves all types of choices and must include within its scope the curriculum, teaching, supervision, and all other activities of the school. The classroom teacher can no more be divorced from guidance than can the counselor; in many ways he is fundamentally more important. On the other hand, to identify all guidance with the teacher would be equally fatal. Adequate guidance requires the cooperation of the whole school staff—administrators, teachers, personnel workers, and specialists.

Areas of Choice Not Provided for by the School

Must we, then, spread the work of guidance throughout the school with no attempt to coordinate it or to provide specialized services? Is there no place for a department of guidance more or less separate from the work of the classroom teacher and the principal but coordinated with them? To the latter question we must emphatically answer that there is such a place. There are areas of problems, choices, and adjustments that are not adequately provided for in schools as now organized. Some of the most important of these arise at crucial places in the educational progress of the pupil, such as (1) the end of the compulsory attendance age; (2) the completion of elementary school; (3) the beginning of junior high school; (4) the completion of junior high school; (5) the entrance to senior high school; (6) the completion of senior high school; (7) the entrance to college; (8) the leaving of school at any time; (9) the taking up of an occupation.

The choices and adjustments at these times are of extreme importance and call for special forms of assistance. Many facts necessary for an intelligent choice are not provided in the ordinary school; many habits, attitudes, and ideals needed are, at best, only indirectly taught. In proportion as the school is reorganized with these needs in view, to that extent will the special work of guidance in providing for information, habits, attitudes, and interests be reduced. If properly planned, any type of reorganization should allow ample opportunity to give special attention to ways in which needed information can be made available and assistance given.

Special Crises Requiring Reorganization of Material

Many choices and problems of adjustment to school and work require a reorganization of information already obtained from classroom activities as well as a selection from among the facts at hand. Such reorganization and selection are often very difficult and, without assistance, beyond the power of the individual to do. They sometimes involve factors other than the individual himself. Difficulties that arise in school or occupation or home not infrequently are due to clash of personalities or to a complexity of conditions. Adjustment involves not only the individual himself but other people and other factors as well; it is not something that he can work out by himself alone. It can be accomplished only by cooperative effort, and this cannot be left to haphazard activity. Such cooperation must be planned.

Problem Cases

The aim of guidance is to develop individuals so that they will be able to solve their own problems as far as this is possible. But even the best efforts of the school will not result in the entire elimination of problem cases. There will always be occasions when every student will need special assistance, and it is probable that some students will continually need help. Special facilities must be provided for meeting these needs.

Scope of an Organized Guidance Program

Some superintendents and principals believe that no specialized personnel is necessary for guidance, that the classroom teacher can provide all the assistance needed, and that it is the function of the principal to provide for coordination of effort. This attitude is due in part to the very real danger that the provision of a separate guidance department may result in the teachers' feeling that *all* guidance functions will and should be performed by the counselors and that they themselves have no guidance responsibilities. In some cases this attitude is due to the failure of the principal or superintendent to understand fully what the function of guidance is. Some of this confusion could be avoided if we called the specialized department "personnel work" instead of "guidance." Guidance is a function of the entire school; the function of the department of personnel work is to coordinate the guidance activities of the school and to supplement these activities by specialized work. This department would also have the responsibility of keeping constantly before the rest of the staff the need for assistance in areas that are likely to be neglected and of stimulating all to more effective action. In some schools and colleges this department is called "student welfare" and is coordinate with administration and instruction. The scope and function of any specially organized department of guidance or pupil personnel in the school system will depend upon the effectiveness with which the system as a whole is organized and administered from the guidance point of view.

We are still in the experimental stage of guidance; we do not yet know just what problems can be most advantageously handled by specially organized guidance departments. As the curricular and supervisory personnel of the school become conscious of the purpose of guidance and are reorganized in accordance with it, more and more of the actual guidance work can be successfully left to these agencies. We cannot accurately forecast exactly when this will be, nor can we determine completely what activities, if any, should always be performed by the special guidance bureau. Organized guidance must do for children what the rest of the system fails to do; it must build upon and supplement the regular work of the school. It may be found, for example, that much of the work, especially that concerned with securing information and developing the habits, ideals, interests, and techniques necessary to intelligent choice, can be done better if organized as a regular part of classroom procedure and not left to the organized guidance department. On the other hand, it will undoubtedly be found that certain kinds of assistance can be most efficiently and economically given by the organized department of guidance.

At present, organized departments of guidance or pupil personnel are concerned chiefly with certain crises, certain areas of problems, certain very important adjustments that the ordinary work of the school either does not provide for at all or does so very inadequately.

SUMMARY

Guidance is the assistance given to individuals in making intelligent choices and adjustments in their lives. The ability to make wise choices is not innate; it must be developed. The fundamental purpose of guidance is to develop in each individual, up to the limit of his capacity, the ability to solve his own problems and to make his own adjustments. Experiences of the individual himself and that of others may be very helpful in making choices, but they may also lead to choices that are unwise and harmful. In order to make experience valuable the individual must learn to analyze the past experiences to see whether the previous problem is like the present one and whether the solution arrived at before was a good one or whether a better one can now be found.

③ Guidance is not confined to any one type of situation. It can involve all types of life situations—personal, social, religious, occupational.

④Guidance is an integral part of the educational process. Although it is most needed and most effective in childhood, adolescence, and early adulthood, for some people it may be a lifelong requirement. The chief responsibility for guidance rests upon the home and the school. In the school every member of the staff is concerned with the guidance of the students entrusted to him. Trained counselors are essential to assist parents and other members of the staff in their guidance responsibilities and to deal directly with special problems of youth.

EXERCISES

1. On February 20, 1920, the National Vocational Guidance Association adopted the following statement: "The purpose of vocational guidance is to assist individuals to choose, prepare for, enter upon, and make progress in an occupation." Make a list of ten important problems of youth which are not included in this statement and which you feel should be the responsibility of the guidance department of the secondary school.

2. Find the meanings of the following: to assist, to lead, to advise, to steer, to guide, to regulate. Compare the definitions of these words and be prepared to discuss the distinctive meaning of guidance.

3. Evaluate the following statements:
   a. We have no need for a counselor because in our school every teacher is a guidance worker.
   b. Our counselor has absolutely nothing to do with discipline.
   c. There is nothing new about guidance; after all, guidance is just good teaching.

REFERENCES

Association for Supervision and Curriculum Development: *Guidance in the Curriculum,* National Educational Association, Washington, 1955.
Johnson, Walter F., Buford Stefflre, and Roy A. Edelfelt: *Pupil Per-*

sonnel and Guidance Services, McGraw-Hill Book Company, Inc., New York, 1961.

McDaniel, H. B., John E. Lallas, James A. Saum, and James L. Gilmore: *Readings in Guidance,* Henry Holt and Company, Inc., New York, 1959.

Mortensen, Donald G., and Allen M. Schmuller: *Guidance in Today's Schools,* John Wiley & Sons, Inc., New York, 1959.

Peters, Herman J., and Gail F. Farwell: *Guidance: A Developmental Approach,* Rand McNally & Company, Chicago, 1959.

PART II

GUIDANCE AND THE DEVELOPMENT
OF UNDERSTANDING

CHAPTER 2

UNDERSTANDING THE INDIVIDUAL

Guidance, like teaching, is a service given by one person to another. We often say the teacher is "teaching a class," but what he is really doing is teaching *each one* in the class—helping each pupil to learn. The counselor often meets pupils in a group, but his purpose is to help each individual in the group. This help cannot be effective unless the teacher or counselor knows the problems faced by each pupil and his characteristics, his abilities, and his desires. On the other hand, if the help offered is to be accepted by the individual, he must know himself, his limitations, and his strengths. Successful guidance, like successful teaching, is predicated on the student's being understood by the counselor and by himself.

IMPORTANCE OF UNDERSTANDING

It would seem to be self-evident that effective counseling toward specific goals is impossible without a clear understanding of the individual by the counselor, the teacher, and the parent, and that guidance should not be attempted unless such understanding is present. But life is full of tragedies in home and in school because of the lack of such understanding. Many parents try to determine the future of their children, especially that of their sons. If the family tradition for generations has been that the first-born son becomes a physician, a lawyer, a minister, then an attempt may be made to fit a boy into the tradition regardless of his abilities or in-

31

terests. Other parents dream that their boys will go to Princeton because the men in the family have "always" gone to Princeton. Mothers want their girls to go to Mount Holyoke because they went to Mount Holyoke. There are certain values in such traditions—common memories, common experiences, common friends that bind families together. However, these decisions are based on the desires of the parents and not on the needs of their children. Such family-centered vocational and educational decisions indicate a lack of appreciation of the importance of understanding the individual.

Students in high school tend to prefer occupations that are of a higher social status than that of their parents. This preference is especially marked in children whose fathers are in unskilled or semiskilled occupations. To understand the meaning of such a preference we need to take account of the desires of the parents which may be finding expression through the vocational selections of the children.

Choices of curriculum in high school are too often made on the basis of the "standing" of the curriculum and not on the needs of the student. The high salaries now paid to subprofessional workers have changed to some extent the relative social status of high-school curriculums, but teachers, as well as parents, are still too inclined to influence the better students to take certain courses because of the prestige involved without sufficient consideration or understanding of the needs, abilities, and interests of the student himself.

It is often said that what the student does, what courses he takes in school or college, what occupation he chooses, should be based on the needs that he, himself, feels. There is no doubt that these are important, but the needs that one feels at any given time may not be based on a clear self-understanding. We often feel a variety of needs at any given time, but some are quite superficial and relatively unimportant. We may feel a "need" for a Cadillac, to "keep up with the Joneses," but an understanding of ourselves and our financial status may make us willing to settle for a used Volkswagen. Assistance in making choices should be based on as thorough an understanding as is possible of the individual, of his basic needs, and of the real circumstances surrounding his decisions.

MAJOR LIFE AREAS NEEDING TO BE UNDERSTOOD

Understanding an individual is dependent upon knowledge of how he acts in different situations. This understanding may come from observations by those who know him in school, at home, or in the community. These observations need to be combined and judgments made regarding the motives and reasons behind the observed acts. This is by no means an easy thing to accomplish. It calls for sympathetic insight into the desires and needs of students and the unusual ability to put aside any preconceived ideas of what the individual may be.

One important key to such understanding is the physical and social environment of the individual. Careful, long-range studies are now being made of the relationship between social environment and behavior. Some very significant results are beginning to emerge. Descriptions of overt behavior are not as important as the "climate" of the social environment, the kinds of behavior that are approved by the community, the home, the school, and especially by the adolescent group of which the individual is a part.

The Individual in His School

A study made recently indicates that the greatest prestige is often given to those students with organizational leadership ability —the ability to get other students to agree on what is to be done and to organize them so as to do it effectively, even if what is planned is not approved by the school authorities. In some schools the value placed by students upon superior attainment is high, in others it is low. Such student values are of extreme importance and can usually be developed by the school itself with the support of the homes and community. This "climate" of the school often becomes traditional. An example of this is the difference between the traditions of Eton and Rugby in England and those of the English "provided" schools—similar to American "public" schools. Recently a father took his son out of a public school that had a very low standard and secured his admission into one of the private schools in the East that traditionally maintained unusually high scholastic standards. In the public school the boy received high marks—B's and A's—but the father found his academic achievement to be very low. In the private school the boy was told that he would be dismissed at the end of the term unless his achievement improved. By hard work, and with the help of outside tutoring, he steadily advanced and eventually was doing the high quality of work of which he was capable. The improvement was due to the climate of the private school and his acceptance of it.

The Individual in His Home

Another life area that is important in our attempts to understand an individual is his home. The socioeconomic level of the home may account for the academic ambition or apathy of the child. Generally speaking, the lower the level of the home, the less education is valued. Subtle psychological forces such as acceptance, rejection, or domination may play important roles in shaping the child. The relationship between parents and children and sibling relationships may provide us with keys to the behavior we observe. The home is often the most important element in the individual's life, and we cannot understand him without knowing about his home. The counselor may be an important bridge between the school and the home and thus help both the parent and the teacher to know the student more completely.

The Individual in His Community

Community conditions are of great importance in securing an understanding of individual students and in developing effective self-concepts. Such conditions are fully as significant as those in the home or in the school. Differences in the social status of families in a community often are reflected in the attitudes of different groups of high-school students toward one another. Differences in dress, in habits of speech, in social manner, in points of view, and in values are often seen. In consolidated schools, rivalries and clannish customs often appear and cause feelings of hostility between groups. In spite of efforts made by the school staff to overcome these unfavorable conditions, they often continue. In the school itself, students in the college preparatory course are likely to look down on those taking industrial courses. This is sometimes shown in the reluctance of boys in the college preparatory course to date girls in the industrial course or of girls to accept dates with boys who are in a different course. Such differences often show themselves in school elections and in committee selections. Even though the school faculty does not approve of such practices, they cannot ignore them if they wish to understand the students. Unpopular students do not understand why they are not dated or elected to office and are bewildered or deeply hurt. A knowledge of community and home conditions and sensitivity to such rivalries in and out of the school are the keys to a real understanding of the student.

It is important to keep in mind that understanding an individual involves much more than an assembly of facts about him and his behavior. Facts themselves are often misleading, and they must be interpreted by reference to other facts and to the circumstances in which they are found. Understanding cannot come merely from observation of what a person does, how he acts, and how he seems to feel. It is important to know the influences that were responsible for his behavior, "how he got that way," what his purpose was in doing what he did. Many times he himself does not understand why he acted as he did.

PSYCHOLOGICAL BARRIERS TO UNDERSTANDING

A meaningful understanding of the individual is not always easy to secure. Certain psychological barriers may impede our progress toward understanding. Young people especially are reluctant to reveal themselves as they really are. Because of the intensely personal nature of our lives, it is difficult—perhaps impossible—to have complete empathy for another person, that is, to feel what it would be like to be in his position. Finally, because individuals change, we can never be sure that our understanding is up to date—the student in October is not the same student that he was in April.

Reluctance to Reveal One's Real Self

Young people in particular are very hesitant to reveal their "true self" to others, especially to adults. This difficulty is described by James Whitcomb Riley in *A Child's World:*

The child heart is so strange a little thing,
So mild, so timorously shy and small,
When grownup hearts throb, it goes scampering

Behind the wall, nor dares peer out at all
   It is the veriest mouse
   That hides in any house
So wild a little thing is the child heart!
   Child heart, mild heart
   Ho, my little wild heart
Come up here to me out o' the dark
   Or let me come to you.

Adolescents often go to great lengths to keep another person from knowing what they really are. They are cruel to keep others from knowing that they are really tenderhearted; they pretend to dislike someone in order to conceal their inner feelings of respect and liking. Many persons, old and young, feel that it is indecent to "bare one's soul and dare the day." It is almost as bad as being a nudist! They also feel that "it is none of your business." This attitude, in itself, reveals something about the individual. A wise and sympathetic counselor or teacher, who has not forgotten his own youth, can look behind this bravado and learn much about the student.

Difficulty in Understanding Another Person

It is difficult for adults to understand the behavior of adolescents; we so easily forget what we thought and did when we were "young and gay." A common danger is that we may read our own present motives, feelings, and aspirations into the expressions and activities of the student. Another serious difficulty is that, although we can secure some information about the individual, what we get sometimes interferes with our understanding of him. "We cannot see the forest for the trees." The human being is a complex organic unit. He is "more than the sum of all his parts." We can gather together all the facts that can be obtained about him—his background, his surroundings, his experiences, his many characteristics—and still not understand him. There is real danger in half-truths and in unrelated information. No one type of information can stand alone; it must be considered in relation to all the other data. Real understanding of another person involves an unusual ability to put oneself sympathetically and intelligently in his place. At the same time one must stand apart and be impersonal. The privacy of the individual must be respected; we must not delve too deeply nor be in a hurry to see what the student is not ready to disclose.

Individuals Change

One difficulty in dealing with the adolescent is that he is constantly changing, even from day to day. As a consequence, by the time data are obtained and recorded, he has changed, and the data are important only as they show a developmental picture of the student. Such a picture is important, but it does not tell us what he is now. A current picture is very difficult to attain. Cumulative records have great value in showing the development of the individual from year to year—his scholastic record, his changing interests, his attitudes toward teachers and fellow students, the changes in his personality patterns. But more important is a truly understanding teacher or counselor who can interpret the conflicting behavior of the developing adolescent. Such understanding is absolutely essential. The past must not be confused with the present. Records tell us what was; only the individual himself can tell us what is. We must take care not to confuse marks, scores, and records of incidents with the living individual we are trying to understand and help.

SOCIAL CHANGES ARE BARRIERS TO UNDERSTANDING

Great and rapid changes in our society increase the difficulty of understanding across the generations. Adults and adolescents live in truly different worlds. The meaning of work, the role of the family, religion, and morals, the philosophy of the schools have all undergone considerable transformation during this century. These changes impede the understanding which is so essential for the function of guidance.

The Meaning of Work Is Changing

During the past twenty-five years there has been a marked change in the attitude of youth toward standards of accomplishment in schoolwork. In most schools the number of high-school students who have the ambition to do their best in studies is small. Some think that one of the causes of this situation stems from the attitude of workers during the depression of the 1930s. Unemployment was high, and the government took the responsibility of providing jobs for all. It was difficult to find or create enough jobs for all who needed the income, and, as a result, much of the work was unnecessary, and there were more men on each job than were needed. There was no incentive to do the job quickly or well. A very common sight was that of workers on road jobs leaning on their shovels. This unfortunate attitude toward work permeated nearly all kinds of public employment and society in general.

Another cause of the change in attitude toward standards of accomplishment is the prevailing emphasis placed on social rather than intellectual attainments. Social-mindedness—ability to get along with others, being a "good fellow"—is often overemphasized by parents. Parents may say to their children, "I don't care whether you get A's, B's, or C's in your work. The most important thing is for you to know how to get along with people."

Still another factor related to this situation is the social pressure not to be different from other members of the group. "Who wants to be a brain?" "I want to be like other people." To many students in high school it is no longer considered important or desirable to get high marks or to do one's best—getting by is enough. A community can have whatever kind of school it wants, but it must agree upon the things to be considered important. It may be a school where each student is stimulated to do his best and where high standards of conduct are maintained, or it may be a school with low standards of achievement and conduct. The climate of the community will determine in large measure what kind of school it will be. Most young people will respond to whatever values are set by their companions, their school, and their homes. To understand the changing meaning of work and accomplishment for our adolescents, we must remember that the adult society created the climate that helped these new and troublesome values to flourish.

The Family Changes

In any consideration of the present difficulty in the guidance of youth the changes in the home and community should be kept in mind. In most present-day homes there is no longer the same amount of intimate interrelationship that once was present. The increased tempo of life has too often materially reduced or even eliminated the time or the opportunity for such relationships.

It is difficult to determine all the causes for this change which has been both gradual and complicated. It was not caused by increased time on the job since the "workday" of the majority of workers has decreased until the forty-hour week is now the standard and pressure is being exerted to make it even shorter. Nor can it have been caused by the increased time necessary for household duties, because electrical appliances of all kinds—for cooking, dishwashing, laundry work, housekeeping, refrigeration—have materially reduced the time necessary for such responsibilities. There is actually more time available for home life and for closer relationships. In some homes this "free time" is being utilized to enrich home life and has resulted in closer relationships between parents and children, but in the typical home this is not the case.

There seem to be two main factors that are largely responsible for this situation. One of these is the increased participation of fathers and mothers in activities outside the home in social, civic, church, and political affairs. Such activities, for example, those of the parent-teacher association, are often very useful and desirable, but they reduce materially the time spent in the home—evenings, Saturdays, and Sundays. These activities make it difficult or even impossible to have the unhurried personal contacts with children which are so essential for effective understanding and assistance.

The second factor is the increased independence of children which results in a decrease in the feeling of need for help or even for association with parents. The many out-of-class activities in the school—athletic, musical, dramatic, school government, social— provide group satisfactions and reduce both the time and the need for companionship at home. At home the children have the radio, the television, and the record player at their disposal, and they need no assistance from their parents to enjoy these facilities.

This new kind of less-intimate family seems to have resulted in much juvenile delinquency, although it is difficult to determine exact statistics in this area.

In any event, in spite of increased efforts to cope with the problem, juvenile delinquency still persists in some of its worst aspects. Stringent laws, more adequate police supervision, heavy penalties, establishment of "homes" and detention institutions where delinquent youth may be separated from adult prisoners have all helped, but they are by no means the solution of the problem. The cause of delinquency is in the home and in the community in which the youth lives.

If juvenile delinquency is ever to be eliminated, the home and the community must be improved. As a first step, there must be closer and more effective cooperation of home, school, and community in securing accurate and significant information regarding the conditions and influences that are responsible for the attitudes and purposes of youth. Once identified, these conditions and influences must be changed to provide an environment more conducive to a wholesome life and respect for law.

Religious Beliefs and Morals: Yesterday and Today

Another area of great importance in the lives of young people in which there have been far-reaching and significant changes is that of morals and religion. The reasons for these changes are difficult to determine. Developments in our social, economic, and industrial life probably have contributed to the change, as has the interaction of different beliefs, customs, and morals brought to America from all parts of the world. Whatever the cause, we cannot fail to understand the great importance of different moral codes and religious beliefs to the development of young people, even though both these areas are considered to be the private concern of the family, the church, and the individual rather than of the school. But if the school is interested in getting an understanding of the child and in helping him to develop adequate goals, it cannot neglect these areas, for they have a profound and often a determining influence on such goals. An understanding of the changes in these areas is of very great importance both to the home and to the school.

Many people believe that religion has a greater hold on people than it ever has had and point out that the growth in church membership in all denominations has steadily increased and many new churches are being built. Evangelists attract great numbers of people, and hundreds come forward and announce their determination to accept religion. Some believe that the fear of destruction by atomic bombs and the ensuing uncertainties have served to increase the interest in religion. Others feel that, in spite of the growth in churches' membership, the real hold of religion on people has perceptibly decreased, that it is no longer as important a factor in our lives as it once was. They say that, although the organized church is still very important, it no longer occupies the position of leadership that it once had. It is certain that family prayers have practically disappeared, and even grace at meals is unusual.

Of one thing we are certain: religious customs have changed. The great majority of people are far more liberal in their beliefs and more tolerant of those who do not believe as they do than they once were. Young people are increasingly thinking for themselves and refusing to accept religious dogmas merely because they have been recognized for centuries. In this atmosphere of controversy, of changing beliefs, and of lack of belief, it is small wonder that young people are confused and often unable to adjust properly and to distinguish between transient and permanent values. Wise assistance is needed. Much of this help must be given by the home and the church, but the school also has a responsibility here.

Our situation regarding morals contains so much that is undesirable that we may even wonder whether our moral standards are not weakening. Racketeering, graft, and corruption are everywhere apparent, in politics, business, industry, government, and labor unions. Some men become wealthy and powerful not because of their contribution to society but because of trickery, clever dealing, influence, control of the political machine, or even theft, intimidation, or murder. Our legal system is slow, cumbersome, and too often ineffective. Criminals sometimes escape just punishment because they have money or influence or because of the work of lawyers who specialize in helping criminals evade the consequences set up by the law. The old virtues of industry, thrift, and honesty have, in some cases, been the actual cause of poverty and suffering. Men who have worked long and hard and who have been thrifty have sometimes been cheated by the unscrupulous and lost their money. They have found themselves poor and ruined not because they were dishonest or prodigal but because they were thrifty and honest.

Standards of good conduct are continually changing. Some conduct that was once considered acceptable is now unacceptable, and what was unacceptable is now acceptable. No longer do all believe that conscience is an infallible guide in deciding what is right. Right conduct is determined not only by the motives of the actor but also by the consequences of the act. In the complexity of modern life it is often very difficult to determine the real effects of an act, and this makes it hard to make right decisions. We need to know the probable effects of the proposed action on others and on ourselves before we can decide intelligently what is best to be done.

Some research has suggested that youth indicate relatively little concern about problems of morals and religion or of home and family. Two opposite conclusions might be drawn from these findings. We might say that young people are well adjusted in morals and religion and to home and family since they apparently have few problems in these areas. On the other hand, it is possible that young people have little consciousness of morals or moral obligations. It may be that church and religion are not vital forces in their lives and that they have little trouble with parents and home because parents are not important guiding and restraining influences in their lives. In other words, young people may not be conscious of problems in these areas because they have little sense of moral obligation and little restraint imposed on them. The mounting delinquency rate among youth might indicate that the second conclusion is correct.

The Changing Educational Philosophy

One of the most important social changes in recent years has been that in our philosophy of education as it concerns the place of the child in the teaching-learning process. This change is so intermingled with the changes in the home and in religion and morals that it is difficult to tell whether the changes in the philosophy of education are responsible for the changes in the home and society or the reverse. Formerly, education was the process of passing on to the young the cultural heritage of the past. It was the process of inculcating in the young those habits, skills, ideas, and knowledges that were necessary to enable them to take their place in adult society. The central figure in this process was the teacher. The student was the recipient and, as far as possible, passive and obedient. He was thought to be too young to have any voice in determining what he had to do or to learn. Discipline was the process of preventing behavior that would interfere with this attitude of docility.

The curriculum was organized by the school, and methods were developed with the purpose of molding the pupil into the kind of individual who would make a good citizen and an exemplary person. This educational philosophy was the prevailing point of view in the schools of all countries until the beginning of this century.

The new educational philosophy places the child at the center of the educational process and is concerned primarily with his development, that is, with what he is now rather than what he may become or what society may demand of him. His needs for personal development, his own interests and desires, are dominant. His impulses for action are of extreme importance and should not be unduly restricted. He should have a large part in decisions regarding what he should do—even regarding what he should study. The extreme of this position is that he should not be made to do what he does not want to do. Failures are considered undesirable and should be avoided. Because punishments and restraints are negative, they should either not be used at all or at least be minimized. The rule of promotion for all is sometimes adopted.

Even though some of the extreme implications of this philosophy have not been generally accepted, its impact has been very great. Probably its most important implication is the emphasis it places upon the enlarged place of the individual in choosing his own way of life and in selecting his own activities. Even young children are allowed and often encouraged to make important choices for themselves. Many of these choices may be unfortunate; but when the choice seems undesirable, instead of arbitrarily refusing to allow the child to do what he has chosen to do, we try to help him evaluate the wisdom of his choice.

The underlying idea of this educational position emphasizes the fundamental purpose of guidance—helping the individual to make wise choices. The necessity for adequate guidance in the very early years of life in order to develop this ability is emphasized. While this emphasis is certainly desirable, the popularity of this new philosophy has also resulted in much confusion, uncertainty, and even bewilderment among teachers and parents. It has been difficult for them to adjust themselves to it, and they are often at a loss to know what to do. Some children have been quick to take advantage of this situation in the home and in the school and have become restive under old restraints. Formerly, it was expected that children, willingly or unwillingly, would do what they were asked to do, but now some of them argue about it and often win. Even when they do not, they have had the fun of arguing. In either case their feeling of importance in choosing for themselves and having their own way has been increased.

Parents and teachers who grew up when a different educational philosophy was in vogue often cannot understand the young people of today and are puzzled by their actions. This puzzlement makes them uncertain about the best methods of dealing with today's students. The usual result is that little or nothing is done to change the behavior of the student or to develop his sense of values. Something of the same situation exists also in the juvenile courts of the country in regard to juvenile delinquency. Many minor crimes, and often even more serious ones, committed by youth are dealt with very leniently; they often are let off with a warning or with "fatherly advice." At most, they are sent to some school for delinquents. Crimes by youth continue to increase as a result of this treatment, yet we know that it is not wise to commit them to jails where they associate with confirmed criminals. We have as yet failed to solve the problem of dealing with delinquent youth. We know that the old method of treating them as criminals is not good; we also know that leniency of the courts does not by itself solve the problem. Some more effective guidance is absolutely essential. Many national and local agencies are working hard to solve the problem, and some of the suggested solutions seem to be hopeful. At the root of any successful plan must be some form of intelligent guidance.

In summary, the last few years have seen great changes in our society. Adults trying to understand adolescents must take account of the fact that the world of their own childhood is gone. It is not likely to return. If you wish to understand today's youth, you must first understand his world—however much a stranger you feel in it, however much you may disapprove of some of its elements—for the youth and his world are so much a part of each other that they cannot be known separately.

AIDS IN UNDERSTANDING

Many techniques are needed to help us understand youth. Such an understanding cannot be attained merely by watching what they are doing. We must know the reasons and motives that impel them to act as they do. This level of understanding requires close and sympathetic personal relationship over a reasonably long period of time. The problem is made more difficult because youth do not understand themselves and therefore cannot give much direct help to adults who are striving to learn more about them.

Mutual Experiences

One of the most effective methods of achieving understanding is by having a shared experience in working together toward a common goal. Father and son may work together making needed repairs on the house or improvements in the yard; mother and daughter may share in some enterprise relating to the improvement of a room or the preparations for a social occasion. Other examples of valuable experiences which may be shared and which may lead to better understanding are hikes, fishing, boating, collecting coins or postage stamps, study of birds, butterflies, trees, insects, or flowers. Sometimes the leader of such enterprises may be the parent, sometimes the youth.

It is a major disaster that parents so often are "too busy" and too much absorbed in their adult concerns to be comrades to their children. Scout leaders and athletic coaches, because of their close relationships with youth, often have very valuable information about them. It is unfortunate that such types of information are not more often assembled and made available to counselors, teachers, and parents. When we wish to understand what a student is really like, we should not overlook the value of sharing a meaningful experience with him; we may even enrich our own lives in the process.

Cumulative Records

A cumulative record is a collection of information about a student and constitutes a picture of his development—physically, academically, and socially. These records, which have great value in showing year-to-year development, include, as we have stated earlier, his scholastic record, his changing interests, his attitudes toward teachers and fellow students, and the changes in his personality patterns. Well-organized anecdotal records—objective statements of significant incidents—may be very helpful if carefully made from time to time. Autobiographies often reveal characteristics and attitudes unsuspected even by the student himself. Valuable as they are, such records are quite inadequate to provide a real understanding of the pupil. What is needed most is a sympathetic and understanding teacher or counselor who can interpret the conflicting behavior of the developing adolescent and look behind and beyond the records themselves to see him as he is. This is essential in any attempt to give guidance to the individual.

Cooperation in the School

The development of the self, the ego, is a gradual process which may continue throughout life, but for most people the period of childhood and youth is by far the most important time in the formation of the self. Understanding of an individual comes from a knowledge of how he acts in different situations and why. It might be that the person best able to understand the youth would be the one who has the closest relation to him for the longest period. Therefore the parents, especially the mother, would seem to be the ones. There is no doubt that the mother can be, and often is, a very knowledgeable observer of how her child acts and how he changes in behavior as he grows, but parental love and pride often interfere with judgment and obscure important elements essential for understanding.

Teachers see children six to eight hours a day, five days in the week, for nine or ten months a year and observe their acts and judge their motives. Teachers, however, see the individual in a more or less restricted situation and are not completely qualified to understand him. Fellow students, on the other hand, observe their classmates in many types of situations which are more varied and lifelike than those seen by parents or teachers. Although the counselor is the person who is charged with the responsibility for bringing together all the data in the school records, including the observations and opinions of teachers and peers, he may have comparatively little personal contact with individual students. Often, however, he can judge more objectively than parents and teachers, even though he might not be able to develop a completely accurate understanding of the whole personality by himself.

It must be conceded that there is no way by which the real self of an individual can be accurately determined, but it seems clear that the only way in which the school can approximate such an understanding is by the cooperation of all the individuals and agencies who come in contact with the individual. This means that, since all the institutions in the community have a responsibility for the education and training of children and youth, they must also cooperate in developing an understanding of them.

Cooperation with the Home

The school and the family share the greatest responsibility for understanding. They are so closely related that there is every reason and need for cooperation, but effective methods to bring this about have as yet not been developed. The major responsibility for initiating such cooperation rests upon the school system. During the past ten years a number of systems have been experimenting with different types of cooperation, some of which seem to be very promising. Efforts are made to clarify the particular responsibility of the school, the family, and the community as well as to eliminate misunderstandings that have arisen among them and to emphasize the need for cooperation and point out ways in which it can be accomplished.

Close personal relations are developed among teachers, parents, business and professional people so that they are known to each other as individuals. Through social occasions and professional meetings they come to know one another better and to realize the necessity for cooperation among friends in all areas, not only in the schools.

In many schools lay people have been invited to come to the school for a variety of reasons so that they can know and understand it better. Some schools are providing "parent" rooms where there are easy chairs and books and pamphlets on school matters and where desirable conferences with teachers, counselors, and administrators can be arranged.

At present the chief means of cooperation with the home is through reports to the parents on the status and progress of the child, but it is difficult to make such reports meaningful to them. The primary meaning is conveyed by the grades received, promotion or nonpromotion, and comments on the child's behavior. At times conferences are arranged between the teacher and the parents to discuss the status of the pupil. In most schools, however, this conference is held only when there is something wrong. If the pupil is getting along well in school, no need for a conference is seen. Likewise, when the teacher visits the home, it is usually because of some problem either in the child's work or in his behavior. The difficulty in providing these conferences is very great; but in the schools where such methods have been adopted, a very definite change has been seen in the relation between teachers and parents not only in their personal contact but also in their friendly cooperation in the solution of problems of pupils and in the improvement of school facilities.

Community Information

Teachers and counselors should know their community if they are to be of maximum help to students. The school needs to know about the community activities of the students. Which ones are active in church work? Which ones are leaders in their neighborhood peer groups? Contacts with service clubs such as Rotary, Kiwanis, and Lions have been found to be very useful in revealing sources of assistance and also in securing information about students who are friends or relations of members of these organizations.

Many schools have found it helpful to initiate some type of community survey, which reveals the resources of the community, such as men and women who are leaders in business or industry and who are willing to talk with students about opportunities and qualities essential to success in life. Such contacts will help students to understand social and economic conditions and to realize how they may prepare themselves for lines of work for which they are especially fitted.

SUMMARY

∧ Effective guidance of youth depends on a sympathetic understanding of the individual. Securing this understanding is a difficult and time-consuming task. It demands close cooperation with the individual, the family, the school, and the community. It demands a vicarious entry into the individual's problems, his failures, and his successes. It attempts to discover what he is as well as how he got that way.

Four things are imperative to effective guidance: We need a

better understanding of children and youth and of their developing problems and needs. We need to have the youth understand himself, his home, his school, his community, and his physical environment. We need to discover, by cooperative effort, effective methods of helping the home, school, and community to adjust themselves to the constant changes in their functions and character and of helping children and youth to learn how to use their extended freedom and wider opportunities. Finally, we need to help youth to develop necessary restraints and to evolve a set of values that will enable them to form self-concepts that are realistic and that will help them in their choice of personal, social, and occupational activities.

EXERCISES

1. Describe instances where the help offered you by parents, teachers, counselors, or others was ineffective or even harmful because they did not know enough about you. If you do not recall any such experiences, describe some instances that you have observed in the case of others.

2. Do you feel reluctant to give information about yourself to others? If so, what are the causes of such reluctance? Describe the situation and the conditions in which you would feel free to give information about yourself.

3. Usually there are differences between the picture we have of ourselves (our self-concept) and the way we are seen by others (our public image). Discuss these differences in the case of someone well known to you. What accounts for such differences? Do you see ways to lessen these differences?

REFERENCES

Bossard, J. H. S.: *The Sociology of Child Development,* Harper & Brothers, New York, 1954.

Frank, Lawrence K., and Mary Frank: *Your Adolescent at Home and in School,* The Viking Press, Inc., New York, 1956.

Havighurst, Robert J.: *Human Development and Education,* Longmans, Green & Co., Inc., New York, 1953.

Ilg, Frances L., and Louise Bates Ames: *Child Behavior,* Harper & Brothers, New York, 1955.

Super, Donald E.: *The Psychology of Careers,* Harper & Brothers, New York, 1957.

CHAPTER 3

SELF-UNDERSTANDING AND THE GUIDANCE OF YOUTH

There are several terms that have practically the same meaning as "self-understanding." They are "self-image," the "ego," and "self-concept." The concept of self-understanding has come into prominence through the studies and publications of Rogers, Snygg and Combs, Super, and others.

It is an interesting and stimulating approach to guidance. It provides a dynamic center around which to group the factors relating to future life activities and especially to the choice of life work. This is in essence the modern version of the old Greek motto "Know thyself," and like this motto it looks to the future and seeks to find the types of activity which will be in harmony with the self-concept. It involves bringing together into consciousness the characteristics, abilities, aptitudes, potentialities, and ideals of the individual and organizes them in such a way as to point to the kinds of activity—personal, social, occupational—which will enable him to meet his basic needs and to secure personal satisfaction.

The importance of the self-concept in guidance stems from the fact that individuals live in separate and constantly changing worlds which constitute the only reality they can ever know. The individual is the center of his world, and we can never completely share his view of things since we can never join him in his private world. To understand our behavior we need to assume that all of us have drives to actualize, maintain, and enhance ourselves and that what we do constitutes an attempt to satisfy our needs in the world as we see it. We all behave in ways that are consistent with our view of ourself and our world. Healthy people admit to consciousness all experience, but others deny or distort whatever is not consistent with their rigidly held notions of themselves and their worlds. In many cases an understanding of the individual's self-concept is a key to understanding his behavior.

It is impossible to overestimate the importance of self-understanding. A well-formulated self-concept that takes into account the realities of the working world makes for an easier transition from school to work than does a hazy or unrealistic one. A major goal of education is the development of clear, well-formulated, and realistic self-concepts. Guidance workers also attempt to help people develop clear and consistent self-images not too opposed to social reality and not too distant from the ideal which we all hold up for ourselves. In summary, if we are to understand the individual, we must strive to see the world through his eyes. If we are to aid an individual, we must help him clarify his self-concept and think through its consequences—personal, vocational, and social.

DEVELOPMENT OF THE SELF-CONCEPT

We are not born with the ability to understand ourselves. The young child is not even conscious of himself as an individual; he is merely a part of his environment. Consciousness of oneself in some cases emerges suddenly, almost without warning. Instances are recorded where a boy walking to school in the morning suddenly realizes "I am myself; I am nobody else." It is a staggering experience and one that is likely to throw the individual off balance for a time. To some it is electrifying and deeply satisfying; to others it is depressing, for it signifies that he is alone in the world. Such a dramatic experience is by no means common; but when it does occur, it may well be the beginning of real self-understanding.

For most youth the development of self-understanding is a slow and relatively unconscious process involving some degree of emotional maturity and readiness. It requires more than the collection of data about oneself. It calls for the ability to interpret these data in terms of self and environment. The individual must come to see himself as he is in comparison with what he wants to be. He must come to grips with himself as he is, as well as with what he thinks he should be; that is, he should have a clear and realistic concept of himself, his surroundings, his obligations and opportunities.

Self-understanding Is Not Related to Age

A realistic self-concept, that is, accurate self-understanding, is not attained at any given age. Some attain it in early youth; some later; some never. An accurate self-concept usually begins to appear in early adolescence, becoming clearer with growth and experience so that it is translated into terms of life work in later adolescence or early maturity. For a limited few the life concept is fairly clear at graduation from high school or even before; with others it may not come until after a year or more in college or even until entering an occupation. Some never attain it.

In view of what we know about the emotional stability and social intelligence of the gifted, it is likely that they will be emotionally ready for self-appraisal and self-conceptualization before others of their age and that, in later adolescence, they will be able to carry out the process at increasingly higher levels. It will usually be possible to share with the gifted youth all available data about his strengths and weaknesses early enough and fully enough so that he can develop or remedy them. He will certainly be able to use this information realistically in planning.

Making Decisions Helps Develop a Realistic Self-concept

If the purpose of guidance is to help the individual solve his own problems and make his own choices as an adult, the responsibility for the choices he makes as a youth must also rest primarily on himself. If he is to make choices that are wise, he must understand himself, his needs, and the choices available to him. High-school students are at the age when many important psychological, physiological, and emotional changes are taking place, and it is no wonder that they do not always understand themselves. It is at this time that the understanding and sympathetic teacher or parent can help the student to accept his new and troublesome desires and attitudes.

In helping the student to understand himself, one must take great care that he does not develop the habit of morbid introspection to the extent that he either becomes the center of everything —the most important person in his world—or shrinks in importance so much that he feels worthless to himself and to others. Either result will make it impossible for him to assess correctly his abilities and aptitudes and will defeat his attempts to reach emotional maturity. ←

Information Is Needed for the Development of a Self-concept

It is difficult to decide how much, if at all, the individual should participate in gathering information about himself. The prevailing feeling is that the school counselor is a person with special training in the methods and techniques of guidance and that he, with the other school personnel, is responsible for securing the necessary information about pupils and recording it in the cumulative folders. After studying these records, he consults with teachers and with the pupil and, on the basis of all this information, helps the pupil to understand himself, to adjust to school, and to plan his future. This approach is quite logical if the counselor is considered to be the center of the guidance process. If, however, the individual student is considered to be the center, the process of securing and interpreting information should be a part of the guidance of the student himself; he should participate in it and, through this participation, learn more about himself. We should also remember that certain important data cannot be obtained without the cooperation of the pupil himself. The pupil needs information about himself as an aid to clear self-understanding.

Current Experiments in the Development of Self-understanding

One school carried out a very interesting project involving the cooperation of the students in learning more about themselves. The students were asked to make out their own cumulative record in which information about grades, test results, attitudes, and interests was included along with comments and interpretations by the pupils themselves based on their own reactions and on interviews with the counselor. It was thought that the process of filling out these records would help them to learn more about themselves.

Another quite similar plan has been the custom in many schools of having each student write his autobiography. This autobiography includes information of various kinds about school progress, results of tests, self-estimates, estimates of teachers and of schoolmates, and statements of his hopes and plans for the future.

Sociograms may help in self-understanding by showing the pupil how he is seen by his fellow students. Even when the judgments of other students about an individual are incorrect, they may help him to ask, "What have I done that makes other students see me as they do?"

In one high school the students who were nominated for various offices were brought together in a number of conferences where they discussed the purposes and duties of the various positions and the kinds of ability and qualities essential for them. Each nominee was stimulated through these group discussions to examine himself and find out whether or not he had the attributes considered essential for the job for which he was nominated.

In another school a still more interesting and daring plan was used. A selected group of seniors engaged in a free discussion of the qualities and characteristics of different members of the group. The teacher sat in the rear of the room and took no part in the discussion except when he was asked for his suggestions. One boy was selected as the subject for discussion, and a student evaluator gave in detail what he considered were the good and bad characteristics of the boy. When he had finished his summation, another student spoke in defense of the individual being discussed. Finally, the boy himself was given an opportunity to speak. To the observer, the procedure was not only cruel but very questionable because of the possibility of the development of animosities. However, there was not the slightest evidence of hurt feelings by any of the students. The teacher in charge was confident that the plan was a very useful one in helping the student to understand himself and in helping fellow students and teachers to understand the individual. Perhaps the secret of the success of this plan was that the teacher had real sympathetic understanding of youth. He had not forgotten his own youth, as unfortunately is the case with many teachers, counselors, and parents.

There are many ways of helping students attain a realistic self-concept. It may be done in face-to-face counseling interviews, in conferences dealing with difficulties in studies or behavior, in the consideration of the choice of an occupation, or in the discussion of plans after graduation from high school. It may be done through informal incidental associations. Counselors sometimes set up situations that will reveal to the student himself characteristics of which he may be quite unconscious.

Such devices are useful in helping the individual to develop an understanding of himself, which is essential for adjustment and for the solution of personal problems. While it is difficult even for an adult to attain a complete understanding of himself, it is still more difficult for an adolescent, for in this period of his life he is experiencing many crises and is often a stranger to himself. He is a strange mixture of boy and man. The entire direction of his future depends upon choices that are made, and wise choices are determined by the degree to which he understands himself. Wise counsel by sympathetic and understanding teachers and counselors can be of great help at this time.

MEASUREMENT OF SELF-UNDERSTANDING

By its very nature the self-concept is so private and deep that it probably cannot be completely communicated to others. Attempts are made, however, to disclose this core of the student's personality so that guidance may be based on the individual's "reality."

Autobiography

The autobiography has been previously mentioned as a device for developing realistic self-pictures, but it is also used for disclosing the self-concept. Through these life stories the student may tell how he sees himself and how the world looks to him. This instrument has especial value because it can be adapted for use at nearly all grade levels and is easily related to the regular work of the classroom. By examining a student's autobiography, the teacher may assess the extent of the understanding which the student has of himself.

Interview

Perhaps the most useful method for disclosing the individual's level of self-understanding is the interview. If we give students a chance to talk in a nonthreatening atmosphere, they will tell us much about themselves, and in the process they may be helped to clarify what they really think and believe. The feelings of the student will be expressed to his and our benefit if we but take time to listen.

Scales and Check Lists

There are a variety of scales and check lists on the market which are sometimes used to help teachers and counselors understand the self-concept of their students. For the most part these instruments are not standardized tests but research devices which are still in the developmental stages.

Teachers may want to construct their own lists of incomplete sentences to be completed by the student. Such "stubs" as the following may be useful: I am . . . ; People say that . . . ; I get nervous when . . . . These approaches should not be thought of as clinical tools but merely as stimuli which may help the student to clarify what he thinks about himself. Lists of adjectives are also used for this purpose. The student is presented with a list of flattering and damaging descriptive terms and asked to underline the ones which he thinks apply to him. So used, devices of this kind may provide us with gross measures of the student's concept of himself.

APPLICATION OF THE SELF-CONCEPT IN GUIDANCE: THE CASE OF JOHN

To see the value of the self-concept as an aid in understanding students, let us examine the case of John M.

John's Family

The M. family consists of

Mother:	Helen, age 36
Father:	Robert, age 40
Stepfather:	Alfred, age 37
Girls:	Audrey, age 17
	Susie, age 8
Twin boys:	Harry and John, age 15

The family lives in a semirural district in the South. Their home is in a lower-class neighborhood near a section which has no sidewalks, electricity, gas, or inside toilets. John's home is in an area only slightly higher on the socioeconomic scale.

John lives in a small house with a tiny yard in front and a large yard in back. A small cement walk leads from the pavement through the yard to a stoop a few inches higher than the ground.

The front door opens into the parents' bedroom. This room contains a bedroom suite and has a linoleum rug on the floor. Off this room is a small living room with a bright blue, heavy, over-stuffed sofa, two armchairs, two cigarette stands, a television set, and a linoleum rug. A stairway leads upstairs to two bedrooms and a bath which is as large as an ordinary room. Beyond the living room is an immaculately attractive kitchen, with a porcelain break-fast set, gas stove, electric washing machine, electric refrigerator, and electric clock. (How might living in this neighborhood and home affect John's self-concept?)

According to the mother, the children have not always been well. All have had the usual childhood diseases—measles, chicken pox, whooping cough. Mrs. M. says that John's twin brother has been through the Cardiac Public Health Clinic, though nothing was found to be wrong. According to the mother, however, he has had rheumatic fever and several heart attacks.

John's stepfather is a sheet-metal worker. He formerly con-tributed to the support of his children from a previous marriage—an older boy, now enlisted in the Navy, and a younger one, who has been committed as a delinquent to an industrial school for boys.

The family attends a Protestant church; John goes to Sunday school, but only under protest, because he cannot go out to play on Sunday unless he does. He does not belong to any organized youth groups of the church.

Neither John's father nor his stepfather completed elementary school, and his mother stopped two months before graduating from high school.

The status of the family in the community is not high. The boys have a reputation for fighting. When neighbors complain, the boys are protected by their mother, who in turn gives the complain-ing neighbor a tongue lashing. Some of these parents have threat-ened to give John a beating and say they are willing to pay a fine for doing so. (How might his mother's reaction to criticism affect John's self-concept?)

Father's Family

Robert M., John's father, was born in a Southern city. He was one of five children whose parents were poor, hard-working people who lived in rather meager surroundings. None of the children completed elementary school, and all have been married and divorced. He is an enlisted man in the Navy and is stationed in Florida at present. After his divorce from John's mother he remarried and has children by his second marriage. He contributes to the support of John and his brother and sisters.

Mother's Family

John's mother is an only child and was born in the same Southern city. Her father was born in Pennsylvania and was an enlisted man in the Navy. He had studied two years for the ministry before he joined the Navy. He retired from the Navy after twenty years' service and then worked at the Naval Academy for many years. He was held in high esteem by his associates. He built a five-room home in a desirable residential section and was very proud of it; he worked diligently to keep the surroundings neat. He was very well read, and it was said that he knew his Bible from "beginning to end."

The father was very severe with his daughter and would not let her entertain her friends at the house. He expected very exceptional work scholastically. He bought a piano for her musical training and also encouraged her work in art. He would not allow her to attend any social gatherings where boys would be invited, so she began meeting boys on street corners without the knowledge of her parents. When this happened, the father realized that he had been too strict, and he tried to remedy the situation; but it was too late because the kind of company that he wanted his daughter to keep would not now accept her as a desirable companion.

John's grandmother was one of several children of a family which was held in high esteem in the community, and she enjoyed a pleasant childhood and marriage. Upon the retirement of her husband they enjoyed a good reputation until the daughter started "running wild."

Since the death of John's grandfather, his grandmother has turned to drinking as did her husband before his death. At the present age of fifty-eight she is well known in ill-reputed taverns. (How might his grandmother's behavior affect John's self-concept?)

Family Culture Pattern

During the first year of his first marriage, John's father began to drink. This behavior continued over a period of five years during which time he did not support the family; there was naturally much strife in the home. Due to their low income they were forced to move quite frequently, and each home was less desirable than the last one.

The mother and father separated soon after the birth of Susie; the mother went to work, and the children were left with the grandmother during the day. According to the mother, the children "ran wild" at this time.

When the parents were finally divorced, the mother kept on working until her marriage to her second husband. During this second marriage the family has lived in several lower-class sections of the city. They have no automobile or telephone. (How might such a family background affect John's self-concept?)

John Himself

John is a healthy fifteen-year-old boy whose appearance is generally neat. His school records tell us little about him except for an occasional comment from a teacher.

Third grade. "John is very trifling. He seems to think he is very funny. He should put more time on his work."

Sixth grade. "John gives up very quickly. If he makes a mistake, he doesn't try again. He needs to stick to his work every minute. Am pleased with his attitude. John needs some help at home on his tables."

The comment in this last grade is very interesting because in the fifth grade John was suspended from school for telling a teacher to "Take your damn hands off of me." The teacher was attempting to force the boy into his seat after a rather wild exhibition in the classroom. There is also evidence of John's frequently getting in trouble for infraction of school regulations. On many occasions he has indicated an utter contempt for school and everything pertaining to it.

In an interview John listed the following hobbies: fishing,

crabbing, woodworking. He said that at one time he belonged to the YMCA but quit because he did not like the leader. His employment experiences to date include a one-year job delivering milk and another assisting a truck driver for an oil company. His present stated occupational preferences are movie-machine operator, fisherman, and sailor.

The subjects that he says he likes best are arts and crafts, athletics, arithmetic, and spelling. Although he has average intelligence (IQ range from 85 to 98), he is two years retarded in reading.

A friendship sociogram revealed that John was selected two times by boys whom he did not select and rejected by the six boys that he selected.

John's mother says that he is a problem at home. When questioned about receiving help from the family with his studies, John declares that he is rejected by them because of his inability to understand his school assignments. He says he is "too dumb to learn." (How might his school status have affected John's self-concept?)

Given John's family, community, and school experiences, what might we expect his self-image to be, and what behavior can we predict? In studying the case of John, we should remember that the attainment of a life that is really successful and satisfying depends upon the development of an understanding of the self. This is a major goal of education and especially of guidance. A study of the home and the community will be of great assistance in understanding conditions that influence or even determine this self-concept. The improvement in conditions in the home and the community is one of the most valuable methods of influencing the development of satisfactory and effective self-concepts in youth.

SUMMARY

If we wish to understand a student, we must consider not only how he appears to adults and to his peers but how he appears to himself. Every individual lives in a world that is his own, that is different from anyone else's world, and that represents reality to him. The self-concept—the picture that a person has of himself—is the key to understanding his behavior, for we all do the things which are consistent with the notions which we have about ourselves.

Our self-concept may be congruent with social reality, or it may be distorted. To help people develop healthy self-concepts we must make them understand themselves, understand their world, and accept themselves with all their strengths and weaknesses. We do this by giving them information about themselves and the world and by providing a situation in which they feel free to examine their feelings and beliefs without pressure or threat.

Although one person can never completely know how another views himself and his world, we may approach such knowledge by techniques like the interview and the autobiography. When we attempt to apply our knowledge of another to explain and predict his behavior, we may want to take special account of his self-concept.

As we said before, it is impossible to overestimate the importance of self-understanding. Here, then, is a major goal of education: the development of clear, well-formulated, and realistic self-concepts.

EXERCISES

1. Ask someone to give ten different answers to the question "Who am I?" Do these answers give you any clues as to the way he views himself? What do you see as the values and dangers of such an assignment in helping you to understand a student?

2. In what ways was your self-concept different during your adolescence from what it is now? How do you account for these changes, and what do they suggest regarding the value of the self-concept as an aid in understanding youth?

3. Much research is being done on the self-concept. Read an article dealing with some aspect of this problem and summarize it for class presentation. (Such articles are most apt to be published in *Journal of Counseling Psychology*, *The Personnel and Guidance Journal*, *Journal of Abnormal and Social Psychology*, and *Journal of Consulting Psychology*.)

REFERENCES

Combs, Arthur W., and Donald Snygg: *Individual Behavior*, Harper & Brothers, New York, 1959.

Leary, T.: *Interpersonal Diagnosis of Personality*, The Ronald Press Company, New York, 1957.

Rogers, Carl R.: *Client-centered Therapy*, Houghton Mifflin Company, Boston, 1951.

Rogers, Carl R., and Rosalind F. Dymond (eds.): *Psychotherapy and Personality Change*, University of Chicago Press, Chicago, 1954.

Wylie, Ruth C.: *The Self Concept*, University of Nebraska Press, Lincoln, Neb., 1961.

PART III

INFORMATION ESSENTIAL FOR
EFFECTIVE GUIDANCE

CHAPTER 4

ACHIEVEMENT AND APTITUDE TESTS

Effective guidance is dependent upon accurate and comprehensive information about the individual. The school is the chief agency upon which we must depend for securing this information and for interpreting it to parents and to the child. The three most important reasons for this are as follows: (1) Children and youth are in school for most of the time during the period of physical and mental development. (2) The school is the only agency established by law whose duty it is to gather and organize this information. (3) Every member of the school staff is required by law to secure training in methods of interpreting this information to parents and to the child. Although there is much room for improvement in this preparation, the school is performing a truly remarkable service in this area of its responsibility.

One of the chief sources of information about students is found in tests. A test may be roughly defined as a device for the determination of the presence or absence, quality or quantity of a trait, characteristic, ability, habit, skill, or knowledge. It is a group of carefully selected samples of the work that an individual might be presumed to be able to do more or less effectively in different stages of his development. Tests may be oral or written. They may be observation of an activity or inspection of the product of an activity, such as a problem in mathematics, an essay, a loaf of bread, a painting, a sewing table, or a jump. Tests are used to estimate capacity as well as actual attainment at any given time; they reveal both deficiencies and strengths. They provide efficient ways of securing data on the educational, social, physical, and economic attainments of individuals. They help to find whether an individual is ready for a certain job, for promotion in school, for entrance to college, or for membership on a football squad or some other type of activity.

ACHIEVEMENT TESTS

Achievement tests are used to find what has been learned, that is, what habits and skills have been developed after a period of study or exercise. They are valuable as a means of determining to what extent the individual has attained a certain degree of progress toward a desirable goal, whether he is ready to undertake the next step, and how his attainment compares with that of other members of his group.

Teacher-made Achievement Tests: Values and Limitations

There are two general types of tests given in the schools: tests made by teachers and standardized tests; each has its own value. At best, teacher-made tests may be better adapted to the needs of the pupil and the goals of the local school. Too often, however, they are hastily constructed and badly worded and have no really definite purpose. In the same examination there may be questions requiring mere memory or skill and others requiring judgment. This makes it difficult to determine what particular objectives have been attained. The results of such tests cannot be compared with the results of tests given by other teachers. Some mathematics teachers grade tests entirely on the correctness of the answer, while others consider the method and the reasoning of the pupil in reaching the conclusion. Another factor that often causes differences in the mark is the appearance of the paper; a neatly typed paper usually receives a higher mark than one that is slovenly, dirty, or difficult to read. Still another variable is that some teachers tend to read "between the lines" and give a good or well-liked pupil the benefit of the doubt, thus giving him credit for what he "meant but did not say." For these and other reasons teacher-made tests usually lack "reliability." Reliability, when used with regard to tests, refers to the accuracy of the results, that is, the degree of consistency obtained between repeated measurements of the same individual.

Such tests may also lack "validity." Validity, in this context, refers to the extent to which tests measure what they purport to measure.

The author once tried an experiment in a university to determine the reliability of a nonstandardized test scored by five members of the department of mathematics. An algebra examination was mimeographed and a copy given to each member of the department for grading with the instruction not to compare notes beforehand. The results were rather startling. There was little consistency in the marks given. The nearest agreement had a difference of nearly fifteen percentile marks. If the student's entrance to college depended on the judgment of one of the instructors, he would have been refused admission; if it depended on another, however, he would have been accepted.

Although most of the tests given by teachers are the essay type, an increasing number are the so-called "new type" that require little writing and can be "objectively" scored. The teacher-made tests are often just as effective as the standardized tests of the same type in revealing achievements and weaknesses of pupils, and they should not be condemned. The results cannot, of course, be compared with those achieved by students in other classes or other schools. Neither can we rule out the essay type of test as being ineffective. Some things that are very important to know about pupils can be revealed better by well-constructed essay type of tests than by standardized tests. Nor can we eliminate from consideration the subjective judgments of capable, well-trained teachers who know their pupils and who can, through this knowledge, interpret their written, and often imperfect, expressions. In addition these judgments often give reliable evidences of the abilities and progress of students.

Values of Standardized Achievement Tests

In a standardized test each question is arranged so that the answers are always scored in the same way and a definite length of time is allotted in which to complete the test. The explanations and directions that are to be given by the teacher or the test administrator are always the same, and definite, detailed directions for scoring the tests are given. Stencils are often used for marking. Such tests are the result of much experimentation, and no test is marked until it has been very carefully revised after many trials. The wording of the questions is selected after various formulations have been tried out in actual examinations. No grades are given on these tests; comparative scores only are used. The results are standardized by collecting the answers from thousands of cases in different parts of the country. They are tabulated, and standards or norms for each grade are constructed. By means of these standards the achievements of pupils in one grade and school can be compared with those in other grades and schools. Such standard tests are now a part of the regular equipment of our elementary and secondary schools.

In the past fifteen years there has been a phenomenal increase in the number and variety of standardized tests. There now are several tests in every school subject for every grade in the elementary and secondary schools and in college. Among these are batteries of tests which include different areas or phases of the same subject, such as silent and oral reading, verbal and abstract reasoning, arithmetic manipulation, solution of problems, and logic. Tests such as these have been used in determining admission to college, in discovering educational attainments of children and youth, and in diagnosing academic weaknesses and strengths.

Limitations of Standardized Achievement Tests

Several weaknesses and limitations have come to light in the indiscriminate use of the results of standardized achievement tests. One weakness is that they do not measure all the desirable outcomes in any subject. No effective standardized tests have yet been devised for the adequate examination of aesthetic appreciation, power to organize, initiative, leadership, or character. Some tests attempt to measure such factors indirectly and are undoubtedly very helpful, but they are acknowledged to be ineffective instruments on the whole for this purpose.

When pupils are given standardized tests and their achievement scores taken as the measure of success of their work and also of the success of the teacher, undue emphasis may be placed on the particular elements that are tested, to the neglect of other equally important factors which may not lend themselves to testing. There is also great danger that in their teaching, teachers will also place the main emphasis on the formal testable elements because these are the ones stressed in the test and neglect other elements that are often of greater importance. When this happens, the educative process is greatly weakened.

Another danger is that of uniformity. Curriculum builders are tempted to put in the curriculum the subject matter that is included in the tests, and since the same tests are used in all parts of the country, the subject matter tends to be uniform and not sufficiently responsive to the special needs of different localities.

There is also a tendency to use the norm as a measure of desirable and undesirable achievement. To be below the norm is to fail or to be unsatisfactory; to be at the norm is satisfactory; and to be above the norm is worthy of praise. But the student who ranks below the norm may be doing work that, for him, is excellent; and the one who is above the norm may be harming himself physically or developing unsocial habits—or he may be copying his answers from a friend who sits near him. The rank of any individual in a test should be considered in relation to his ability, his health, and his other personal needs. A standardized test can only tell us what a group has done, not what it should have done. Furthermore, it is sometimes forgotten that a norm is an average score, and like all averages, it must by definition have as many children scoring below it as above it.

Use of Achievement Tests in Guidance

The values of achievement tests for guidance are many. Any accurate instrument by means of which we can compare the achievement of one person with that of others, with the averages of groups in widely different sections of the country, and with his own previous achievement will be of great help in the diagnosis of his weaknesses and strengths. School progress can be measured, the need for remedial measures determined, and the entire program of the school improved. An arithmetic test may help diagnose whether the weakness of a given pupil is in the fundamental operations, in decimals, in the analysis of the problem, or in carelessness. Tests may show that the cause of failure in physics was due to difficulty in understanding the meaning of the question or weakness in arithmetical computation. French tests have shown whether the difficulty was a weakness in knowledge of vocabulary or in grammatical terms. Such tests, if properly used, help in securing definite data by which improvements can be made. Standardized tests enable us to learn the points of weakness and of strength.

APTITUDE TESTS

Aptitude has been defined by Bingham as a measure of the probability of the success of an individual, with training, in a certain type of situation—a job, in school, or in such activities as playing the violin or learning a language. Traxler called aptitude a condition, a quality, or a set of qualities which is indicative of the probable extent to which an individual may be able to acquire, under suitable training, some knowledge, understanding, or skill. In other words, it is a present situation that indicates the potentialities for the future. An aptitude is not an ability, but it helps to predict the probable development of certain abilities. A test of aptitude may reveal abilities as well as skills, but the significance of the test is in revealing *potential* abilities and skills.

An aptitude is not inborn; it is a combination of inborn capacities and developed abilities, skills, etc., that makes the person what he is at any given time and predicts what he may become. The terms "achievement," "ability," and "aptitude" are often used synonymously, but they have differences in meaning which are important to keep in mind in the discussion of types of tests. Achievement looks to the past; it indicates what *has been done*. Ability is concerned with the present; it indicates the combination of skills, habits, and powers which an individual *now has* and which enables him to do something. Aptitude looks to the future and, on the basis of the habits, skills, and abilities that an individual now has, predicts what he, with training, *may become* and what success he may have in a given occupation or position.

Relationship to Intelligence Tests

The tests described here as aptitude tests include some that formerly were called "intelligence tests." This term has been largely discarded because the meaning of "intelligence" is often misunderstood and because, even when it is defined as "the ability to solve new problems or to meet successfully new situations," it is very difficult to find problems or situations to include in the test which are equally new to all. An interesting illustration of this dilemma was found in experience with the Army Alpha test that was used with the armed forces in World War I. It was discovered that the scores of women who took this test were, on the average, lower than those of men. This led to the "unfortunate" statement that women were inferior to men in intelligence. But when the problems and situations used in the tests were analyzed, it was found that they had been chosen because they were within the experience of most men but less familiar to women. When this bias was eliminated, the scores of women compared favorably with those of men.

The establishment of the validity of aptitude tests is a difficult task. Ideally we might like to use the tests to predict who will be successful in an activity, but the problem of determining the qualities and characteristics of a "successful" person is a very difficult one. Two people considered to be equally successful in the same type of occupation may be very different in character and in types of ability. The problem then is to determine what makes them both successful.

There are two approaches to the solution of this problem. One is to study successful people in a certain occupation and formulate descriptions of them in terms of general abilities that they all have. The other approach is to analyze occupations and find the different activities, skills, attitudes, and abilities essential to a satisfactory performance. Among the types of test representing the first approach, that of general ability, are the following: academic or scholastic aptitude, social intelligence, clerical aptitude, musical talent, and artistic ability. Tests of this kind are now available representing several hundred different occupations. The second approach has resulted in several types of tests based on the concept of "factor analysis." Each general ability, like intelligence, is considered to be made up of certain, more or less separated or different, factors. By the statistical process of factor analysis these clusters or factors are identified, and tests are designed to measure them in the most efficient fashion. Such tests are generically known as "multifactor" tests. Some very helpful tests of this type have been constructed and are being used extensively.

Examples of Aptitude Tests

It is not possible or desirable within the limits of this book to describe in detail all the tests that are used in securing useful information about pupils. These are treated in detail, and more authoritatively than could be done here, in research reports, monographs, journal articles, and books entirely devoted to tests and measurements.

The General Aptitude Test Battery (GATB), which was developed by the United States Employment Service, is intended to give information useful in the prediction of success in different occupations or fields of work. The GATB yields the following ratings: G—Intelligence, V—Verbal Aptitude, N—Numerical Aptitude, S—Spatial Aptitude, P—Form Perception, Q—Clerical Perception, K—Motor Coordination, F—Finger Dexterity, and M—Manual Dexterity.

These tests are used very extensively and have proved to be helpful in many cases. There is a difference of opinion regarding the accuracy of their prediction for success on the job. Some authorities believe that they are better for prediction of success *in training* than for success on the *actual job*. They seem to differentiate between certain types of occupations but not between others: for example, they do not differentiate between physicians and engineers, but they do differentiate between these occupations and those of draftsmen and technicians. If the subscores of the GATB are combined, an estimate can be made regarding the student's aptitude for the job under consideration. Many schools have made arrangements with their state employment service to make this test available to their students.

Another such test is the Multiple Aptitude Test (MAT) published by the California Test Bureau. This test yields the following subscores: Verbal Comprehension (word meaning, paragraph meaning, language usage), Perceptual Speed (language usage, routine clerical ability), Numerical Reasoning (arithmetic reasoning, arithmetic computation), and Spatial Visualization (applied science and mechanics, spatial relations—two dimensions, spatial relations—three dimensions). The MAT has been used more for educational guidance than for vocational placement and is typical of the newer multifactor tests.

There are many other kinds of aptitude test. Perhaps the most important are those that are concerned with help given in the choice of an occupation. This help requires a study of the occupation to find the abilities, skills, and personality traits which seem necessary for success and then the construction of a test to find out whether the individual has, or can develop, these characteristics. This process of matching the requirements for success with the traits and potential development of the individual will be discussed in detail in a later chapter on vocational guidance.

Values of Aptitude Tests

An examination of the "aptitude" tests clearly shows that many of them are not tests of aptitude as defined by most authorities. They test for the possession of abilities only and not for readiness to acquire ability or for the various personality and emotional factors that are so important to success on the job. It is very difficult to arrive at any conclusion regarding the accuracy with which prediction may be made on the basis of these tests. Some reasons for this are as follows:

1. Most tests do not measure all factors important for success and do not consider the relationships between factors, that is, the pattern of factors.

2. Those who seek to evaluate the tests differ regarding the criteria used for success on the job. Some consider only the ability to hold the job; others, production rates; and still others, such various factors as interest, effort, personality.

3. The weight attached to various factors in efficiency rating may differ with the investigator.

4. Many tests make no attempt to find the extent to which the factors tested are really crucial on the job.

5. The range of potential ability of groups tested varies greatly.

6. The statistical measures used to express the accuracy of prediction are fairly satisfactory for groups but quite unsatisfactory when applied to individuals.

From the above it seems evident that the study of aptitudes must, in the future, proceed on a more individual and clinical basis than is true at present and employ methods that will reveal the integration of the various factors rather than each factor separately. Aptitude for any task consists of a constellation of factors. An adequate aptitude test would be one that would measure all the factors necessary for success; this goal is practically impossible. The complete determination of aptitude for any job would require tests of specific abilities, personality, general mental ability, observations by skilled observers, and mental and physical records. Emphasis should be given not to weaknesses and to lack of abilities so much as to strengths and to presence of abilities.

The estimates of the accuracy of these tests for purposes of prediction vary greatly with the authority making them. Some claim a very high degree of accuracy, others are more modest and restrained. Taking all the facts into consideration, we are probably safe in saying that the tests are helpful if used with care and in connection with other data. Practically all of them are very useful in group prediction. If registrars or directors of admission of colleges or vocational schools wish to reduce the number of probable failures among those who enter, they would be quite justified in making their selection on the basis of some of these tests; there would most certainly be failures among those admitted, but not so many as with random selection. In any case there would still be many excluded who would have been successful.

Aptitude tests that are reasonably valid for workers on the job may not be valid for guidance into an occupation; aptitudes for work cannot adequately be determined on the basis of success in or aptitude for success in the training program.

Aptitude tests of various kinds are used extensively in secondary schools and colleges as helps in counseling students regarding choice of occupation and in commerce and industry for placement of individuals in jobs suitable to them. They are very intensively used in secondary schools to assist in admission to college. Such college admission tests may be useful in indicating areas of strength and weakness in students, thereby helping in the selection of courses or curriculums in high schools and colleges and suggesting the need for remedial work. Primarily, however, college admission tests are used to identify the important factors in determining admission to and success in college. They are most likely to be given in the last two years of high school. The scores in these tests, together with the rank in the test scores and in class and the recommendation of the school, are the determining factors for admission in a large number of colleges.

There is a great difference of opinion regarding the predictive value of these tests for determining admission to college. Some colleges rate them very high and practically require them for admittance. They also advocate their use in high school for selecting different courses, such as courses for those who plan to major in mathematics or science or in literature or languages. Other authorities, admitting that they are valuable in reducing college risks, feel that they often eliminate many who have such qualities as high potential for leadership and who would be greatly helped by college training but who may lack some of the elements stressed in the tests. The tests emphasize the ability to do the work required in college, but they neglect the even more important elements that indicate the sane and progressive leadership in society which we have a right to expect in college graduates. For this reason many colleges are asking secondary-school principals to report on evidences of leadership, attitudes, participation in extracurricular activities, and other contributions to school life. No doubt this practice is sometimes used primarily to justify securing star athletes who will bolster up the college prestige in football, but even this goal has some possible merit.

Limitations of Aptitude Tests

The limitations of aptitude tests are generally well understood by those who construct them but not always by those who attempt to interpret and use them. Great care should be taken in the interpretation of these tests, and no one who is not trained should attempt to explain the results to students.

One obvious limitation of these tests is that the physical, social, and emotional environment when the test is taken is often different from that on the job or in college. The general atmosphere in college or on the job may and often does contain elements so different as to reduce materially the predictive value of the test. Predictions of success in college based on these tests fail because, for example, college students are forced to study in the midst of the noise and interruptions that freshmen usually have when there are two or more housed in the same room. It is often said of a successful housewife that her success is due to her ability to fulfill her many obligations in spite of, or in the midst of, constant interruptions—the incessant ringing of the telephone, the call for help from her small children, the care of the dog or the cat at the time when some important duties demand her attention. It would be an interesting experiment to administer a college admission test in such a way that there would be frequent interruptions instead of ordered silence and see what would happen. A test so given might measure the prospective student's ability to study *in the environment* which he will have.

Another comment on the use of these tests for admission to college is that they are especially useful when dealing with groups but not so useful when dealing with individuals. One can select with great accuracy the group in which most of the good prospects lie; that is, the college can reduce materially the risks of failures by choosing those who are near the top, but one cannot be sure that all these will succeed. It is also probable that there are a few in the lower group who will make good students, although most of them will fail.

We must not forget that an aptitude test gives us a prediction of the probability only; there is never any certainty of prediction when we are dealing with human beings. Some students who are high in the scholastic aptitude test have failed in college, and some who are below the standards set for admission, but who, for various reasons, were admitted, attained satisfactory standings.

Recognizing the limitations of the tests now used for admission to college, the College Entrance Examination Board is conducting experiments to discover more effective factors for use as criteria for admission to college. Less emphasis is being placed on scholastic aptitude and more on what is called "developed abilities." Aptitude is considered to indicate or measure the probability of developing the abilities necessary for success. This probability (aptitude) remains relatively constant, whereas ability changes and develops. The factor that is most important in college admission is whether the applicant *now* has the ability to do college work. Emphasis is placed on the depth of understanding and the ability to apply knowledge and principles to the solution of problems. There is less concern with factual knowledge and more with evidence of mature thinking. One committee working to improve testing in social studies has identified five aptitudes that it considers important to measure: (1) Ability to recall basic facts and terms; (2) ability to perceive relationships among facts or concepts; (3) ability to draw inferences when the factual knowledge is given; (4) ability to draw inferences when understanding and information from the student's background must be applied to the problems presented in the test;

and (5) ability to reveal understanding and knowledge in clear and coherent language.

Another study aims to construct instruments capable of measuring a college's psychological and social environment, which is a part of its "culture." Colleges differ in the nature of their culture, and these differences may be important elements in the success of the student. Because the culture and social character of the home and community from which the student comes is also different, the culture of one college may be better suited to one student than to another. The nature of the relationship between college and home culture and its effect on success is not now known, but in the selection of a college a comparison of these two cultures would seem to be helpful.

THE USE OF ACHIEVEMENT AND APTITUDE TEST DATA
IN GUIDANCE: THE CASE OF HENRY

This fourteen-year-old boy is in the eighth grade of Hoover Junior High, where, at the end of the first semester, he has come to the attention of the counselor because he had many low marks on his report card: English—F, history—F, science—D, industrial arts —C, physical education—C, music—D.

Henry came to this school in the fall from the village of Clarien, 200 miles away. His personal data blank indicates that he has one brother, Joe, who is twenty, living in Clarien. His sister Mary is sixteen; another sister is two. Both live at home. His father is an auto salesman, and his mother does not work outside of home.

One week after Henry entered Hoover Junior High School, he disappeared from home and went to Clarien where his brother Joe lives. Joe, who is unmarried and who is an auto mechanic, allowed Henry to stay with him three days before he returned him to his home. Recently Henry told his parents that he hated school and that he intended to run away again and join his brother. This prompted his mother to call the principal and report the incident. She said, "Henry agreed to stay in school through the semester, but he insists that he doesn't like it. I hope you can find some way of helping him." (At this point what hypotheses do you have regarding Henry's poor marks?)

Henry missed three days just before Christmas vacation. When the nurse called at his home, she reported: "Henry was at home when I called. He had a slight head cold but no fever nor other signs of illness. He seemed to be in a depressed mood and obviously not very enthusiastic about school. It was difficult to get him to explain his attitude." His mother, who was home with Henry, did not appear much concerned over the situation. She dismissed the matter by stating that he would feel better after Christmas vacation and would probably be eager to get back to school.

Henry is quite careless about his appearance and usually prefers a faded gray coat, old corduroy trousers, and a shirt open at the neck. His red hair is slightly curly and always seems in a definitely rumpled condition.

It appeared that Henry needed someone to help him, and an appointment was arranged with the counselor. Some of the notes which the counselor made during his first interview with Henry are as follows:

> Likes to read about the care and protection of animals. Often wishes he could equip a chemical laboratory of his own at home. Remarked: "I'd like to go into animal husbandry if I could get the training."
>
> Stops occasionally at city library on way home from school and reads *Popular Mechanics* and books on wildlife and on the breeding of fine horses. Wants to travel, "just anywhere, but mainly to South America." Wants to go simply because "it would be educational." "School just doesn't get me anywhere; I'd criticize it, but I don't know what to put in its place."
>
> On social interests: Claims to prefer a few close friends but likes "most people." Finds it difficult to make a few close friends in a new school; worries somewhat because "the boys I'd like seem to be getting girl crazy. I don't think I understand girls."
>
> On recreation: As in earlier report, he mentions hiking and taking pictures as main choices. He has "a very ordinary camera," but hopes to buy a good one soon if he can "earn some money at odd jobs."
>
> Concerning siblings: Enjoys being with his older brother. Gets along well with his sisters except that "Margaret would be happier if I learned to dance and if I seemed more polite in society. It worries me some."
>
> Regarding his parents: "Everything is fine, only I guess

Mother isn't pleased with my schoolwork. Dad treats me fine—about like any boy's dad would treat him."

Preferences in school activities: Science experiments and geography. Wants to know more about nature study.

After explaining to Henry about the desirability of securing more information about him, the counselor arranged with the boy to take some tests. Here are some of the results:

Differential Aptitude Test	*Percentile*
Verbal Reasoning	50
Numerical Ability	85
Abstract Reasoning	93
Space Relations	80
Mechanical Reasoning	72
Clerical—speed and accuracy	15
Language Usage:	
Spelling	4
Sentence	8

The counselor next gave Henry an achievement test:

Iowa Every-pupil Tests of Basic Skills	*Percentile*
Silent Reading Comprehension—total	5
Reading Comprehension	2
Vocabulary	10
Work Study Skills—total	20
Map reading	60
Use of references	5
Use of index	3
Use of dictionary	3
Graphing	80
Basic Language Skills—total	5
Punctuation	3
Capitalization	5
Usage	10
Spelling	3
Basic Arithmetic Skills—total	60
Fundamental knowledge	75
Fundamental operations	50
Problems	65

With this information available, the counselor arranged for remedial work in reading and language for Henry in an effort to make school a more meaningful experience for him.

SUMMARY

The construction of standardized tests in achievement and aptitude and their wide use in schools and colleges as well as in industry have inaugurated a new era in guidance. This has been of great service in the improvement of teaching as well as in occupational choice and adjustment to the job.

Standardized tests are not intended to replace teacher-made tests since both have unique values. Standardized tests permit comparisons from one class to another, from one place to another, and from one time to another. If we wish to study a student's development, we will find the results of standardized tests most useful.

Achievement tests tell us what a student knows. Aptitude tests tell us his potential for learning more. While we separate these two kinds of tests for the purpose of discussion, they actually have much in common. A student's achievement may tell us about his aptitude, and his aptitude is usually indicative of his achievement. One way of describing the relationship between these types of test is to remember that achievement tests are apt to be concerned with a narrow—often school-centered—aspect of learning while aptitude tests are more apt to deal with a broader—life-centered—aspect of learning.

While the values of these tests have been shown, they do have limitations which should be kept in mind by all users.

EXERCISES

1. We do not have all the facts in the case of Henry, but we do know some things. You are asked, therefore, to indicate what you think of the following assumptions by putting the appropriate letter after each of the statements listed below.

Put a *W* if you consider an assumption to be definitely warranted by the data.

Put a *T* if you think an assumption seems tentatively supported;

the evidence is not conclusive, but it does, nevertheless, point in the direction of the assumption.

Put an *I* if you consider that there is insufficient evidence to justify an opinion one way or the other.

Put a *C* if you think that an assumption is contradicted by the evidence.

1. Home life unhappy
2. Friction between parents and children
3. Feeling of inferiority when compared with his older sister
4. Feels lost in new school
5. Concerned because he thinks his mother does not understand him
6. Worried over his own health
7. Is rejected by other boys of his age
8. Desires more attention from girls of his age
9. Physical immaturity interferes with his satisfactory social adjustment
10. Requires more help in adjusting socially to his new school environment
11. Lacks ability to do average eighth-grade work
12. Is lazy
13. Present school work is not "geared" to his main interests
14. Has more mental ability than is required to do the work of his present grade in school
15. Emotional instability is basic to his trouble

2. Study the case of Henry and comment on the tests that were given him. Are they adequate or inadequate for effective guidance? Could you suggest other types that would be helpful? What additional information about Henry would be helpful?

3. Secure a copy of an achievement test in your teaching field. Examine the items, and, by reference to your own beliefs regarding what should be taught in your subject area, discuss the validity of the test.

REFERENCES

American Personnel and Guidance Association: "Use of Multifactor Tests in Guidance," reprint from *The Personnel and Guidance Journal*, 1958.

Anastasi, Anne: *Psychological Testing*, The Macmillan Company, New York, 1961.

Buros, Oscar Krisen: *The Fifth Mental Measurements Yearbook,* Gryphon Press, Highland Park, N.J., 1959.

Goldman, Leo: *Using Tests in Counseling,* Appleton-Century-Crofts, Inc., New York, 1961.

Rothney, John W. M., Paul J. Danielson, and Robert A. Heimann: *Measurement for Guidance,* Harper & Brothers, New York, 1959.

CHAPTER 5

PERSONALITY ESTIMATES AND INTEREST INVENTORIES

Although there are many difficulties in testing achievement and aptitude, "testing" personality and interest is an even more complex task because of the indefiniteness of the concepts of "personality" and "interest."

Estimates of the probability of success in any line of work must take into consideration factors other than the specific ability to perform the various kinds of operations required by the job. Skills and abilities will always be important, but it is becoming apparent that other factors profoundly affect success in occupational life, in school, in social life, and in the performance of our obligations to society. Personal qualities and interests are fully as important as intelligence and technical skills.

MEANING OF PERSONALITY

It is generally accepted that an individual's personality is that core element which makes him different from all other people, but the nature and essence of that core element are a matter of dispute. Psychologists have not been able to agree on what constitutes personality. There are at least three somewhat different meanings in common use: (1) Personality is the combination of the physical and mental qualities, ideals, aspirations, ambitions, aptitudes, and interests that characterize a person. (2) Personality is the structure and pattern of the total behavior of the individual. (3) Personality is the social and psychological impact one makes on others.

Personality Means the Inner Sources of Behavior

From the first point of view personality is something that an individual has within himself that causes him to act in certain ways. It is the "inner" sources of his behavior, the causes of his conduct. From this point of view motives, ideals, purposes, and goals are of supreme importance as sources of actual behavior. Such a definition leaves personality necessarily hidden and unknowable. While this concept may be useful to those desiring abstract theoretical explanations of behavior, it makes any real measurements impossible.

Personality Means Characteristic Behavior

From the second point of view "inner sources" are not personality but important factors in determining future personality. They might be called "personality aptitudes." Personality is how one *behaves*. This is the popular meaning of personality. We say that the glamorous actress *has* personality; the ineffective teacher *lacks* personality. The term "split personality" has something of the same basic meaning. We also say that someone does not always *show* his personality to others, but, rather, his *true* personality is revealed only when conditions are favorable. He may seem to his business associates in the office to be cross, crabbed, and miserly, but when he leaves the office and gets home in the evening with his loved ones, he becomes genial, sympathetic, and generous. The advocates of this meaning are more and more including in "behavior" elements that are not visible to others, such as thoughts, plans, purposes, and even emotions. When these elements are included, there is little difference between this meaning of personality and the first one.

Personality Means the Social Consequence of Behavior

From the third point of view personality is thought of as one's effect on others. This definition has some merit, but, strictly speaking, how another person reacts to you indicates his personality, not yours. But, you say, since it is I who cause him to react as he does, it indirectly provides clues about my personality. It is, however, dangerous for anyone to infer his personality from the way another reacts unless he knows the kind of person the reactor is and unless it is the customary reaction of many people. It is easily possible that ten people might react in ten different ways to exactly the same thing that one says or does.

It will be generally agreed that in some way the Great Stone Face in Hawthorne's story was a very important factor in changing the wistful, undeveloped boy into the strong, self-reliant, influential man. From the first point of view regarding personality, it was the thoughts, ideals, and purposes that came to him when he gazed at the Stone Face which were his personality and which caused the change in his behavior. From the second point of view, his personality was constantly changing; that is, his behavior changed as he tried to make it correspond to his ideals and carry out his purposes. From the third point of view, the Great Stone Face, being a mere block of stone, could not be affected by the boy and therefore had nothing to do with his personality. His personality would appear in the reaction of members of his family or his friends and neighbors. In the story they thought of him as a dreamer, a queer fellow, possibly an idler. If we accept the third point of view, this was his personality.

The first concept is more effective by far than either of the others, for it makes personality a dynamic factor in development. It was not the negative reaction of his friends and neighbors nor the Stone Face itself that made him what he was as an adult; it was the ideals, purposes, and plans that came to him after observing the face, that is, something within himself, that made the change. No doubt hundreds of other boys of the same age looked again and again at the same Stone Face but had no such thoughts and ideals. The Great Stone Face was just an odd-shaped piece of stone to them.

"A primrose on the river's brim, a primrose was to him and nothing more." This meaning of personality, and the method of discovering it, described by Longfellow, is in many respects similar to various projective techniques for assessing personality. Each method presupposes that there is something within the person that causes him to react as he does and that his reactions will reveal his personality.

ESTIMATING PERSONALITY

Whether personality is considered to be "characteristic behavior" or the "inner sources" of such behavior, the only means of estimating it is by observing how the individual behaves in different situations, what he says, what he does, how he acts, that is, by his behavior. The instruments used for the appraisal of personality may be roughly divided into two classes, although some are quite interesting mixtures. One is the "atomistic" method, the other is called the "global" method. The atomistic method assumes that bits —atoms—of behavior may be added together to construct a total picture of personality. The global method believes that bits of behavior have no meaning in themselves and that only the totality should be examined.

The atomistic method seeks to get descriptions of an individual's behavior in all sorts of situations. Records of his behavior may be made by the individual himself or by others, such as his playmates, his fellow students, fellow workers, or by parents, teachers, or guidance specialists. The behavior reported may be in social occasions or in situations organized especially for the purpose of discovering significant traits and characteristics. Autobiographies and anecdotal records are often helpful in revealing behavior and sometimes indicate aspirations, attitudes, and beliefs unsuspected by others. Choices of leaders for homeroom, class, or school, for captains and managers of athletic teams are also helpful. It is now common practice for teachers to report characteristic behavior of students. Such estimates are required in the application for admission to college and to other types of educational institutions. They are also used in the Army and Navy for indicating fitness for promotion and fitness for group participation.

The global method seeks, often through projective devices, to assess the total personality. In this the individual is stimulated to project his personality into the test exercises which attempt to arouse responses that are a projection of the "inner self," of motives and personality traits that are usually hidden, often unsuspected by the individual himself. This global assessment may then be used to explain and predict behavior. Psychologists subscribing to this point of view are more interested in the dynamics of the meaning of behavior than in the overt acts themselves.

Scales Are Used in Estimating Personality

The use of scales in this regard is based on the belief that those who know a student well—teachers, peers, parents—may be able to contribute valuable information about his personality if they are helped to focus and systematize their observations and judgments. The forms used to guide observers who are estimating personality range from words or descriptions indicating desirable or undesirable traits to definite weighted scales for various items. They vary from small cards with short lists of traits to long, involved lists covering several pages and requiring extensive observation of the individual. Typical of forms used in personality estimating are the usual school report cards which include such items under the headings of "Character" or "Citizenship." The most common items are (1) cooperation, (2) initiative, (3) reliability, (4) promptness, and (5) neatness or orderliness. Sometimes the items are grouped under certain headings as "Social Attitudes" and "Work Attitudes," or "Traits Affecting Behavior," "Traits Affecting Learning," and "Traits Affecting Social Efficiency." In school reports the forms are likely to be characterized by descriptions of the traits listed, three or five degrees for each rating, cumulative records in order to show growth or change, and the requirement that teachers record only those traits that are very evident to them.

A report that has been used rather widely is the Personality Record of the National Association of Secondary-school Principals. This record, which is reproduced in Form 1, explains itself for the most part. Seven general traits are given and five spaces allotted for checking each trait; each of the five divisions or spaces is described by appropriate words or phrases. On the permanent record both the modal behavior and the variations in teacher rating are noted. This gives a much more complete and accurate picture than the modal rating alone, for it often shows variations in behavior with different teachers.

The Behavior Description of the Reports and Records Committee of the Progressive Education Association is an elaborate and comprehensive folder including record forms for each teacher, a permanent cumulative folder for each pupil covering the grades 7 to 12, and a manual of descriptions and directions for each teacher. The following headings of general types of behavior or traits are included: (1) Responsibility, Dependability; (2) Creativeness and Imagination; (3) Influence; (4) Inquiring Mind; (5) Open-mindedness; (6) Power and Habit of Analysis, the Habit of Reaching Conclusions on the Basis of Valid Evidence; (7) Social Concern; (8)

FORM 1   Personality Record of the National Association of Secondary-school Principals

PERSONALITY RECORD (CONFIDENTIAL)

Room...............
Grade...............

PERSONAL CHARACTERISTICS OF...............

Last Name   First Name   Middle Name

School............... Town or city............... State...............

The following characterizations are descriptions of behavior; they are not ratings. It is recommended that where possible the judgments of a number of the pupil's present teachers be indicated by use of the following method:

Example SERIOUSNESS OF PURPOSE

	1	M (5)		2
Purposeless	Vacillating	Potential	Limited	Purposeful

M (5) indicates the most common or modal behavior of the pupil as shown by the agreement of five of the eight teachers reporting. The location of the numerals to the left and right indicates that one teacher considers the pupil *vacillating* and that two teachers consider him *purposeful*. If preferred the subject fields or other areas of relationship with the pupil may be used to replace the numerals.

1. SERIOUSNESS OF PURPOSE	Purposeless	Vacillating	Potential	Limited	Purposeful
2. INDUSTRY	Seldom works even under pressure	Needs constant pressure	Needs occasional prodding	Prepares assigned work	Seeks additional work
3. INITIATIVE	Seldom initiates	Conforms	Varies with conditions	Self-reliant	Actively creative
4. INFLUENCE	Passive	Retiring but cooperative	Varying	Contributing	Strongly controlling

5. CONCERN FOR OTHERS

| Antisocial | Indifferent | Self-centered | Somewhat socially concerned | Deeply and generally concerned |

6. RESPONSIBILITY

| Unreliable | Somewhat dependable | Usually dependable | Conscientious | Assumes much responsibility |

7. EMOTIONAL STABILITY

| Hyperemotional / Apathetic | Excitable / Unresponsive | Usually well-balanced | Well-balanced | Exceptionally stable |

Significant school activities:

Special interests or abilities:

Significant limitations (physical, social, mental):

Additional information which may be helpful such as probable financial needs or work experience:

Principal's recommendation (specific statement concerning the applicant's fitness for acceptance):

Date.......... Signature.............................. Title..............

This Personality Record is available as a separate form, i.e., the Secondary-school Record is omitted, leaving one side blank.

FORM 2 Excerpt from Behavior Description of the Reports and Records Committee of the Progressive Education Association

Last name _____ First _____ Middle _____ School _____

BEHAVIOR DESCRIPTION*
(Experimental Form)

This report describes the characteristic behavior of the student in a number of important areas. *It should not be interpreted as a rating.* Instead one should read the descriptions and attempt to get from them an understanding of the person described, and of his fitness for particular opportunities and understandings.

Directions:

(1) In general the initials of subject or activity fields are used in the recording in order to identify the relations between the observers and the student. A complete key is given at the top of the folded over sheet.

(2) The spaces from left to right, being chronological, show the changes or continuity in behavior during the period covered by the record.

(3) While agreements in description may show a student's most common behavior, they may not be more important than an isolated judgment, which often has great significance because of a better basis for judgment, or because it indicates a response to some particular condition, field, or personality.

	Type	Grade 7	Grade 8	Grade 9	Grade 10	Grade 11	Grade 12
SOCIAL CONCERN							
Generally Concerned: Shows an altruistic and general social concern and interprets this in action to the extent of his abilities and opportunities	1						
Selectively Concerned: Shows concern by attitude and action about certain social conditions but seems unable to appreciate the importance of other such problems	2						
Personal: Is not strongly concerned about the welfare of others and responds to social problems only when he recognizes some intimate personal relationship to the problem or group in question	3						
Inactive: Seems aware of social problems, and may profess concern about them, but does nothing	4						
Unconcerned: Does not show any genuine concern for the common good	5						
EMOTIONAL RESPONSIVENESS							
To Ideas: Is emotionally stirred by becoming aware of challenging ideas	1						
To Difficulty: Responds emotionally to a situation or problem challenging to him because of the possibility of overcoming difficulties	2						
To Ideals: Responds emotionally to what is characterized primarily by its personal or social idealism	3						
To Beauty: Responds emotionally to beauty as found in nature and the arts	4						
To Order: Responds emotionally to perfection of functioning as it is seen in organization, mechanical operation or logical completeness	5						

* Used by special permission of the publisher.

Emotional Responsiveness; (9) Serious Purpose; (10) Social Adjustability; (11) Work Habits; (12) Physical Energy; (13) Assurance; (14) Self-reliance; (15) Emotional Control. In order to show the general features of the blank, the heading and several complete items are given in Forms 2 and 3.

FORM 3 Excerpt from Behavior Description of the Reports and Records Committee of the Progressive Education Association

A markedly high (H) or low (L) degree of the following behavior characteristics is shown by recordings in the appropriate spaces. No implication is assumed as to desirability or undesirability for the particular individual. Any qualifications or further comment should appear under General Comment.

			Grade 7	Grade 8	Grade 9	Grade 10	Grade 11	Grade 12
Physical Energy	Behavior in relation to vigor and endurance	H						
		L						
Assurance	Ability to meet situations and people easily	H						
		L						
Self-reliance	The habit of depending on one's self rather than on others	H						
		L						
Emotional Control	Ability to retain poise and self-control	H						
		L						
		H						
		L						

Use H (high), U (usual for age), or L (low) to indicate the success this student has had in dealing with
- Abstract ideas and symbols...
- People.....................
- Planning and management...
- Things and manipulation.....

General Comment: The following space is to be used for specific instances of behavior and for additional information that amplifies and synthesizes the description of the student.

Problem Check Lists Are Used for Estimating Personality

An important approach to the study of personality is the inventorying of the felt problems of students. Many teachers and counselors have made such lists and have found them very helpful in providing the opportunity to prepare for meeting the needs suggested therein. There are problem check lists which are available through commercial channels, and some schools have used them as aids in counseling or in surveying the concerns of the student body. For the second purpose they may be filled out anonymously. A problem check list or inventory consists basically of a list of problems which research has suggested are common to a population of the age being studied. The student doing the inventory indicates which of these problems are bothering him. Although a student, for a variety of reasons, may not be willing to admit that a problem is concerning him, these check lists, if interpreted properly, furnish interesting and helpful data for counselors. They may reveal unsuspected problems and, in many cases, their hidden causes. Their greatest value is as a basis for a counseling interview.

The conclusion regarding the personality of the individual based on information obtained from this type of inventory will depend upon the concept of personality held. If personality were considered to be characteristic behavior, all the responses would be carefully examined, and characteristic behavior would be inferred from this. The process would end there because the individual's characteristic behavior is his personality. If personality were considered to consist in his motives, attitudes, ideals, etc., the attempt would be to infer from his behavior what his ideals, attitudes, and motives would be, for they are his personality.

All the preceding attempts to uncover the personality of individuals approach the problem from what is called the atomistic point of view; that is, they attempt to find the elements that together constitute personality.

Projective Techniques Are Used for Estimating Personality

In contrast to the previous measurement techniques, the global approach to the appraisal of personality attempts to study personality as a whole. This method is often called the "projective" technique because the individual is stimulated to project his personality into the test exercises. The stimuli used in projective techniques attempt to arouse responses that are a projection of the "inner self"—of motives and personality traits that are usually hidden and often even unsuspected by the individual himself. The subject may be asked to respond to a series of pictures, ink blots, or similarly ambiguous stimuli. The interpretation of the responses re-quires a long period of training and should be done only by those who are specially qualified. Strictly speaking, every test may in-volve the projection of the self in some degree, but projectives rely more completely on the signs of the personality disclosed.

Autobiography and Other School-centered Techniques Are Used for Estimating Personality

The use of autobiographies for personality and interest esti-mates was quite common several years ago, but recently their use has fallen off considerably, although many counselors still consider them very valuable. One of the limitations of autobiographies lies in the possibility of unauthorized people reading them. Many stu-dents have a natural reluctance to reveal to others, especially adults, what they think and feel and what they really would like to be. This reluctance may be especially great if they suspect that the adult would disapprove of their goals or laugh at them. "A boy's will is the wind's will, and the thoughts of youth are long, long thoughts."

In spite of these and other limitations the autobiography may have many values. It aids in the interpretation of facts obtained by objective methods and permits the client to participate actively in the counseling process and in the development of self-understand-ing. The autobiography encourages the presentation of experi-ences too intimate to be revealed in a face-to-face situation by shy students. Most important for busy teachers, it is an easy method for recording information which might be imparted in an inter-view, but which the teacher might not have time to record ac-curately. It is invaluable in developing the longitudinal histories that are needed to supplement our cross-sectional techniques. Finally, autobiographies can be obtained in groups with a mini-mum expenditure of the time of the counselor or teacher. This guidance technique has much to recommend it, but it suffers, of course, from the reticence which characterizes many adolescents in their dealings with adults.

Because of this reticence, reliable information about the thoughts and the feelings of youth is usually best secured indirectly. Some teachers use a character in literature or history as topics of themes and ask students to discuss what sort of man he was, what his purposes and ideals were, what he liked and disliked, and in which respects was he a success and in which a failure. The student may reveal his own ideals and ambitions by what he finds in others. Another device used is to have students write themes on more personal experiences and reactions such as their goals and fears, what they really want in life, or the person in the community whom they admire most.

Sociometric devices which have been used in many schools with varying results are methods of determining friendship patterns and other social and psychological interaction in a group. These devices are difficult to construct and often not easy to interpret. One fundamental requirement is that the responses of individuals be kept confidential by the teacher or counselor. Types of questions like the following are used: "Who would be your choice to take the leading part in the school play?" "Who would you like most to be your partner in the laboratory experiments?" "What boy or girl would you like to have sit next to you in school?" "Who do you think would make the best captain for next year's football team?" "Who in your class seems to agree with everything that is proposed?" "Who always disagrees with what the majority wants?" The questions used should be those that are considered to be important by the group.

Such devices are useful in determining which students would be congenial as working companions for certain jobs. They are also helpful in finding the characteristics of individual students as determined both by their own responses and by the reaction of other students to them. Sociometric techniques have been very useful in the Army and Navy in organizing groups of men in airplane crews who are congenial when in close contact for many hours at a time. Anecdotal records also aid in disclosing personality because they give not only a definite description of the observed behavior but also a statement of the conditions and circumstances surrounding it. They may also include suggestions by the observer regarding the cause of the behavior or the use to be made of the trait revealed.

MEANING OF INTEREST

Closely related in both purpose and method to the personality estimates just described are the various interest finders or inventories now so extensively used. In fact, it is difficult to find any clear distinction between personality and interests because any adequate description of personality must include the interests of the individual—intellectual, physical, cultural, social, occupational, and recreational. Likewise, interests are closely related to aptitudes. Interests are elements in the total personality and aptitude patterns.

The term "interest" is rather loosely used in guidance, but it may be defined somewhat technically as a feeling of liking associated with a reaction, either actual or imagined, to a specific thing or situation. Since it is a feeling, it cannot be objectively measured or determined, for its presence or absence can be revealed only by the statement of the individual himself. Although there is no way by which this self-report can be completely validated, we can make estimates that are, for practical purposes, very helpful.

Interest May Be Extrinsic or Intrinsic

Psychologists classify interests as "extrinsic" and "intrinsic." Extrinsic interests are pleasurable emotions that are connected with the purpose or goal of an activity; intrinsic interests are those connected with the activity itself. Extrinsic interests may involve the solution of a problem, the successful completion of a task, a victory over others, or money, praise, etc. An intrinsic interest, which is centered on the activity itself, is a more basic or real interest. In many cases it is difficult to determine whether an interest is extrinsic or intrinsic. In playing golf intrinsic interests are involved in the pleasure of swinging the club, hitting the ball, walking in the fresh air, and talking with friends. Extrinsic interests are involved in hitting the ball where you want it to go, making a hole in one, making a score under 80, beating the other person, or winning money.

Each type of interest has its value. An extrinsic interest provides a constant incentive to continue an activity until the goal is reached even after pleasure in the activity itself is gone. This incentive may continue to operate throughout one's life. Competitive sports and nearly every other activity where competition is involved have extrinsic interest, but they also usually have intrinsic interest. One danger in connection with extrinsic interest is that the goal may be so artificial that, after it is reached, the interest is gone. Therefore worthwhile activities are better supported by intrinsic interests because the pleasure continues even if the goal is not reached. With the different types of instruments used in the discovery of interests it is often impossible to determine whether the interest revealed is intrinsic or extrinsic.

Successful Experiences May Develop Interests

There is a common belief that ability and interest are closely related and that one who has high ability in some activity will have a high interest in it, while one who has low ability will have a low interest. Observation indicates, however, that this relationship is not always present. A man may perform some job in which he has little interest, but he does it to make a living. On the other hand, one who has low ability in some activity may have a deep interest in it. The most important element in success is ability, not interest. Interest acts merely as a stimulant and does not ensure effectiveness of performance.

ESTIMATING INTEREST

There are three methods used in the attempt to discover the interests of people. The first method is to ask individuals what they like to do. This has some value, but answers to questions about interest may indicate only a very temporary interest, may come from the desire to please the one who is asking the questions, or may be based on the belief that certain occupations are higher than others on the social scale. The second method is to analyze the activities that a person performs. Nearly all cumulative records have spaces for indicating the interests of students as suggested by their extra-curricular and out-of-school activities. The difficulty with this method is that what one is doing may not be what he would like to do but what he has to do to make a living. All acts are not free choices. When this method is used, it should be restricted to those activities that have been freely chosen by the individual himself. The third method of measuring interest is by the use of interest tests and inventories. There are many instruments now in use, and the great majority of them deal with occupational interests.

Typical Instruments for Estimating Interests

Nearly all these instruments use some form of self-report or questionnaire and cover a wide range of interests. They vary in complexity, with the simplest merely giving a detailed list of occupations and asking the student to check those in which he is interested. The more complex instruments involve the analysis of activities common in different occupations and attempt to reveal the attitude of the student toward conditions surrounding various kinds of work. Regardless of their degree of complexity, they are all directed toward the location of occupational interests or preferences. Some attempt to determine interests in specific occupations or in the activities and conditions characteristic of occupations or of families of occupations. An example of this approach is the Kuder Preference Record. Other instruments attempt to assess personality factors considered to be important in various occupations. An example of this type of instrument is Strong's Vocational Interest Blank.

Although the methods used in the various blanks are fundamentally very similar, there are certain important differences. Some restrict the questions to the liking or disliking for certain types of activity and to the interest or lack of interest in different occupations; others include subjective estimates of degree of interest or ability, such as "How much do you like it? How good are you at it?" Still others attempt to find how much the individual knows about the occupation or activity.

One of the most widely used of the interest inventories is Strong's Vocational Interest Blank, which measures the extent to which one's interests are like those of successful men in a given occupation. In addition to the page of general information about the individual, the inventory is divided into eight parts as follows: (1) Occupations, (2) Amusements, (3) School Subjects, (4) Activities, (5) Peculiarities of People, (6) Order of Preference of Activities, (7) Comparison of Interest between Two Items, (8) Rating of Present Abilities and Characteristics.

The Kuder Preference Record is another widely used interest inventory in which the scores are based on answers to carefully worded questions indicating liking for various activities common in certain occupations. Occupations are grouped under nine general heads indicating areas of interest or preference: (1) Mechanical, (2) Computational, (3) Scientific, (4) Persuasive, (5) Artistic, (6) Literary, (7) Musical, (8) Social Service, (9) Clerical. The grouping of the occupations under the various heads is based upon the judgment of the author regarding the similarity of the activities listed in the scale to the known duties of the worker. This blank is intended to serve as a means of making a systematic approach to the problem of selecting an occupation. The specific aims of the record are considered to be:

1. Pointing out vocations with which the student may not be familiar but which involve activities of the type for which the student expressed preference

2. Checking on whether a person's choice of an occupation is consistent with the type of thing he ordinarily prefers

It is recommended that, after the individual's profile has been obtained, the occupations that seem to be indicated by the profile be discussed with him. The areas that are particularly high may be noted, and occupations thus indicated may be selected for further investigation. The author emphasizes the fact that the scores on the record should not be taken as evidence of ability. Evidence of ability must be obtained from other sources.

Limitations of Interest Inventories

Interest inventories have proved to be valuable instruments in locating general and special interests of secondary-school students, but they should be used with a clear understanding of their limitations as well as their values. Among the limitations are the following:

1. It is not possible to determine the accuracy of the statements made by the individual reporting his interests. Apparently the truth of the statements varies with the form of the question.

2. Although Strong has found patterns of interest that distinguish men from women and those engaged in certain occupations from those in other occupations and from "Mr. Average Man," there is considerable overlapping among the interests of these groups; therefore we cannot be certain that a given pattern is necessarily characteristic of a given occupation.

3. The interest of the adult worker in his activities may have been attained after he secured the job; he may not have had this interest when he was in school.

4. Meaningful interests of high-school students are, naturally, confined to those activities in which they have had experience actually or vicariously. Since one of our tasks is to broaden and create

interests, the interest of a student at a given time may not be indicative of what occupation he should choose.

5. Interests are not to be confused with abilities. A person may have an interest, superficial or deep, in some activity for which he has little ability. The converse is also true. Present interest does not necessarily predict success in the occupation.

6. Interests of high-school students may not be sufficiently permanent to warrant using them even as general indicators of occupational selection.

7. No satisfactory method has been developed for grouping occupations into "families" which represent similar activities. Radically different occupations may involve the same or similar activities. The important element in an occupation is often not merely the activity itself but the pattern of duties and responsibilities involved in that occupation.

8. The families, or patterns of interests, as found by Strong are not necessarily related to success in the occupation. They are the interests of those engaged in the occupation, but we do not know whether these interests are necessary for success in the occupation.

Values of Interest Inventories

Such inventories have value in that they require the pupil to review and analyze his interests and to find those occupations about which he knows very little and which he should investigate more fully.

The interests, the likes, and the dislikes revealed by these blanks are, in most cases, *real present* interests and as such have a great deal of value even though they are often not safe guides for the future choice of an occupation. These interests should be utilized by teachers and counselors as a means of widening and enriching the knowledge of the pupil and developing in him an understanding and appreciation of different types of occupational life.

Counselors who use the results of these interest inventories find that they are especially helpful as an introduction to the interview itself. The interest inventory helps the counselor understand the student and permits the counseling to start with a relatively non-threatening topic—the interests of the student.

USE OF PERSONALITY AND INTEREST IN GUIDANCE: THE CASE OF PEG

Personality and interest estimates prove their value only in specific guidance situations. Let us look at a girl, and as we study her case, we can consider whether personality tests or interest inventories would have been helpful to teachers attempting to work with Peg, to Peg herself, or to the counselor gathering information about Peg.

Peg's Background

Peg is a high-school junior who was adopted by a teacher. She is a fine example for study of "background versus heredity." Peg and her twin sister were adopted at the age of four months by a childless couple who gave them every advantage. Their mother, who died several days after their birth, had fourteen children. At five, their foster father died, and at that time their foster mother revealed to them that they were adopted. (Peg feels proud and fortunate to have been selected.)

The foster mother has acknowledged that the "balance wheel" of the family was removed with the death of her husband. She has been overambitious for her girls scholastically and feels that they have let her down. The girls know that they have fallen below their mother's expectations, and their attitude is a combination of shame and resentment. This summer the girls met members of their own family for the first time and learned that their real father, who is exceedingly poor, is rearing another family and drinks heavily. He was proud of his daughters when he met them. None of the rest of the family has turned out well. One brother is now AWOL from the Army. One of the sisters has had three illegitimate children. Peg feels fortunate to have escaped this sordid background.

Peg and her foster mother get along very well, and Peg seems very fond of her; but she does not live amicably with her sister, and they were finally given separate rooms. Peg's sister was recently dismissed from a private school and is now employed as a clerk. Peg, however, is eager to complete high school. Peg sings in the church choir, plays the piano quite well, enjoys movies and reading. She apparently has few or no dates.

Personality and Interest Data

After an interview with Peg the counselor made the following notes:

> Present subjects: Spanish—A, U.S. history—C, home art—C, chemistry—C, physical education—B. Regular attendance and no tardy marks. Favorite subjects: English, history, music. Least-liked subjects: math, chemistry. Member of the Dramatic Club. Hobbies: knitting, movies, reading. Belongs to: church choir, Job's Daughters, Tri Hi-Y. Reading: fiction. Magazines: largely movie magazines. Peg expresses an interest in music and drama. Employment experience: store clerk and beauty-shop helper. She likes the beauty-shop work best because "it is interesting. You meet an awful lot of nice people."

Additional information about Peg comes from a list of occupations which she made for a report in one of her classes:

Occupation	Reason for Interest
Nursing	It is a wonderful opportunity to help people.
Dramatics	I love to act.
Make-up artist	It is a wonderful way to meet various kinds of people.
Singer	I'd love to be able to sing well.
Write	I'd love to write.

Her present vocational choice is nursing. She made this decision about five years ago. Peg feels very certain that this is the career that she would want to follow, but adds that within a ten-year period she would like to be the mother of two children. She is especially interested in social-service work, and secondly, in occupations requiring special artistic abilities. On an adjective check list Peg characterized herself as being friendly, patient, stubborn, self-confident, quick-tempered, and cheerful. She also listed herself as being nervous and given to headaches but with no physical disabilities.

Outlook for Peg

Peg has read many books about nursing and is very interested in it. Her interest was first aroused when she was a patient herself several years ago. Her mother wants Peg to be a teacher or a hairdresser. She does not believe that Peg has the stamina to see a nursing course through to the end.

Peg has found out that she can be admitted on her present grades into a hospital in which she is interested and appears to be well acquainted with the rigorous life of a nurse.

The school adviser feels that Peg has a good chance of making a success of nursing. Peg has raised some questions, however, which suggest that her mind may not be completely made up. She wonders if her personality is one that would help or hinder her as a nurse. She has heard that some nursing supervisors and doctors are hard to work for and that a nurse has many bosses. Furthermore, she wonders if her interest in nursing would sustain her during the long and rigorous training.

As a school counselor, what are some things you could do to help Peg assess her personality and interests in a way that would help her decide if nursing would be a satisfactory goal for her?

SUMMARY

To most people personality means individuality—what makes an individual. Beyond this, there is little agreement on what constitutes personality, but there are three different meanings in common use.

1. Personality is the combination of all the physical, mental, and social traits, qualities, ambitions, aptitudes, and interests that characterize the individual.

2. Personality is the structure and pattern of the total behavior of the individual.

3. Personality is how the individual affects others.

The most common method used in assessing personality is observation by teachers, counselors, and fellow students. Similar methods and instruments are used in assessing the interests of students.

Most cumulative school records will have a section dealing with observed characteristics, and teachers may here record their observations and judgments about students. Similar observations are also used in business and industry in connection with the selection of workers and with promotion. This method may be called "atomistic" since it focuses on specific traits and, on the basis of the combination of these traits, some conclusion is reached regarding the personality of the student. Contrary to this is the global method that attempts to study the personality as a whole. Although neither method is completely satisfactory in describing the personality of individuals, they may be the basis for the development of instruments which would be useful in the hands of well trained and sympathetic counselors.

Interests are very important both for vocational choice and for useful and satisfying participation in the activities of the home and the community. With wise guidance, school life and community activities can be very effective tools in the development of interests that will lead to realistic occupational choices and satisfying life adjustments.

EXERCISES

1. One commonly used interest inventory classifies interest into six fields—personal-social, natural, business, mechanical, the arts, the sciences. From what you know about Peg, what two fields do you think would be her strongest interests? Why?

2. One commonly used personality measurement purports to describe the level of adjustment in four areas—home, health, social, emotional. How would you characterize Peg's adjustment in each of these areas? Why?

3. Read a research article making use of a personality test or an interest inventory, and be prepared to report to the class on the study. (Such articles are most apt to be found in *The Personnel and Guidance Journal, Educational and Psychological Measurement, Vocational Guidance Quarterly*, or *Journal of Educational Research*.)

REFERENCES

Froehlich, Clifford P., and Kenneth B. Hoyt: *Guidance Testing*, Science Research Associates, Inc., Chicago, 1959.

Hall, Calvin S., and Gardner Lindzey: *Theories of Personality*, John Wiley & Sons, Inc., New York, 1957.

Marzoff, Stanley S.: *Psychological Diagnosis and Counseling in the Schools*, Henry Holt and Company, New York, 1956.

Noll, Victor H.: *Introduction to Educational Measurement,* Houghton
    Mifflin Company, Boston, 1957.
Super, Donald E.: *Appraising Vocational Fitness by Means of Psycho-
    logical Tests,* Harper & Brothers, New York, 1949.

CHAPTER 6

SCHOOL RECORDS AND REPORTS

The effectiveness of the guidance program is dependent upon a comprehensive and smoothly functioning system of records and reports. In gathering information essential for proper guidance, it will be necessary to make much use of records and reports. It is not an exaggeration to say that the success of the information-gathering service—and, by extension, the success of the guidance program—is dependent upon an effectively carried out record-keeping plan.

Making records and keeping them up to date are probably the most tedious and uninteresting duties of teachers and counselors. The time spent in making these records often seems so fruitless to teachers in comparison with the time devoted to their basic function of helping children. In many schools record keeping actually does seriously interfere with these duties because so many detailed reports are required that the time necessary for preparation for teaching and counseling is insufficient. This "mania" for records and written reports seems to have swept the country and is clearly evident in government services and in business and industry. "Reportitis" is a disease that is universal and highly contagious. Nearly everyone regards it as a nuisance, but no one does anything about it. However, records are essential to the improvement of teaching and counseling, and they cannot be eliminated; but their preparation should be as efficient and effective as possible with a minimum of detailed writing.

Although every member of the school staff is responsible for keeping records relating to his special responsibility, those kept by the teachers are the most important for they deal primarily with the students themselves in their learning activities. Teachers' records are the basis for promotion and for remedial work. Some of these records are personal and private, important only to the teacher himself and never appearing on the cumulative record. Others form the basis for items in the permanent school records which are open to various staff members. Among the most important teachers' records are those of daily attendance, lesson assignments, achievement of objectives attained by the class as a whole and by individual students, individuals needing special help, and notes regarding the progress, needs, attitudes, and interests of pupils. Some of these records may be symbols known only to the teacher and, with other items of a temporary nature, may well be kept in a notebook that is his private property. Nevertheless they often form the basis for estimates made by the teacher, and these are essential for effective guidance.

THE CUMULATIVE RECORD

The great importance of adequate records can best be understood when we realize that such records constitute the only systematic, detailed history in existence of individuals from the time they enter school at the age of five to the time when they graduate from high school at eighteen. This is the formative period of their lives; character is shaped, and the trend of their development occupationally, socially, and morally is largely determined during this time. Records are history and do not, in themselves, contribute to the development of the individual; however, they do provide data that reveal the special needs of students as they progress through adolescence. They also provide a means of understanding students and their growth and development. They are useful in planning more effective instruction and in selecting and organizing educational procedures and facilities.

Importance of the Cumulative Record

Teachers in secondary schools and in departmentalized elementary schools see only a segment of each pupil. They know him chiefly as a student in English, mathematics, or science, but not as an individual. Each teacher may meet 125 different students for a forty-minute period every day for one semester and then meet entirely different students the next semester. As recorded, the marks given by teachers constitute only isolated bits of information and, by themselves, do not provide an adequate basis for understanding the individual student.

A cumulative record is a permanent record of a student which is kept up to date by the school; it is his educational history with information about his school achievement, attendance, health, test scores, and similar pertinent data. Usually the cumulative record will be kept together in a folder or envelope especially designed for this purpose. The term cumulative record is often used interchangeably for the data alone and for the form on which the data are written. This record, being a continuous report of each student by different teachers, provides the only basis for a real understanding of the growth of the individual—physically, socially, intellectually, and emotionally. It is also the basis for reports to parents, to schools and colleges, and to prospective employers. The data recorded in the cumulative record are a very small part of the records kept in the school and include only items that are considered to be of permanent value to the school or to the individual pupil. The information in the record is copied and condensed from many special reports made by various members of the school staff.

Principles to Be Used in Building Cumulative Records

There are certain basic principles which should be used when making up cumulative records. Cumulative records serve as the core of the guidance program. They are essential for the proper functioning and improvement of both instruction and administration. Because the record will be continuous over the entire history of the student, it should be simple and well organized, containing only data which are pertinent, reliable, and valid. In setting up a system of cumulative records, careful advance planning will assure that the record is in harmony with the nature and purpose of the school and has uniformity throughout the local school district with a minimum of repetition of information. To accomplish this desired uniformity a manual of directions may be needed. Because the record is frequently used as a basis for reports to parents, employers, and colleges, it should be organized with this function in mind, perhaps by cooperative planning of those who will be working with it. The less clerical time and ability needed to keep the record up to date, the better. Because it is primarily designed to help teachers understand children and thus is a basis for improving teaching, the cumulative record will need to be housed in a place where it will be easily accessible to teachers. Finally, a degree of control will have to be exercised over some or all of the information in the records because of their confidential nature.

Confidential Information and Record Keeping

Confidential data about students which, in the opinion of the counselor, should not be kept routinely in the cumulative folder for use by all staff members should be kept in a separate confidential file. Some interview notes, special test results, confidential information about home and family problems, and certain other clinical data may have meaning only to the counselor and should be shared by him with other personnel only where, in his judgment, the best interests of the student are served. People to whom such data may be given might include the parent or guardian of the pupil or a person designated in writing by his parent or guardian. Certain data might be released to an officer or employee of a school the pupil attends, has attended, or intends to enroll, or a government official seeking information in the course of his duties. Still other kinds of confidential information might properly be given to a public or private guidance or welfare agency of which the pupil is a client or to an employer or potential employer.

If a school keeps too much information confidential, however, teachers will not know the student's situation and will not grow in their ability to evaluate and incorporate such data into their judgments. On the other hand, if the school does not exercise some precautions regarding the release of information, the interests of the pupil may be damaged by gossiping or moralizing teachers. A balanced, fair policy on confidential data is as desirable as it is difficult to develop.

Typical Cumulative Record

Cumulative records are sometimes developed by the local districts, sometimes more or less standardized throughout a state, and sometimes distributed nationally by professional organizations or commercial sources. Typically, a record contains identification data, often including a photograph; courses taken and marks, including the satisfaction of local or state graduation requirements; psychometric data; information about the family, including membership, employment, and language used; and teacher judgments and comments about such matters as interests, accomplishments, maturity, and vocational plans. When maintained properly for several years, such a record gives a longitudinal and developmental picture of the student. It changes him from a unit in a class of thirty to an individual.

Form 1, in this chapter, shows a cumulative record widely used in the state of Michigan. Its organization and coverage are typical of most such records. Properly maintained and used, a record such as this one makes possible some individualization of instruction by providing the teacher with the information he needs about each child.

ANECDOTAL RECORDS

It would be a mistake to assume that all the useful information about a student comes from the vital records in the cumulative folder, class recitations, and tests and examinations. The daily observations of other teachers are often very revealing but are too frequently forgotten or overlooked by the teacher in the rush of his daily work and overcrowded classes. A student who meets a teacher forty-five minutes a day, five days a week, for four or five months is almost certain to be involved in some very significant incidents during this association. In order to provide some means of capitalizing on such experiences, the anecdotal report was devised. It may be defined as an "on-the-spot" description of some incident, episode, or occurrence that is observed and recorded as being of possible significance. When these reports are gathered together, they are known as an anecdotal record.

In practice the distinction between report and record is not always observed, and the two terms tend to be used interchangeably. The report itself, however, should be a clear, precise statement of what happened and of the circumstances surrounding the incident and should avoid any projection of the observer's person-

NAME

NO. OF CHILDREN IN FAMILY	TOTAL	BOYS	GIRLS	NO. OLDER CHILDREN IN FAMILY		
ECONOMIC STATUS OF THE HOME	GOOD	LOW	MODERATE	UNKNOWN		

MALE / FEMALE — YOUNGER CHILDREN IN FAMILY — BOYS — GIRLS

PLACE OF BIRTH — RACE WHITE / NEGRO / OTHER — DATE OF BIRTH — CHURCH PREFERENCE — CODE

ELEMENTARY SCHOOL RECORD

YEAR										
SUBJECTS	KDG.	1ST GRADE	GRADE	GRADE	GRADE	GRADE	GRADE	GRADE	GRADE	GRADE
ARITHMETIC										
ENGLISH — READING										
ENGLISH — LANGUAGE GRAMMAR										
ENGLISH — HANDWRITING										
ENGLISH — SPELLING										
SOCIAL SCIENCE — HISTORY										
SOCIAL SCIENCE — GEOGRAPHY										
SCIENCE — GENERAL SCIENCE										
SCIENCE — AGRICULTURE										
SCIENCE — PHYSIOLOGY HYGIENE										
ARTS AND CRAFTS — HOUSEHOLD ARTS										
ARTS AND CRAFTS — INDUSTRIAL ARTS										
ARTS AND CRAFTS — ART										
ARTS AND CRAFTS — MUSIC										
DAYS PRESENT										
DAYS ABSENT										
TIMES TARDY										
REMARKS										

SECONDARY SCHOOL RECORD

7TH GRADE / 8TH GRADE

YEAR	WEEKS IN SCHOOL YEAR SUBJECTS	MARK 1ST / 2ND	GRADE ELIMS	YEAR	WEEKS IN SCHOOL YEAR SUBJECTS	MARK 1ST / 2ND	GRADE ELIMS	YEAR	WEEKS IN SCHOOL YEAR SUBJECTS	MARK 1ST / 2ND	GRADE ELIMS

UNITS FOR THE YEAR
HALF DAYS ABSENT

YEAR	WKS. IN SCH. YR. SUBJECTS	HRS. PER WEEK	MARK 1ST / 2ND	GRADE ELIMS	...

UNITS AND POINTS FOR YEAR
UNITS AND POINTS TO DATE

YEAR	WKS. IN SCH. YR. SUBJECTS	HRS. PER WEEK	MARK 1ST / 2ND	GRADE ELIMS	...

UNITS AND POINTS FOR YEAR
UNITS AND POINTS TO DATE

PHOTOGRAPH

FAMILY DATA

	FATHER	MOTHER
NAME OF PARENTS		
HOME ADDRESS		
COUNTY OR STATE		
NATIONAL DESCENT		
OCCUPATION		
LANGUAGE IN HOME		
EDUCATIONAL STATUS		
DATE NATURALIZED		
CAUSE OF DEATH		
STEPPARENT		
GUARDIAN		
MARITAL STATUS		
WITH WHOM DOES CHILD RESIDE		

GRADUATION FROM SENIOR HIGH SCHOOL

NAME OR SIGNATURE OF HIGH SCHOOL PRINCIPAL

GRADUATION DATE — NO. IN CLASS — RANK IN CLASS — COURSE COMPLETED — DATE TAKEN — AGE — GRADE

NO. OF HONORS

CODE FOR BIRTH INFORMATION:
CERTIFIED COPY OF BIRTH CERTIFICATE=BC
CHURCH RECORD=CR
FAMILY BIBLE=FB
CERTIFIED COPY OF BIRTH CERTIFICATE=SC
SCHOOL RECORD=SR
PASSPORT=PP
PARENT'S STATEMENT=PS
LIFE INSURANCE POLICY=I
IMMIGRATION CERTIFICATE=IC

* RECORD IN PENCIL.

FORM 1. Typical Cumulative Record Folder

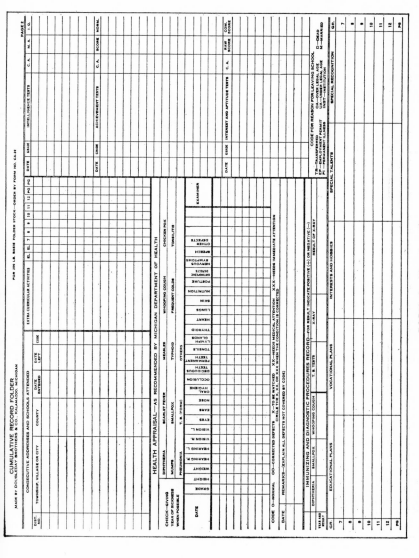

FORM 1. (Continued)

111

NAME   ADDRESS   MARRIED NAME

EDUCATIONAL FOLLOW-UP RECORD

DATE	NAME OF INSTITUTION	COURSE OF STUDY	REPORTED PROGRESS

EMPLOYMENT RECORD (WHILE ATTENDING SCHOOL AND AFTER LEAVING SCHOOL)

GRADE IF IN SCHOOL	AGE	YEAR	LENGTH OF JOB	NAME AND ADDRESS OF EMPLOYER	TYPE OF WORK	WAGES OR SALARY	REMARKS

OTHER SIGNIFICANT EXPERIENCES

OTHER WORK EXPERIENCES			HOME DUTIES		EXCEPTIONAL EXPERIENCES (TRAVEL, ETC.)	
YEAR	TYPE OF WORK	TIME SPENT	YEAR	TYPE OF DUTY	YEAR	PLACES, ETC.

FORM 1. (Continued)

CUMULATIVE RECORD FOLDER CA-39

SUGGESTIONS FOR ADDITIONAL DATA WHICH MAY BE FILED IN THIS FOLDER:

1. Correspondence with Parents.
2. Records of Home Visits, Parent Interviews, etc.
3. Records of Pupil Interviews or Counseling.
4. Anecdotal Records or Behavior Journals.
5. Diaries, Autobiographies, etc.

6. Copies of Pupil's Long-Range Course Elections.
7. Special Data on Health, Attendance, Discipline, etc.
8. Profile Sheets from Interest Inventories.
9. Personality Rating Sheets.
10. Vocational Themes, Career Booklets, etc.

RECORD OF TRANSCRIPTS SENT:

DATE	TO WHOM SENT	REASON

MEMORANDA:

FORM 1. (Continued)

ality. Anecdotal records, on the other hand, may consist only of a description of the incident or may include an interpretation of the observed behavior and a recommendation for action. Such records are often properly listed under "personality records" because these observations of behavior are important in revealing the personality. The description of the behavior is the most important part of the record, and some authorities say that the interpretations and recommendations should be made only by qualified experts in psychology, not by teachers.

Types of Anecdotal Records

As indicated above, there are various types of anecdotal records which are in general use. The first type contains only an objective description of behavior with no comment or interpretation. The second has a description of behavior and some comment or interpretation. The third type has a description of behavior with comments and interpretation and a statement of treatment. And, finally, a fourth type may contain a description of behavior with comment, interpretation, and recommendations for desirable future treatment.

An example of the first type is as follows: "When Henry came to class this morning, he seemed very tired and just slouched into his seat. He took no part in class discussion and seemed to have no interest in what was being discussed. This was very unusual, for he has always been eager to participate and often monopolizes the discussion time."

An example of the second type is as follows: "Mary came to me before class today to say that she had written to the state department of agriculture concerning their bulletin on mammals. She had just had a reply stating that they had none on hand but would send them as soon as they were available. Mary has shown a real interest in biology since she studied the subject of birds. She is reporting her own observations to me and looking up outside material."

The following is an example of the third type: "I have found Edward day after day in the library reading magazines, yet he never has time to correct errors in his papers or to work carefully on his English assignments. He likes to read but not to work on his schoolwork. I have taken library privileges from Edward until he brings his work up to a satisfactory level. The librarian has agreed not to admit him to the library during his free periods."

The following is an interesting example of the fourth type: "John has dropped off to sleep in class three times this week. He is so obviously conscientious about his work and so helpful and cooperative that I wonder whether he is ill or spending too much time on athletics. Someone should inquire more definitely into his case and find what is the real cause of his unusual behavior."

Values of Anecdotal Records

Anecdotal reports dealing with the same student but made by several different teachers are very valuable, for they indicate whether the behavior described by one teacher is characteristic or caused by a reaction to the teacher himself. Anecdotes by one teacher about the same pupil over an extended period of time are also important for showing growth and change.

Many schools find it helpful to distribute to teachers and counselors cards prepared especially for such records. Headings for the name of the student and the observer, time of day, and description of the incident and the circumstances surrounding it are typed on the cards for the convenience of the teachers.

Some schools are experimenting with reports by students of their fellow students. This plan has definite dangers as well as possible values, for, although fellow students often have more accurate understanding of other students than do teachers, the plan may engender jealousy and tattling. Whenever this practice is used, there should be very definite supervision. In some schools all these records are placed in the hands of the counselor and are not open to every teacher.

In summary, anecdotal records provide a variety of descriptions concerning the unconstrained behavior of pupils in diverse situations and thus contribute to an understanding of the core or basic personality pattern of each individual and of the changes in patterns. Properly used, they substitute specific descriptions of personality for vague generalizations and direct the attention of teachers away from subject matter and class groups and toward individual pupils. They stimulate teachers to use cumulative records and to contribute to them. The counselor secures information which he needs for conferences with individual students. The personal relationship between pupil and counselor is improved by these records, for they show the pupil that the counselor is acquainted with his problems and also point out the need for better work and study habits as well as growth in these respects. An appropriate summary of anecdotes is valuable if it is sent with a pupil when he goes to another school. Finally, a collection of anecdotal records may provide the necessary validation of various evaluative instruments.

Principles to Be Used in Preparing Anecdotal Records

Anecdotal records should not be considered as substitutes for other records but as supplements to them. The form, which should be short and informal, should provide space for all pertinent information, especially the objective descriptions of behavior separated from the subjective comments and interpretations. Reports are of most value when they deal with significant episodes showing a marked deviation from the normal behavior of the individual or his group. An attempt should be made to secure anecdotes about all types of students and not just those who are disciplinary problems. Because people behave differently in different settings, anecdotes should go beyond the classroom and the school to include any significant behavior wherever it is observed. Any behavior that will help in understanding a student should be noted whether it is favorable, unfavorable, or neutral. The anecdote should be written as soon after the incident occurred as possible to prevent distortions caused by memory lapses. There should be no requirement for teachers to prepare a definite number of anecdotes for any given length of time because such a requirement often results in inferior records, since incidents worthy of recording do not happen at any given time.

Conclusions drawn from the anecdotal records are often written in the permanent record, but the report itself should not be a part of the cumulative record but should be placed in a separate folder included in the record. The writing of anecdotal reports is a skill which needs developing, and teachers need in-service training in making and using such records. Staff members who are expected to write anecdotal records should have a period of instruction under an experienced person who would help them to understand the purpose of the records and to make proper use of them.

REPORTS TO PARENTS

Reports to parents are often considered to be a "necessary evil" and are frequently unsatisfactory to parents and to the general public. With greater public concern for the progress of education, we may expect a continued desire on the part of the parents to know how the schools are functioning. Schools, therefore, will need to face the criticism of their previous reporting methods and strive to improve them.

Difficulty of Communication between School and Parent

A recent newspaper editorial in one of our large cities stated what it considered to be some of the basic problems and inadequacies of the usual systems of school reports. The board of education in this city had just announced that extensive changes were being made in the systems of records and reports. After wishing the authorities well in their efforts, the editorial continued:

> This is a subject that is doomed to perpetual controversy. For there will always be some parents, perhaps many, who do not understand the cards, or who do not like the reports, or both. And there will always be some teachers, perhaps many, unqualified to produce an understandable report.
>
> At the very least, however, the local study should turn public attention to the reporting system, and this is all to the good. For example, even its announcement should give parents and teachers cause to reflect on the basic purpose of the cards. They are, as their name implies, "reports" from the teacher to the parent, from the school to the home, on the school performance of the child. Practically all parental complaint about the grading system—and there can be no doubt that it is widespread—can be boiled down to this: the parent cannot tell from the report card how his child is doing in his school work. In short, the report has failed in its primary purpose.
>
> Chief target of such complaints is the card that seeks to advise the parent of his child's scholastic accomplishments, not in relation to other students, but in relation to the student's own ability. The catch here is that few teachers are actually qualified to judge accurately the ability of even one or two pupils, let alone each of the members of a class of thirty or more.

To put his faith in the reporting system now in general use in elementary schools, the parent must first have faith in the teacher's qualifications to judge his child's potential ability. That is asking a lot.

It is the theory of the promoters of this system that the old-style method of grading a pupil in relation to specific standards of accomplishment, and in competition with his fellow pupils, is likely to have an undesirable effect on children in their formative years. The bright child may find that he can coast and still get good grades. The dull pupil or the slow starter may become discouraged. Everyone agrees, however, that eventually the pupil must emerge into the harsh world of competition, where his accomplishment will be stacked up against that of others, not against what some teacher thinks he is capable of doing. But when does this come? In the first grade, the fourth, the seventh, the high school? Opinions, to understate the case, differ.

Nearly every parent can sympathize with the point of view expressed in this editorial. It is extremely difficult to solve the problem of satisfactory communication with parents. There can be no question of the inherent right of the parents to know how their children are getting along in school and of the desire of the school to give this information in such a way that the parents can understand it. Teachers know that the efficiency of the school depends in large measure on the helpful cooperation of the parents, but this is hard to get. In some cases such parental cooperation interferes with the efforts of the school. Even when most parents have gone to schools much like the one to which their children are going, they often have forgotten their own experience, or the schools have changed so much that the parents are quite ignorant of present conditions and methods.

Most of our schools are very conscious of this need for helpful cooperation between school and home but have not yet devised effective methods to secure it. Practically all schools send cards to the home on which are indicated students' grades in different subjects, often with some notation regarding the general character of his progress and his behavior. But as the writer of the above editorial indicates, the parent does not understand what the notations on the report card mean. A mark of A or D, of 90 or 60, means very little, for in some cases it indicates his achievement relative to his ability and gives little information regarding his actual achievement. This condition shows clearly the need for more effective communication between school and home.

Typical Reports to Parents

Many schools send brief letters to parents which describe in simple terms how the student is getting along in school—his grades, his attitudes, his study habits, and his progress. The two blanks used in the Radnor schools, reproduced here as Forms 2 and 3, are good

FORM 2 Sample Report Regarding Class Failure

Radnor High School
Wayne, Pennsylvania

Date_____

Dear _____,
We wish to bring to your attention the following concerning the scholastic achievement of _____.
He, she failed to receive credit in (subject) _____.
It is recommended that he, she:

1. Do work over the summer, according to the direction of the teacher, and submit it to him before September, _____.
An examination *may* be necessary.
2. Repeat the subject
or
Discontinue the subject and make an acceptable substitute for the credit lost.
3. Earn the credit for the subject in an approved summer school.
4. Tutor in the subject during the summer (a minimum of _____ hours is necessary) with an approved tutor and take our re-examination before September, _____.

We are especially desirous that this decision receive your careful consideration and thank you for your cooperation.

Sincerely,

Guidance Counselor, Upper School
Guidance Counselor, Middle School

examples of information blanks that give meaningful descriptions of personal characteristics, study habits, and school progress. They lay the foundation for effective conferences between parents and teachers. The special report sent at or near the end of a term (Form 2) gives suggestions on several ways in which the student might make up the deficit and obtain credit for the work in which he had failed.

FORM 3   Excerpt from

PERSONAL CHARACTERISTICS		Date of Evaluation			
		November 15	January 31	April 15	Final Eval.
Citizenship	Above Average				
	Average				
	Below Average				
Initiative	Above Average				
	Average				
	Below Average				
Interest	Above Average				
	Average				
	Below Average				
Responsibility	Above Average				
	Average				
	Below Average				
Work Habits	Above Average				
	Average				
	Below Average				

RECORD OF
ATTENDANCE   Sept. Oct. Nov. Dec. Jan. Feb. Mar. Apr. May June

	Sept.	Oct.	Nov.	Dec.	Jan.	Feb.	Mar.	Apr.	May	June
Number of Days Absent										
Number of Days Tardy										

Sample Report Card

NAME: _____

INTERPRETATION OF MARKS

"A"—excellent work   "D"—below average work, barely
"B"—good work   passing
"C"—average work   "F"—little or no progress, failing

Students who do not earn an average of "B" or better in grades 9–12 will experience difficulty in securing entrance to college.

PUPIL'S PROGRESS

Subject	Teacher	First Quarter	Second Quarter	Third Quarter	Fourth Quarter

Marks in Radnor High School are cumulative: that is, the last mark recorded indicates the quality of work done from the beginning of the year to the present.

TEACHER'S COMMENTS

First Quarter

Second Quarter

Third Quarter

Fourth Quarter

Trends in Reporting to Parents

The two major problems in any reporting system are making the report useful and meaningful to parents, to students, and to the school itself and at the same time making it as simple as possible in order to reduce the amount of work required of teachers and the clerical staff. Many school systems are experimenting with various types of systems to solve these problems. A procedure that is being used in the Washington High School at Massillon, Ohio, looks promising. This school is using a new punch-card style of report card developed by the Royal McBee Corporation. Application of the new reporting system to punched cards not only reduces over-all clerical work from the previous grade-card requirements but also assigns the bulk of this work to office secretaries, thus leaving teachers with more time for their actual teaching duties.

Office secretaries type and punch sets of cards for each student so that they contain all necessary information. After the typing and punching are completed, the sets are key-sorted alphabetically by grades, subjects, teachers, and class periods. Teachers receive their cards arranged alphabetically by classes. Each teacher then marks the subject grade and records all class absences. Space is also provided for comments and citizenship ratings.

The marks are recorded on all parts of the grade-report set by means of a wax spot on the back of each card. The copy used for the last reporting period, of course, contains the complete record for the year. After teachers have recorded their marks and comments, the sets are returned to the office secretaries who arrange them alphabetically by grade level. Each student's sets are gathered together by key sorting.

One copy is mailed to the student's home. Another copy remains in the principal's office after the school term has ended. All records except personal comments can be obtained from the card, and valuable research studies can be made on grade distribution by teachers and subjects and by attendance, tardiness, and citizenship ratings. After all records have been recorded and research studies conducted, each student's key-sorted punched cards are placed with other guidance material in his counselor's files.

This promising trend toward mechanization of record keeping

and reporting may do much to improve school-home communication and consequent cooperation. Only by freeing the teacher for professional work can his talents be best used. The schools need to follow the lead of industry in assigning clerical work to clerks and machine operators, reserving professional work for professionals.

SUMMARY

School records are one of the most essential elements in guidance and, at the same time, one of the most troublesome. At their best, they contain the most extensive and valuable history of each student from the kindergarten through the high school as well as information about parents and home conditions. There are no similar records in any other part of our social system. They are a running account of a child's growth and development from infancy to adulthood. They contain records of physical growth, of health and sickness, of mental and social developments, of special weaknesses and strengths, of problems, of hopes for the future, and often experiences after graduation from high school.

Much clerical work is involved in keeping these records accurate and up to date. Therefore, unless ample clerical assistance is provided, record keeping may interfere with teaching itself, thus posing an even greater problem. Much study has been given to the development of concise, well-organized cumulative folders which are invaluable for effective teaching and guidance.

In addition to the cumulative record, anecdotal records may be used to describe instances of significant behavior from time to time. These records are usually kept on separate loose-leaf sheets slipped into the folder. In some cumulative folders, there is a place for recording judgments or estimates by the teacher which are often very revealing.

It is difficult to report to parents in such a way as to promote cooperation between the home and the school in the education of the student. Considerable progress is being made through parent-teacher associations and through conferences between teachers and parents held in the home and in the school. Finally, mechanization and job simplification may relieve teachers of the onerous clerical chores associated with record keeping and reporting.

EXERCISES

1. Write five anecdotal reports of the kind that you think would help someone understand the student who is the subject of the report. Be prepared to discuss them in class.

2. Should all the information about an individual student be accessible to all teachers? To parents? If not, what types of information should not be given to all teachers? To parents? Give your reasons.

3. Secure a report card and/or cumulative record to serve as a basis for a group discussion of the values and limitations of these two forms.

REFERENCES

D'Evelyn, Katherine: *Individual Parent-Teacher Conferences*, Bureau of Publications, Teachers College, Columbia University, New York, 1956.

Hymes, James L., Jr.: *Effective Home-School Relations*, Prentice-Hall, Inc., Englewood Cliffs, N.J., 1954.

Langdon, Grace, and Irving Stout: *Teacher-Parent Interviews*, Prentice-Hall, Inc., Englewood Cliffs, N.J., 1954.

McDaniel, Henry B., and G. A. Shaftel: *Guidance in the Modern School*, The Dryden Press, Inc., New York, 1956.

Warters, Jane: *Techniques of Counseling*, McGraw-Hill Book Company, Inc., New York, 1954.

PART IV

SCHOOL GUIDANCE
ORGANIZATION

CHAPTER 7

GUIDANCE IN THE
ELEMENTARY SCHOOL

Anna R. Meeks*

The growth of the elementary school from the days of the simple colonial-dame school, devoted to ABC's and the primer, to the modern school, which strives for the best total development of each individual pupil, has been nurtured under the American democratic goal of adequate standards of health and decency for all. Over the years the elementary school has modified its organization to meet changing demands, but essentially it has been organized to meet the needs of childhood, looking toward the future development of the adolescent in the secondary school.

The number of years of elementary schooling varies over the nation. The most generally used organization includes the years devoted to kindergarten and grades 1 to 6. Some schools provide prekindergarten experience and others include grades 7 and 8. The elementary school is essentially designed for middle childhood, with some overlap into early and later childhood. Strictly speaking, it completes its function for most children at the end of grade 6 because grades 7 and 8 are more properly geared to late childhood and early adolescent needs. In many schools in the United States grades 7 to 9 constitute the junior high school, but, regardless of where grades 7 and 8 may be housed, guidance procedures for this

* Guidance Supervisor, Baltimore County Public Schools, Towson, Md.

age are more closely allied to secondary than to elementary programs.

The elementary school is charged with the development of skills in the fundamental processes, but of equal importance is its responsibility for the encouragement of initiative, creativity, and leadership. In these early years of the school experience children develop self-concepts and values which determine their motivation for learning and personal development in the secondary school as well as in the later years of their lives. The primary grades 1 to 3 demand a most skillful and understanding approach to individual differences in needs, interests, and potentialities, for what the child will become depends in no small manner upon the way the primary school meets his educational and personal needs. Building upon a sound foundation, the teacher in grades 4 to 6 emphasizes both the development of skills and the transition from childhood education, with its close teacher-pupil relationship, to the junior high school, with its demand for increasing self-responsibility. The gradual cutting of some "apron strings" in the later years of the elementary school is an essential aspect of successful progress in growing up and must precede satisfactory adjustment in the junior high school.

It has long been the role of the elementary-school teacher to bear the chief responsibility for knowing the child and giving help in personal and social development. Many factors have contributed to an increasing demand for organized guidance services in the elementary school, and there is a definite trend toward such services that will enhance the guidance role of the teacher and at the same time provide more adequately for the great diversity of pupil needs.

IMPORTANCE OF GUIDANCE IN ELEMENTARY SCHOOLS

Significant developments in recent decades have brought a recognition that organized guidance programs are as important on the elementary as on the secondary level. Guidance is an integral part of the total educational program, serving as a positive function rather than a corrective force, and to be most effective it must be a continuous process from the child's first contact with the school until he is ready for placement on a job or in some type of post-secondary education. Emphases may change as the growing child's needs change, but the essential process of helping each child to understand himself in relation to his own needs and to those of his environment must begin long before he is ready for secondary school. Early guidance which helps the child to make adjustments to each new situation can strengthen his ability to apply his self-understanding to the solution of problems in his later years. Guidance is no longer based on a concept of services designed to meet crises but rather on a concept of continuous development. This view emphasizes prevention and good mental hygiene and demands organized guidance services in the earliest years of the educational experience.

Preventive Measures Can Be Taken

The present emphasis upon the development and utilization of human resources is bringing increased demands for earlier and more effective identification of individual differences. This demand for earlier identification is gaining impetus with the growing recognition that guidance services in the elementary schools are especially effective because (1) the child is flexible and has had less time for problems to become deep-rooted; (2) the parents are more actively associated with the school; and (3) many years of more successful development lie ahead for the child who can be helped to understand himself and to find acceptable approaches toward the solution of his problems. When the major guidance concern was only for the serious behavior problems, the school could look to outside agencies for assistance in providing therapeutic measures; but with the present emphasis upon prevention of serious maladjustment and upon the establishment of learning climates which encourage maximum total personal development, there is an imperative need for organized guidance services which are an integral part of the total educational program of every elementary school.

Readiness Can Be Developed

Research findings and developments in the curriculum field point up the necessity for increased guidance services in these early years of the school experience. The concept of readiness for learning includes the recognition that educational stumbling blocks may appear if curriculum experiences are offered too soon or too late. This concept demands the earliest and best possible identification of individual differences and calls for greatly improved systems of pupil records. The emphasis upon continuous educational development, as opposed to isolated strata of educational programs which demand arbitrary common levels of development at each transition, calls for better articulation of elementary- and secondary-school experiences. Interest in greater motivation for learning and in the development of learning situations which produce creativity and leadership must result in systematic counseling for parents and pupils. This concern also calls attention to the school's responsibility to provide consultation services for the teacher in this most complex educational program. In short, time, energy, and money spent in the earliest years of the child's school life pay larger dividends in the conservation of human resources than can be expected from remedial and corrective processes offered in later years of the pupil's school experience.

THE NATURE OF THE CHILD IN THE ELEMENTARY SCHOOL

All growth follows a pattern, and each child has his own built-in growth pattern and "timetable." Some mature very rapidly in all areas, and others lag behind their age group in one or more of the four areas of development—physical, mental, social, or emotional. Research shows that children exhibit every conceivable combination and variation in their growth patterns. Some grow at the same rate in all four areas, while others grow unevenly. Children may show rapid physical development with slow mental development. In addition, the same child may show both spurts and lags in his growth and development. These differences are mainly the result of the built-in growth pattern but may be influenced to a limited extent by disease, nutritional deficiencies, or other extreme environmental deprivations. Olson and Lewellen[1] say that "if we are aware of this many-sided and exciting process of growth as it occurs in them, we will be better equipped to help our children mature."

Children in the kindergarten and in grades 1 to 6 span three periods of growth and development. The kindergarten child is usually completing early childhood development, and the child in grades 5 and 6 is probably in the period of later childhood. Between these two periods is the stage of middle childhood. Each of

[1] Willard C. Olson and John Lewellen, *How Children Grow and Develop*, Science Research Associates, Inc., Chicago, 1953, p. 43.

these periods represents a specific stage in the systematic process of child development.

Because of the great variety of developmental patterns we would expect to find many different levels of development in any year of the elementary school, although in general children of any given age period will exhibit certain characteristics of growth and similar levels of development. For purposes of orientation then we need to look at the characteristics of middle and later childhood.

The Child from Six to Ten

Middle childhood usually covers the years between six and ten. In this period the child is growing in all parts of his body but less rapidly than in early childhood. Muscular growth and coordination are uneven and incomplete, but manual dexterity and eye-hand coordination have developed sufficiently to allow the child to use his hands and fingers for writing, drawing, sewing, and playing musical instruments. He still has better control over the large muscles than he does over the small. The child needs opportunities for active play to release pent-up energy and a balance of rest and relaxation to meet the increasing demands which school places upon him.

The mental development in middle childhood is characterized by learning to read and by the acquisition of many other knowledges and skills. Olson[2] says there is evidence that these children learn best when they can be active while learning.

This is the period when children begin to recognize differences in how boys and girls are expected to behave. Socially and emotionally, they are developing sexual feelings, but a divergence in interests between boys and girls results in less play together. These children are becoming more independent, are learning to take more responsibility and to show increasing control of emotions. This is a period of emerging values with some concern about right and wrong.

The Child from Ten to Thirteen

Children in grades 4 to 6 have received only limited attention in research and in the study of human growth and development. A recent bulletin, *Educating Children in Grades Four, Five, and*

[2] *Ibid.*

Six,[3] has summarized the available research on them. The educators who prepared the report of this period, which is usually referred to as one of "latency," speak with praise about the characteristics of these children. The lack of research, they believe, is a tribute to the fact that children of this age have failed to give concern to educators.

These children are active and want to be on the move. Physical growth is slow, and health is good. Some, particularly the girls, may be maturing more quickly and may advance into the more rapid growth phase of prepubescence. The child of twelve or thirteen may show evidence of physical ungainliness and awkwardness of movement. Enlarging hips, breast development, and menstruation may present problems of adjustment for those girls who are earlier maturers. Voice changing and characteristic sex changes and developments in boys may appear in grade 5 or 6. These pupils want to be making things, want to be doing and performing in response to their need to try out their own powers.

This is the period when children are showing a tendency to draw away from adults and to turn toward their peers for companionship and for modes of living. Independence in ideas and activity is normal behavior at this age. These children need support from both adults and peers, for both help in defining acceptable limits of behavior. In many cases children show fears and worries which center in developing independence, parental and school expectations, and home problems. Competition may also be a threat to emotional well-being.

Later childhood is characterized by a desire to learn and by a wide variety of interests. The child is developing an understanding of cause and effect, forming concepts, and beginning to solve simple problems. Value judgments of right and wrong are not as well defined for the child in grade 6 as they were in grade 4. This seems to be the age when the child develops some tolerance and the ability to see things as gray rather than as black or white.

Implications for Education

Knowing about individual growth patterns and how a child grows as a whole can be of immense value. Olson and Lewellen[4]

[3] U.S. Department of Health, Education, and Welfare, *Educating Children in Grades Four, Five, and Six*, Office of Education Bulletin 3, 1958.

[4] Olson and Lewellen, *op. cit.*, p. 4.

say that "no pushing can make him do more than his capacities permit. But it is true that in order to fulfill his latent promise each child must have the *opportunity* to develop and learn as fast as his growth pattern allows him to. . . . That is why a child's environment—the situation in which he is placed—is so important to his total development." We can help our children grow to greater social and emotional maturity. Understanding the growth process can reduce much of the worry and tension besetting parents and teachers. Children can be happier when adults recognize certain modes of behavior as normal steps in the process of growing up.

In a summary of studies of how human beings grow and develop,[5] we see the following:

> Children are both similar and different.
>
> Each individual grows according to his own time schedule and in his own style.
>
> Growth takes time; it can be encouraged but not forced. Both nature and nurture play a part.
>
> Growth of abilities in the same individual often varies.
>
> Growth is continuous, following an orderly sequence in each individual.

We also learn that conditions in the environment which encourage the proper development of human beings are (1) those which support physical well-being and stimulate growth—food, warmth, air, light, activity and rest, and safety; (2) those which support emotional well-being—giving a sense of security and of worth or self-respect; and (3) those which lead to increased ability to cope independently with life situations.

Finally, the emotional needs of all human beings must be kept in mind when we attempt to understand the nature of elementary-school children. These are the need for belonging, achievement, economic security, love and affection; the need to be free from fear and relatively free from guilt; the need for self-respect and self-understanding.

The major goal for education is to help children meet the developmental tasks imposed upon them by their innate growth drives and by the society in which they live, that is, to help them

[5] U.S. Department of Health, Education, and Welfare, *op. cit.*

to grow up capably and happily as individuals and as thoughtful, contributing members of society.

THE ROLE OF THE TEACHER IN GUIDANCE

The interrelation between guidance and instruction in the educational process emphasizes the key role of the teacher in guidance. The teacher is uniquely responsible for the climate of learning in which the class as a group, and each pupil as an individual in the group, finds opportunity for learning and for personal development. Johnston, Peters, and Evraiff[6] say, "The school must be conceived of as the setting for learning experiences, and everything which helps to make that setting educational is a concern of the teacher." Teachers affect the lives and personalities of children, and their influence goes far beyond the academic area and what can be measured by achievement tests. Ohlsen[7] says, "If the teacher will accept each pupil as he is, with all his strengths and weaknesses, and will help him to improve where he needs to improve, the teacher will have many opportunities to help pupils understand and accept themselves and to aid them in defining reasonable life goals—two major aims of guidance. He may also influence the attitudes and feelings which contribute to making independent choices either easy or difficult."

Gordon's[8] summary of some general principles of learning emphasizes the significant guidance role which the teacher must assume if learning is to take place. He says, "Learning, then, is a dynamic process strongly subject to the background of experiences of the learner, his organism, and his interpretation and integration of his experiences, his goals and aspirations, his tensions and anxieties, and subject too to the total situation in which he finds himself." The teacher functions primarily in his guidance role as a worker with groups of pupils and their parents; but he is also concerned about individuals in the group, and he cooperates with other

[6] Edgar C. Johnston, Mildred Peters, and William Evraiff, *The Role of the Teacher in Guidance*, Prentice-Hall, Inc., Englewood Cliffs, N.J., 1959, p. 4.

[7] Merle M. Ohlsen, *Guidance: An Introduction*, Harcourt, Brace & World, New York, 1955, p. 66.

[8] Ira J. Gordon, *The Teacher as a Guidance Worker*, Harper & Brothers, New York, 1956, p. 180.

persons vital to the guidance function. To provide an educational setting in which learning will take place, the teacher studies both the individuals in a group and the group itself, so that he can recognize how one group differs from another. By cherishing individual differences and by developing dynamic group processes, the teacher offers each pupil in his class an opportunity to learn.

The Teacher Studies Children

Child study is a basic guidance function and is accomplished through the use of both formal methods involving tests and cumulative records and informal methods based upon observations of the pupil in his classroom and in other settings. The teacher learns much about the child as he studies the pupil's production, his oral and written work, his art work, and his reading record. The teacher seeks to observe hobbies and interests as an aid to motivation through understanding. Observations of behavior systematized through the use of the anecdotal record provide a rich source of data for child study. The teacher in an elementary school is in a strategic position to conduct child study, for he sees the child in many differing situations and has frequent opportunity for contacts with parents.

Children enter school with wide differences in chronological age, mental maturity, physical coordination, health conditions, social and emotional readiness for formal school experiences. Children in the first grade range in age from five years and eight months to seven years. A first grade may have children whose mental ages range from three years to ten years or more. The range in physical maturity will be comparable with additional differences introduced through birth injuries, disease, or nutritional deficiencies. The differences in familial patterns and in cultural and economic backgrounds will account for wide levels of maturity in peer relationships and socialization and emotional readiness for learning. Early identification of individual differences is an essential aspect of any attempt to provide meaningful educational experiences for children. Failure to recognize levels of readiness in the early years of school life may be a major factor in the problems of underachievement, school dropouts, and even juvenile delinquency. When children begin school in a kindergarten, the teacher has an opportunity, before more formal education begins, to study levels of maturity through observations, parent conferences, health reports, and developmental records of progress in adjusting to school.

The first-grade teacher who must provide more formal learning experiences for children entering school for the first time faces a big task in studying the individual pupils in his class. Too frequently a reading-readiness score is the only objective evidence of individual differences. This score is too often interpreted as a measure of general mental maturity. The need to establish other levels of readiness and maturity must be met in order to provide a learning situation in which the child can find the satisfaction which will lead to more learning.

Readiness for learning depends upon physical and mental factors, situational factors, and the self-system of the child. The child must see what is to be learned as meaningful and useful as it relates to his needs, goals, and self-concept. The teacher must first look at the individuals in his class in order to determine each child's readiness for learning, the degree to which individual needs are being met, and how each child sees himself. The teacher also looks at himself and raises the question, "How do I feel about each of these pupils? What are my personal needs which may influence my relationship with the group or with individuals within the class?"

The Teacher Collects Data about Children

Early identification of individual needs makes educational planning more valid. Identification and planning, however, must be continuous and not a one-time experience.

Identification involves observation in many areas of behavior, a study of developmental records, and interviews with parents and children. Kough and DeHaan[9] provide teachers with techniques and procedures for observing behavior. Their handbook provides descriptions of behaviors which can be observed as a basis for recognizing children with special interests, abilities, or problems. One of the most useful techniques for informal study is the anecdotal record together with the roster of observations kept by the teacher. Such records, if they represent accurate and objective reporting of

[9] Jack Kough and Robert F. DeHaan, *Identifying Children with Special Needs*, Elementary-school Edition, Science Research Associates, Inc., Chicago, 1955, vol. 1.

incidents, can help the teacher better to understand individual pupils and to recognize more clearly the relationships within the class group. Teachers need help in developing skill in this type of reporting. An excellent discussion of this and other informal methods of collecting data is found in *The Role of the Teacher in Guidance*.[10]

The teacher will also participate in the collection of data by more formal methods and will utilize all the data in the cumulative record of the child. Such data usually cover personal and family background, health, attendance, scholarship, and activities both in and out of school. The standardized test, inventories, and rating scales may all be used in the elementary school to provide essential information for understanding children.

A test program in a school involves the selection, administration, and use of test results. Teachers should have a say in the selection of tests to be used. If the teacher is to help administer standardized tests, a program of in-service education should be provided to ensure valid testing procedures. The teacher's most important role, however, will be in the interpretation of test results. Test data can be utilized to suggest curriculum changes, procedure changes, and even changes in teacher-pupil relationships. Teachers may need help to ensure a professional and objective use of test data. There is a responsibility to give parents and pupils realistic interpretations of test results, but it is important that the school accept the further responsibility of helping to resolve emotional conflicts which may arise from such reporting of test results.

The cumulative record which the school develops is designed to help teachers function more effectively by grouping the data collected so that conclusions are more easily drawn. Effective use of pupil records is possible only when the information covers all the fundamental areas of human development and when it is so organized that developmental patterns are evident. Then the record can be analyzed with a reasonable expenditure of time and effort. Cassell [11] offers a plan of organization for recording developmental data on a profile which makes it possible to recognize growth in

[10] Johnston, Peters, and Evraiff, *op. cit.*
[11] Russell N. Cassell, *The Cassell Developmental Record*, C. A. Gregory Company, Cincinnati, Ohio, 1955.

some six areas of physiological, emotional, psychosexual, intellectual, social, and educational development. This or some similar plan lends continuity to records.

As the teacher studies the individual children who make up his group or class, he recognizes a multiplicity of differences based upon unique growth patterns and environmental pressures and motivations. Then he acts upon his knowledge to modify experiences to make learning more meaningful for pupils with widely varying needs. Skillful and valid planning in the light of individual needs helps each child to work on his developmental tasks in a climate conducive to greater success. Later academic achievement will be deterred or enhanced by what happens in the early years of school. Erikson[12] says, "The danger in these early years lies in a sense of inadequacy and inferiority which may cause the child to despair of his tools and skills or of his status." When this happens, his ego boundaries suffer, and he abandons a developing sense of industry and is thrown back on more primitive aspects of development. Thus the underachiever is born! The teacher in the primary grades can do much for children whose parents have not been successful in aiding the child through these critical adjustments.

The Teacher Counsels

The teacher works with individuals as well as groups, and there is a kind of counseling which is a legitimate function of the classroom teacher. Johnston[13] feels that the teacher's relationship with pupils in this class often leads to possibilities for establishing good counseling rapport. Only in the classroom climate which is really conducive to learning can such a rapport be established, because it is based on respect for the individual and reflects attitudes and not processes. Gordon[14] reminds us that "the teacher-counselor cannot be all things to all students. He must be closely aware of his limits and use referral processes when the counseling situation seems to be going 'out of his depth.'" Johnston[15] says, "The teacher's counseling role is not a therapeutic one, but he does aim at of-

[12] E. H. Erikson, *Childhood and Society,* W. W. Norton & Company, Inc., New York, 1950, p. 227.

[13] Johnston, Peters, and Evraiff, *op. cit.*

[14] Gordon, *op. cit.,* p. 279.

[15] Johnston, Peters, and Evraiff, *op. cit.,* p. 105.

fering the student assistance in making more effective personal and environmental adjustments." When the pupil is unable to relate to the classroom teacher, or when the case calls for techniques beyond the ability of the teacher, the child should be referred to the school counselor.

Many teachers are including courses in guidance in their graduate programs, and these teachers often possess skills which make for effective counseling. If a teacher finds it difficult to accept the basic philosophy of counseling, he cannot be expected to do counseling, as such, in his work. Each teacher will have to decide for himself what limits for counseling are imposed by his own personal values and needs, his professional development, and his group or class responsibilities. He has the responsibility for using all available counseling resources as they are needed; for example, he may ask for help in recognizing the special needs of individual children. Counselors can serve as consultants to teachers, thus providing in-service education in the area of referral procedures. The case conference involving teacher, administrator, nurse, counselor, visiting teacher, and school psychologist offers an excellent opportunity to increase the teacher's skill in looking beneath symptoms to problems which need to be referred.

Besides studying children and counseling them, the teacher has other guidance responsibilities. He will study his group to discover the dynamics which are operating therein in order to improve communication, to utilize desirable areas of influence, and to relieve pressures. Johnston[16] provides a discussion of techniques to be used in understanding group behavior; these are as important as the techniques for understanding individuals within the group. The teacher also works with parents in helping to promote cooperative relationships which will enhance both school and home efforts to contribute effectively to each child's development. Teachers study the school environment as it affects the educational program and utilize resources and persons in the community to help them in their guidance work.

Although the teacher is the key guidance worker in the elementary school, he needs to recognize the guidance roles of other school personnel. The teacher is a member of a team whose func-

[16] Johnston, Peters, and Evraiff, *ibid.*

tion is to obtain the maximum development of each child in the school. Johnston[17] says, "No school is effectively staffed guidance-wise when there isn't someone in the school who can function as a counselor and handle the kinds of cases which are referred by the classroom teacher."

THE ROLE OF THE COUNSELOR

The counselor, a regularly assigned member of the elementary-school staff, is specifically charged with the responsibility for developing those aspects of the guidance function which demand an expenditure of time and the use of specialized competencies which the teacher ordinarily does not have. He is directly responsible to the principal and has only a staff relationship with the teachers and other members of the school staff. Principal and counselor working together plan an organized program of guidance services which include the following: (1) in-service education for teachers, (2) consultation services for teachers and parents, (3) counseling services for children, (4) referral services for children, (5) follow-up and research activities, and (6) evaluation studies.

The Counselor Gives In-service Education

An effective program of guidance services provides in-service education for teachers in the development and interpretation of pupil records. Since the average teacher will have neither the time nor the training to develop records which are complete and so organized that an analysis can be made with reasonable expenditure of time and energy, the counselor must provide assistance in the collection of data, in the methods of recording, and in the interpretation of the developmental record.

The development of a sound test program is another aspect of the elementary guidance services. Counselors can provide in-service education for teachers and can act as consultants in the development of the program and in the interpretation of results. Counselors can do some testing of pupils in the spring before the child enters the first grade. An inventory such as the one by Banham[18] can provide data which will enable the teacher to group

---

[17] Johnston, Peters, and Evraiff, *op. cit.*, p. 197.
[18] Katherine M. Banham, *School Readiness Inventory*, Educational Test Bureau, Educational Publishers, Minneapolis, Minn., 1950.

pupils according to levels of maturity by considering physical co-ordination, reading readiness, social and emotional development. Administering such an inventory requires much more time than the teacher can possibly find. The counselor also does supplementary testing for purposes of verification when results on any test seem to be illogical.

The Counselor Counsels

The counselor's chief responsibility is to provide counseling for all children with unusual interests or needs. Teachers can be helped to recognize these needs so that the children may be referred to the counselor. The per cent of time devoted to counseling for personal adjustment will be greater in the elementary school than in the secondary school, and this is probably the greatest difference in guidance at the two levels. Children, whether self-referred or referred by parents or teachers, may need help in many areas of personal development. The excessively shy child, the socially inept child, the child whose self-concept interferes with learning, the child whose behavior interferes with work in the classroom, the child with educational deficiencies, and any child whose progress in school seems unsatisfactory—all find their way to the counselor's office.

The counselor's office should be an attractive, even if small, room, with toys, books, and manipulative materials readily available to the child. Here a youngster who is overwhelmed by the experiences he is handling or who has reached "an explosion point" may work off tensions with clay, finger paints, darts, punching bags and return to class ready to try again. Toys play an important role in helping children verbalize and communicate. Teacher and child, sitting back to back, may hold "conversations" over toy telephones even if the child is too shy to communicate in a face-to-face interview. Furnished classrooms and doll houses, erector sets, dump trucks, fire engines, and a host of other toys provide opportunities for a child to play and talk as he works with the counselor. Dominoes, checkers, and chess offer an opportunity to help the child learn more about limits, rules, and regulations. Whether the counselor works with the individual child or with small groups, his office represents a neutral setting with many aids to help the child evaluate himself, set goals, and make choices. Here the counselor uses every competence he can muster. Training which includes a knowledge of how personality develops, an understanding of counseling theories and techniques, and some supervised practice in counseling is essential if the counselor is to meet the needs of the children who find their way to his office.

Research indicates that many underachieving pupils have emotional problems and that counseling provided on a systematic long-term basis is essential before the pupil can begin to use his potentialities. Pupils respond more readily if counseling is available in the early years of school at the onset of underachieving. Shaw and McCune[19] in a summary of a recent study of achievers and underachievers indicated that male underachievers had been obtaining grades below their ability level since grade 1. The female underachievers had been performing below their ability level since grade 9 and had tended to do so since grade 6. This study gave support to the hypothesis that academic underachievement is not an easily modifiable surface phenomenon. With the onset of underachieving occurring in the earlier years of school, there is a need to identify and provide counseling at the earliest possible time. Counseling in the secondary school is probably of little help in modifying patterns of underachievement.

The Counselor Makes Referrals

The counselor makes referrals of pupils to other school services and utilizes the resources available in the community. He helps to provide continuity of the educational experience through articulation services at the time a child leaves the elementary school to enter junior high school. Adequate counselor services should contribute to the curriculum through carefully planned research and follow-up activities which reveal the needs of children in the school and which provide evidence of the success with which the school is meeting these needs.

THE TEAM APPROACH

A definite trend in guidance is toward a coordinated team approach under the leadership of the principal. Principals, teachers,

[19] M. C. Shaw and J. T. McCune, "The Onset of Academic Underachievement in Bright Children," *Journal of Educational Psychology*, 51:102–108, 1960.

counselors, and other staff personnel working as a team should evaluate the guidance needs within the school and assess the effectiveness of the services designed to meet these needs. Many staff people, including school social workers, school psychologists, nurses, doctors, speech correctionists, reading specialists, supervisors, and consultants, are available to the modern school. Their services can be most effectively used if the principal arranges systematic case conference procedures. In such case conferences the teacher and the counselor share with other team members the problems of children which they have identified by their close contact. Teachers get some support and consultative help in planning for these children. Referrals for other services which are the result of these case conferences are usually more valid than referrals made without such conferences. The referral report is more detailed and often more accurate, and therefore the referral services will be more effective.

Guidance in the elementary school is the responsibility of every member of the school team. Under the leadership of the principal the team constantly evaluates its objectives and plans for more effective guidance services. Follow-up, research, and evaluation activities are essential aspects of the attempt to provide an educational climate in which each child works toward a healthy personality capable of achievement commensurate with ability.

SUMMARY

Guidance is an integral part of the total educational program and to be most effective must be a continuous process from the child's first contact with the school until he is ready for placement in a job or in a post-secondary school. Guidance in the elementary school is based on a concept of continuous development, emphasizing prevention and good mental hygiene. Traditionally the teacher has borne the responsibilities for guidance in the elementary school, but recent concern for conservation of human resources has given impetus to a demand for organized guidance services which utilize both teacher and specialist.

The major goal of education is to help children meet the developmental tasks imposed upon them by their innate drives and by the society in which they live. The chief goal of guidance is to help provide an educational setting in which learning is enhanced. Valid planning based upon identified needs, interests, and aptitudes is possible when all staff members accept their guidance roles.

The teacher is the key guidance worker in the elementary school. The teacher functions as a worker with groups of children and their parents, but he is also concerned about individuals in the group. He studies the individuals in his group using both formal and informal methods. The teacher provides counseling for individuals within the limitations imposed by time and professional and personal readiness. He works with parents, helping to plan for the development of each child. When necessary the teacher utilizes other school and community services for counseling or therapy. He works cooperatively with other members of the school team.

The counselor, as a regularly assigned member of the elementary-school staff, is responsible for developing those aspects of guidance functions for which the teacher does not have time and specialized competencies. His chief function is to provide systematic counseling for children with special needs or interests. An elementary-school counselor usually devotes a greater percentage of his time to counseling children and parents than does the secondary-school counselor. The counselor also provides in-service education for teachers in the collecting of data, in the development and use of cumulative records, and in the test program. Finally, an important aspect of the counselor's work is to contribute to curriculum development through follow-up and research activities.

Guidance in the elementary school can only be effective if it is carried on through a coordinated team approach in which all school staff members work together to provide resources for helping children with special needs. Principal, teacher, counselor, school nurse, school psychologist, and visiting teacher plan together in case conferences devoted to children with problems or unmet needs.

Guidance in the elementary school differs from that in the secondary only in points of emphasis which are dictated by the levels of development which we find in the elementary school. The goals are the same; the procedures must be adapted to the needs of childhood.

EXERCISES

1. The principal of an elementary school has asked his faculty to evaluate the guidance needs of the school and to make recommendations for improving the school guidance program. The school, located in a small industrial town, has an enrollment of 540 pupils. The staff has the services of a school social worker when the principal asks her to give assistance. The public-health nurse is available for limited consultant and referral services. The test program for the school consists in a reading-readiness test in grade 1, a scholastic aptitude test in grade 4, and an achievement battery in the spring of grade 6. The town has no mental hygiene clinic. Illegal absences, underachievement, and discipline problems plague the school. Discuss the recommendations which you think the staff might offer. Keep in mind goals, program, personnel, services, and procedures.

2. James was nine years old when he returned to the fourth grade in September. According to his test record he has an IQ of 126 and on a standardized achievement test in October received grade placements of 5.0 in reading, 4.8 in arithmetic, and 5.2 in language. Now, in May, the teacher is recommending retention for James because he is doing nothing in classwork. Discuss the guidance procedures which should be followed in working with James and his teacher.

3. You are a teacher in the fifth grade of an elementary school. The pupils listed below seem to need special help. Tell how you would handle each case. Be specific, mentioning procedures and resources to be used and giving some possible explanations for the observed behavior.

a. Timmy's achievement is showing a downward trend. Lately he seems to be always alone on the playground and in other periods of free time.

b. Helen is absent from school so frequently that she finds it difficult to keep up with her group.

c. Sammy had another fight on the playground this morning. He tore up Betty's arithmetic paper. The "chip" on Sammy's shoulder always seems to be in evidence.

REFERENCES

Cottingham, Harold D.: *Guidance in Elementary Schools*, McKnight & McKnight Publishing Company, Bloomington, Ill., 1956.

Gordon, Ira J.: *The Teacher as a Guidance Worker*, Harper & Brothers, New York, 1956.

Lloyd-Jones, E., R. Barry, and B. Wolf (eds.), *Guidance in Elementary Education: A Case Book*, Bureau of Publications, Teachers College, Columbia University, New York, 1958.

Sarason, S. B., K. S. Davidson, F. F. Lighthall, R. R. Waire, and B. K. Ruebush: *Anxiety in Elementary School Children: A Report of Research*, John Wiley & Sons, Inc., New York, 1960.

U.S. Department of Health, Education, and Welfare: *Educating Children in Grades Four, Five, and Six*, Office of Education Bulletin 3, 1958.

CHAPTER 8

GUIDANCE IN THE SECONDARY SCHOOL

The secondary school in the United States has developed to meet the changing needs peculiar to this country which grew from a somewhat loose confederation of a few states to a united nation of fifty states which is a powerful influence in the affairs of the world. As now constituted, the secondary school extends from the seventh grade through the twelfth grade and includes students who range in age from about twelve to eighteen years. There is at present a tendency to consider the two-year junior college as a part of the secondary school, but this will not be discussed here. The dominant purpose of the elementary school, grades 1 to 6, is the development of skills in the fundamental processes; that of the junior high school, grades 7 to 9, to continue the development of those skills and to prepare for the limited specialization which is characteristic of the senior high school, grades 10 to 12. Throughout, from the first to the twelfth grade, great attention is given to meeting physical, social, and emotional needs as they arise. Although many of the fundamental needs remain constant throughout the elementary and secondary school, the changes in the individual and in the character of the school require somewhat different methods of approach as new problems appear.

IMPORTANCE OF GUIDANCE IN THE SECONDARY SCHOOL

Preventive Guidance Is Needed

The need for guidance is universal; it is not confined to the period of childhood and youth. It is present whenever, at any age, help is needed in making choices or adjustments or in solving problems. The recognition of this truth is shown by the increasing efforts to provide guidance for older people who have retired or who are about to retire. It is also seen in the phenomenal development of all kinds of assistance to the handicapped of all ages. Guidance should be a continuous process throughout life for those in need of help. However, it is very apparent that the most important and effective period for such help is at the time when habits, attitudes, and ideals are being formed and when techniques for self-help are being developed. Guidance given at this time will greatly reduce the need for help later and will increase the ability to choose occupational, civic, and social activities wisely in adult life. Preventive guidance in the secondary school lessens the need for remedial guidance later.

Developmental Tasks and Guidance

Among the special tasks which our society imposes on the adolescent are those of selecting and preparing for an occupation and preparing for marriage and family life. These tasks necessitate making important decisions which will do much to shape the entire course of the student's life. If guidance is to play a part in increasing the individual's happiness and effectiveness, it must do so at this time. Adolescence is the period of choice making, and guidance is the systematic effort to improve the quality of choices; therefore it is important that the secondary school have a program of guidance for the adolescents it serves.

NATURE OF THE SECONDARY-SCHOOL STUDENT

Adolescents Are in a Period of Change

The period represented by students in grades 7 to 12 is that of adolescence, when the transition from childhood to adulthood takes place. It is a period of profound physical, mental, social, and emotional change and growth, the nature and significance of which the youth himself does not understand. He is often a stranger to himself as well as to others. It is a period of rapid growth in height, weight, and physical strength and of a broadening of vision of the physical and social world. There is an increasing feeling of personal independence which is mixed with a consciousness of the need—which he sometimes denies and tries to suppress—for companionship and help. It is so difficult for the adolescent to know himself that, even when offered help that he needs and knows that he needs, he often rejects it.

Adolescents Differ in Growth and Development

Adolescence begins with puberty, which is the stage of development at which the reproductive organs mature and the secondary sex characteristics develop. The onset of puberty is not uniform for all youth. It begins at different ages and lasts for different lengths of time. Because school attendance laws and customs are based on chronological age and because of the lock-step method of promotion from grade to grade, there are, in all grades from the seventh to the twelfth, students in all stages of physiological development—immature, maturing, and mature. In spite of these differences, however, in the seventh grade nearly all are immature, and in the twelfth grade nearly all are mature. There are also great differences in mental age in each grade.

Another factor making for differences is that "spurts" of rapid growth—physical, mental, and social—come at different ages, and there are "plateaus" that are not uniform in time of beginning or in length of duration. The problems due to differences among students in extent of maturity are further increased because girls begin and complete the period of maturation before boys.

Misunderstanding often results from the use of tables showing the ages of maturing boys and girls. In most discussions the average ages of beginning and ending this period are considered to be key points and the fact that there are great differences within as well as between the sexes is overlooked. Nor is there any clear evidence that a student who begins this period earlier or later than the average is "abnormal" in the sense that something is wrong with his development. He may be "unnormal" without being "abnormal." Because of these differences in development and the fears and embarrassments associated with them the secondary-school student is in special need of guidance.

Adolescents Differ in Attitudes and Interests

During adolescence there are changes in mental and social characteristics, in attitudes toward school, toward teachers, toward parents, toward peers, and toward authority. Interests and attitudes toward literature and society change rapidly, and individuals in the same grade may not have the same interest or the same comprehension.

In the same class in English, students with different interests, outlooks, and abilities may study *Treasure Island, Lady of the Lake, Ivanhoe, Macbeth, Julius Caesar,* and *Hamlet.* They cannot and should not be expected to get the same meanings or value out of these experiences. The same is true with social studies and science. These differences make the task of the teacher a very difficult one. When marks are given, they are usually based on the attainment of certain interpretations or points of view that are approved by the teacher and, presumably, were intended by the author. Little consideration is given to the fact that students are in different periods of maturation. Conduct, too, is often judged by standards generally suitable for the grade in which the pupil is enrolled but not necessarily suitable for his particular stage of maturation.

GUIDANCE NEEDS RELATED TO EDUCATION

The guidance needs of students in the secondary school are basically not very different from those in any other part of the educational system. What differences there are stem from the degree to which the student is able to participate in the solution of his problems, their urgency, and the facilities available for help.

Adjustment to Secondary School

Although the change from the six-year elementary school to the junior high school is not so abrupt as that from the eighth grade of the old elementary school to the first year of high school, there are several very important differences between the two schools. Because of the departmental organization usually found in the junior high school, the pupil must adjust himself to a variety of teachers instead of to only one teacher. Instead of remaining in the same room for all classes, he moves from room to room. The character of the junior-high-school building itself is often quite different from that of the elementary school. The student is plunged into a different type of school life and school discipline. There are various types of clubs and group activities; there is usually some form of student government; the school library and the school gymnasium provide new experiences. The student is expected to take more responsibility both for his own activities and for some elements in the life of the school.

The junior high school is so organized that in the first year there is likely to be little or no choice of subjects because nearly all students are required to take the same work. Starting with the eighth or ninth grade, however, the student must make decisions about courses which may have lasting results for his occupational adjustment. Out of this situation many important problems arise which require that the student have guidance.

Many of these same problems arise in the transition from the junior high school to the senior high school. Where the entire six years of the secondary school are housed in one building and considered as a six-year school, there is no problem of adjustment to a new building, but other more important problems remain. For example, a student may need help in deciding whether to leave school at the end of the compulsory attendance age or to remain for graduation. In certain areas it is the custom of some parents to transfer their children from a public to a private school for the last two years. When this happens, there is need for some help in preparing the student for the changed life in the private school, especially if it is a boarding school.

Decisions about Leaving School

Soon after starting secondary school some children will begin to reach the place where further schooling of the kind available may not be desirable because each year brings them diminishing returns. How long to remain in school becomes an important problem for these students. Research indicates that the 40 per cent of our students who do not graduate from high school are at a disadvantage for the rest of their lives, particularly with regard to employment. It is essential, then, that every possibility of adapting the school program to serve the individuals be explored before the reluctant conclusion is reached that leaving school is the best available method of "continuing education."

Learning Problems

Although the learning problems encountered in the secondary school are not always new, many now become of increasing importance. Reading difficulties; rate of reading and comprehension; likes and dislikes of studies, teachers, and types of literature; differences in aptitude for different school subjects—all are very important factors in the student's adjustment to the secondary school. A guidance program will help diagnose the learning difficulty and plan steps to overcome it. The student may need remedial reading, help in arithmetic, a different course of study, a change of teachers, or perhaps prolonged counseling to overcome emotional barriers to learning.

Decisions about College

At graduation from the secondary school a decision must be made regarding enrollment in some type of post-high-school institution, such as business school, technical school, or college. Such a complex and crucial decision should be made with adequate guidance from teachers and counselors. At present it seems likely that, with the limited facilities of colleges and with the great increase in the number applying for admission, the problem of being accepted for college work will be a very serious one. This means that the marks earned in the last two or three years of the secondary school and the quality of work done there will be of extreme importance. The unprecedented demand for trained men and women in science and mathematics and the millions of dollars provided by the Federal government, the states, and private enterprises for increased educational facilities and scholarships place an added responsibility upon the schools for the guidance of students who have the abilities to succeed in such specialized training and who have the desire and the ambition to enter this specialization.

The choice of a college is one of the very important problems facing parents and high-school students, and it merits far more consideration than is usually given to it. Colleges are not all alike in entrance requirements, cost, atmosphere, or opportunities offered. Proximity to the home of the student is often a controlling factor. Some students do need a continuance of home influence, but others need to get away from home and learn to be independent. Some need a small college; others, a large one.

Some colleges have developed an aura of respectability, a halo of superiority that is often mistaken for unusual merit. This halo may be the result of long tradition, difficulty of entrance, long waiting lists of candidates for admission, or propaganda. The recent attempts to rate colleges according to certain predetermined elements are, in many ways, helpful, but the ratings do not take into account the elements that are of greatest importance—the quality of instruction, the personal influence of the faculty on the students, and the atmosphere of the college. Because some employers may consult these lists in selecting employees, the rating of a college may have some practical value in helping the student in securing a position after graduation. Most employers, however, are not unduly influenced by the character of the applicant's college because they do not take for granted that attendance at a certain college necessarily implies fitness for a particular job.

Institutions do differ in real effectiveness of instruction, and some that have high prestige really merit it, but others do not. Leaders in all walks of life are by no means confined to graduates of so-called "high-ranking" institutions. There are hundreds of good small colleges scattered about the country where a student may secure a really fine education. Indeed, some of the men and women who have received their graduate training in large universities of high reputation and are, therefore, claimed as their product have taken their undergraduate work in a small college. It is often a blessing, rather than a tragedy, that a student finds himself unable to gain admission to a college that has a high reputation. Much depends upon what the student brings with him, and admission by itself guarantees nothing in the way of learning and success.

Two of the most frequent reasons for the choice of a college are that the father or the mother graduated from that particular college or that some friend, possibly the teacher or the counselor, did. These reasons are emphasized by the propaganda organized by nearly every college and broadcast by the alumni. "Harveton University wants the best. Alumni, be on the lookout for good strong men: scholars, athletes. Get hold of them, send them to Harveton." This activity may be entirely legitimate, but the result is that Mr. Brown, an alumnus of Harveton, principal of the Jonesboro High School, picks out the best students and the finest athletes and tries to influence them to go to Harveton. Now Harveton may be a good university, but it may not be the best place for these particular boys. Alumni are very likely to want to send the best candidates to their own university, saying, "Let the others go to Podunk College." Colleges and universities do differ in spirit, offerings, and suitability for certain types of young men and women. No choice of a college should be made without a very careful study of the institution and of the student to determine the suitability of one for the other. The decision should be made on the basis of the needs of the student and the degree to which the institution meets these needs. When two institutions are equally suitable and equally good, other reasons may then properly enter into the decision. The question is altogether too vital, and means too much in the life of the young man or woman, to be decided upon any other basis than the needs of the individual.

Information about college entrance requirements should be known by students and parents long enough in advance of graduation from high school so that subjects necessary for entrance may be taken. The parents of a young man may plan for years to send him to a certain university, only to find when he is a senior in high school that he cannot qualify because he has only two years of Latin and four years are required. Such a situation is entirely inexcusable.

At present the unprecedented demand for college education and the limited facilities throughout the country have changed the question for many from "What college shall I choose" to "What college will take me?" This condition has made it necessary to begin making plans several years in advance and to make application to several colleges instead of to only one. The competition after a student enters college is also so great that much emphasis is placed on meeting the scholastic demands of the college and on adjustment to college life. This situation places an added responsibility on the secondary school for considering more carefully the type of college which is best suited to a student's ability and needs and for preparing him to adjust himself to the scholastic and social life of the college. The difficulty, importance, and complexity of decisions about college argue strongly for the need for guidance services in secondary schools.

GUIDANCE NEEDS RELATED TO PERSONAL DEVELOPMENT

Emotional Development and Guidance

Emotional disturbances may occur in any stage of a person's development and in any part of the school system. Some have their origin or at least become more pressing in the secondary school. Physiological development, bringing with it increased size and strength, sex impulses, responsibilities resulting from approaching maturity—all are very important causes of emotional changes and emotional instability. Such emotional conditions are often the causes of much maladjustment and unhappiness. The student needs help in his growth toward "emotional maturity," that is, in the ability to direct his strong basic emotions into channels that lead to the attainment of ends that are socially desirable and individually satisfying.

Physical Development and Guidance

The physical needs peculiar to secondary-school pupils center around the period of rapid growth and physiological maturation. Along with these changes we frequently find lowered vitality, fatigue, lethargy (often mistaken for laziness), impaired coordination and awkwardness due to unequal growth of different parts of the body, and physiological changes caused by maturing of the sex organs. Serious maladjustments often result from these conditions. Students undergoing such development need information, understanding, and guidance to help them adjust to their changing bodies.

Social Development and Guidance

The special social needs of the young adolescent arise partly from expanding vision resulting from more extended experience, wider contacts, and approaching maturity. Timidity, self-conscious-ness, overagressiveness, dislikes, "crushes," and "wanderlust" are among the difficulties often apparent in the adolescent. He needs help in the establishment of wholesome relations with the opposite sex. He needs to be understood and accepted even when his con-duct cannot be approved. What he does and what he thinks should be viewed with an understanding of the physical and mental changes that are taking place in him. He needs to have a sense of belonging to some group, a sense of being needed and wanted. He needs help in freeing himself from the fears and the sense of guilt that beset him. The narrow personal loyalty that he feels toward his gang should be respected, but he should be helped to widen this loyalty to a larger group—to his school, to society, to an accepted ideal. He needs to understand more clearly his responsibilities toward others and toward constituted authority. He needs help in the develop-ment of responsibility and independence of judgment.

The purpose of education is to help young people acquire the knowledge, develop the habits and skills, and attain the attitudes and ideals that are essential for adjustment to modern life and for its progressive improvement. Although individual instruction may be more effective than group work in the acquisition of knowledge and in the development of useful habits and skills, providing such instruction is quite impossible. Moreover, there are some distinct advantages in class or group organization in learning to live and work together, to accept restrictions essential to effective learning, to respect the rights of others, and to cooperate with others in enterprises that are planned by the group and have value for all. Group work utilizes the social instinct of human beings.

Guidance has a major responsibility in assisting youth to or-ganize or choose groups that have useful objectives and that are suited to the desires, needs, and abilities of the individuals of the group. Assistance to youth in social adjustments is a function of the entire school. The administrator, librarian, teacher, and counselor all have a definite responsibility for giving such help. Every pupil should feel that he is accepted by his teacher and by every other member of the school staff who has contact with him. The entire atmosphere of the school should be permeated with this spirit even though corrections, restrictions, and punishments may be necessary.

Pupils should always feel free to come to any member of the school staff for help. The desire to be accepted by someone is universal. We all want to have a feeling of belonging, to be needed and wanted. Nonacceptance or open rejection often results in reprisals and in destructive activities.

Guidance can also help in assisting in the organization of such activities as student clubs in the secondary school. Very often the organization of clubs that are constructive and useful prevents the formation of clandestine groups that have undesirable objectives. In many schools certain clubs are purely traditional and, although once useful, do not now meet real needs. Such clubs should be eliminated or their purposes changed. A pupil who wishes to be chosen for a certain club should be helped to realize the necessity for developing the qualifications required by the club he hopes to join and of being the kind of person who will be accepted by the members of the group.

The members of clubs should also be helped to realize their responsibility for the selection of new members. A member should not be chosen or rejected merely for personal reasons or because he lives on a certain side of the railroad track, nor even entirely for the contribution he can make to the club. The help that the prospective member can get by membership in the group should also be a factor in a decision about his selection.

It has been suggested that the choice of a new member of any club be based on his mental ability as compared with that of the members of the group, that is, that a club made up largely of pupils of high mental ability should choose only those students who have high mental ability. In some cases where the activities of the club demand high ability, this might be desirable; but in most cases this is not the case. Studies seem to indicate that the selection of a new member is more often based on personality traits than on mental ability. Student organizations should be helped to realize that they are very important elements in the overall school program and should be so organized and administered that they will be of maximum value to the entire student body and not merely self-perpetuating clubs for certain types of students.

The problems occasioned by organizations and other elements in the school program designed to increase social adjustment call for guidance services. The finest program of clubs, classes, and activities will not help the student who has not been guided in making best use of his available opportunities.

SUMMARY

However effective the guidance given in the elementary school, it will not eliminate all the problems that appear in the secondary school. The period of the junior–senior high school presents a challenge for guidance workers. The differences among secondary-school students in height, weight, physiological maturity, and social and emotional characteristics are very great. All are approaching maturity, but there are often mixtures of immaturity and maturity not only among the pupils in a class but also in the same pupil.

Just ahead are important choices regarding education, occupation, and marriage. Study, discipline, social life, and available school activities are quite different from those found in the elementary school and must be varied for different students in the same class. This is the last opportunity for the school to give the majority of students any material help in learning to make wise choices.

When we consider the nature of the secondary-school student, we see that our culture makes great demands on him. Basic decisions must be made at this time which will have lasting repercussions. Guidance must be available to increase the quality of the vocational, educational, personal-social experiences which the school offers the adolescent.

EXERCISES

1. List some decisions you made in high school that have had lasting effects on the course of your vocational or personal development. How might guidance have helped you with these decisions?

2. There is much controversy regarding the extent of the school's responsibility for the personal-social development of its students. What is your position with regard to this problem?

3. Interview three secondary-school students regarding guidance. Ask to whom they go to discuss (1) personal-social concerns, (2) edu-

cational decisions, (3) vocational plans. Be prepared to discuss the implications of your findings.

REFERENCES

Bennett, Margaret C.: *Guidance in Groups*, McGraw-Hill Book Company, Inc., New York, 1955.

Frank, Lawrence K., and Mary Frank: *Your Adolescent at Home and in School*, The Viking Press, Inc., New York, 1956.

Casell, Arnold, Florence Ilg, and Louise Ames: *Youth: The Years from Ten to Sixteen*, Harper & Brothers, New York, 1956.

Jersild, Arthur T.: *The Psychology of Adolescence*, The Macmillan Company, New York, 1957.

Warters, Jane: *High School Personnel Work Today*, McGraw-Hill Book Company, Inc., New York, 1956.

CHAPTER 9

VOCATIONAL GUIDANCE

Organized guidance in the United States began in an effort to get jobs for youth. Success in this effort depended, in large measure, on finding jobs that were suited to the abilities of different individuals or on finding individuals suited to different jobs. This effort met a real need not only of industry but of youth. Choices relating to occupations are of extreme importance and often are the dominant problem facing youth in high school and college. As the vocational guidance movement developed and the important factors came to light, the concept of vocational guidance was crystallized in the following statement: "Vocational guidance is the assistance given in choosing, preparing for, entering upon, and making progress in an occupation." This is still its accepted definition.

HELPING STUDENTS MAKE VOCATIONAL DECISIONS

Due largely to the increased emphasis upon the individual as the center of the entire educational process, the scope of guidance has been enlarged and now includes help given to the individual in all his problems and choices. However, occupational decisions are still the central problem facing many youths. It is profoundly true, however, that "life is more than meat," and the occupation is by no means all there is in life. Family life and social, civic, religious, and recreational aspects cannot be neglected. The life goal—the objective that provides the center of all activities and gives meaning to life—is very important, but a satisfying and successful life is often dependent on the wise choice of an occupation and a reasonable success in it. The job itself is often the aspect that gives meaning to life just as it is true that a satisfying life goal is frequently what gives meaning to the occupation. The two cannot be separated.

Aims of Vocational Guidance

The specific aims of vocational guidance may be stated as follows:

1. To assist the student to acquire such knowledge of the characteristics and functions, the duties and rewards of the group of occupations within which his choice will probably lie as he may need for intelligent choice

2. To enable him to find what general and specific abilities and skills are required for the group of occupations under consideration and what are the qualifications, such as age, preparation, and sex, for entering them

3. To give opportunity for experiences in school (tryout courses) and out of school (after-school and vacation jobs) which will give such information about conditions of work as will assist the individual to discover his own abilities and help him in the development of wider interests

4. To help the individual develop the point of view that all honest labor is worthy and that the most important bases for choice of an occupation are (a) the service that the individual can render to society, (b) personal satisfaction in the occupation, and (c) aptitude for the work required

5. To assist the individual to acquire a technique of analysis of occupational information and to develop the habit of analyzing such information before making a final choice

6. To assist him to secure such information about himself, his abilities, general and specific, his interests, and his powers as he may need for wise choice

7. To assist economically handicapped children who are above the compulsory attendance age to secure, through public or private funds, scholarships or other financial assistance so that they may have opportunities for further education in accordance with their vocational plans

8. To assist the student to secure a knowledge of the facilities offered by various educational institutions for vocational training and the requirements for admission to them, the length of training offered, and the cost of attendance

9. To help the worker to adjust himself to the occupation in which he is engaged; to assist him to understand his relationship to workers in his own and related occupations and to society as a whole

10. To enable the students to secure reliable information about the danger of alluring short cuts to fortune through short training courses and selling propositions, and of such unscientific methods as phrenology, physiognomy, astrology, numerology, or graphology, and to compare these methods with that of securing really trustworthy information

Methods of Vocational Guidance

Because many factors influence people in choosing an occupation, various methods may be used in helping them choose wisely. The factors responsible for the choice of an occupation are many and often complex. Very often people are not conscious of the influences that were responsible for the choice of their present occupation. Sometimes occupational heredity—family tradition and pride—may influence the choice. People may drift from one occupation to another until finally, almost by accident, one occupation, which was the only one available at the time, becomes permanent. Great admiration for some person who has been very successful or one who has made some outstanding contribution may influence the choice, or the individual may respond to what he conceives to be a direct call from God to enter some service.

There can be no doubt that, in many cases, the occupations chosen on the basis of any of these factors have been quite suitable to the interests and abilities of the individual, but in other cases it has been disastrous for the individual and for the service itself. None of the factors listed can be relied on as adequate means of help in the choice of an occupation, although they may be, in some cases, important auxiliary elements.

Organized vocational guidance assists the individual by providing him with all the data that indicate his interests and abilities and all that are essential to an understanding of the type of work.

He is helped to learn about the duties and responsibilities of various occupations, the conditions of work, the wages or salaries, and other benefits and to organize all this information in such a way as to enable him to make choices suited to his abilities and needs. Of course, it must be freely conceded that the best-organized and best-equipped program of guidance will sometimes fail because of the inadequacy of our present methods and techniques and because the individual may refuse to accept the evidences of his abilities and interests.

Difficulties of Vocational Guidance

In this country there are practically no hereditary occupations, no occupation that passes down automatically from father to son for many generations. Theoretically, any youth with sufficient ability can aspire to enter any occupation regardless of the social status of his parents. Every year boys and girls whose parents are desperately poor obtain the education and training that enable them to attain success in medicine, law, social work, education, research, government work, and many other high-level occupations.

One of the most startling evidences of freedom of choice has been the great number of women who have entered occupations previously staffed only by men. Women have now amply demonstrated their ability in many skilled occupations and in all the professions. In America choice of occupation is not limited by the social or financial status of parents, by race, sex, or place of residence. This very freedom of choice, however desirable, constitutes one of the major difficulties in vocational guidance.

Another difficulty arises from the slow, gradual process of an individual's vocational development. Guidance for choice of an occupation cannot be done in a hurry because it is a process of development which often requires many years. Special abilities and interests that are crucial in vocational choice develop slowly and appear throughout the life of youth. Research indicates that readiness for choice of an occupation is a gradual process. There are stages of vocational maturation, and it is unwise for parents and counselors to urge youth to make choices when they are not yet ready to do so. It also seems clear that such maturation, like physiological maturation, may come at different times with different individuals. Guidance practices are too often concerned with help given at the time of crisis when the choice must be made. Guidance would be much more effective if it were concerned with preparing the individual to meet the crisis before it comes. Guidance should be a developmental process and suited to the stages of development of each student.

What is essential is a concerted and planned program in which parents, counselors, teachers, and fellow students are of real help both in facilitating the development of maturation and in choosing the occupation. Furthermore, special abilities and ambitions may appear throughout the early life of youth and be revealed in various ways to different people not connected with the school. Men and women in the community engaged in business and industry or in various professions can be utilized in the vocational guidance program. Among citizens in the community who should be of special help in the discovery of abilities and interests are workers in churches, because of their basic interest in building character and their service to society.

THEORIES OF VOCATIONAL CHOICE

In the last few years attention has been turned to developing theories that would account for vocational choices. Some theorists have seen vocational choice as a response to economic conditions and therefore dictated largely by external circumstances. Others seem to believe that social determinants are paramount and that the socioeconomic level of the family largely determines one's occupation.

Most theorists, however, view vocational choice as but one aspect of total behavior and therefore look for a more complete explanation within a broad personality theory. For example, psychoanalytically oriented psychologists explain vocational choice as a response to unmet and largely unconscious needs. Behaviorists believe that vocational choice is conditioned by experiences which reinforce certain ways of behaving at the expense of alternative possibilities. Perhaps the most developed theories dealing with an explanation for vocational choice are those of Anne Roe and Donald Super.

Anne Roe: Childhood Determinants[1]

Anne Roe's contribution has two major components—a scheme for classifying occupations and an explanation for vocational decisions. Occupations are first divided into eight groups—service, business contact, organization, technology, outdoor, science, arts and entertainment, and general cultural. Next she divides each group into levels from 1 (highest) to 6 (lowest).

One group will serve to illustrate her scheme of classification. Within the service group she lists social-work supervisors as an example of workers in level 1; social workers for level 2; police sergeants, level 3; barbers, level 4; taxi drivers, level 5; and elevator operators, level 6. All these workers have in common the fact that they serve others, but the training needed for each job is quite different, and the gap in ability between high and low is great.

Roe next considered the characteristics of workers in the eight groups and came to the conclusion that there were certain elements that distinguished each group. Service workers have few intellectual or artistic interests and are not dominating in the personal interactions which are so large a part of their jobs. Business contact workers (public relations counselors, salesmen, peddlers) also lack intellectual and artistic interests but differ from service workers in being strong and exploitive in their personal interactions. Organization workers (industrial tycoons, union officials, accountants, foremen, clerks) have few artistic or intellectual interests but have strong economic values and high persuasive scores. Technology workers (engineers, electricians, truck drivers) have less concern for interpersonal relations, have the highest mechanical aptitudes and interests of any group, have low aesthetic values, are object-oriented, and are marked in the upper levels by intellectual interests.

Outdoor workers (landscape architects, foresters, miners, farm laborers) come almost entirely from families engaged in similar work and are characterized by little concern for interpersonal relations. Science workers (research scientists to veterinary hospital attendants) have the highest intellectual interests of any group but

[1] Anne Roe, *The Psychology of Occupations*, John Wiley & Sons, Inc., New York, 1956.

low aesthetic interests. General cultural workers (college professors, teachers, librarians) are dominant in interpersonal relations, verbally oriented, with high intellectual and artistic interests. Workers in the arts and entertainment tend to be narcissistic, to have few intellectual interests, and to possess special talents and physical abilities.

Roe further concluded that personality and interests are more related to the group in which the worker is found than to his level within the group. Intelligence and socioeconomic level conversely are more related to level than to group.

Roe believes that the characteristics that indicate the group and level that will be chosen by an individual begin to appear very early, at least in the adolescent period, and should be taken into consideration in occupational choice. She is convinced of the importance of "life patterns." These patterns are determined largely by the early family and home situation. The psychological warmth felt by the child is related to the extent to which he was accepted, rejected, or dominated by his parents, and this relationship in turn resulted in the child's being concerned with people or things. People-oriented workers find satisfaction in certain occupations; thing-oriented workers, in different ones. Her theory puts primary emphasis on childhood determinants of vocational choice.

Roe's classification may be very useful in helping a student make a choice of occupations. In using it, one might begin with making an inventory of the student's interests through the use of a standardized instrument supplemented by a counseling interview. Next might come a study of the occupations listed by Roe in each *group* to determine such things as the requirements in age, education, training, the opportunities for employment, salaries, and advancement. With this information would come a consideration of the different types of activities in each *level*. Such a procedure might be a great help in making a choice of an occupation.

Donald Super: Implementation of the Self-concept[2]

In developing a theory of vocational choice, Donald Super has made studies of the course and cycle of the working life and the time dimension of occupational behavior. He describes the

[2] Donald E. Super, *The Psychology of Careers: An Introduction to Vocational Development*, Harper & Brothers, New York, 1957.

stages in what he calls "vocational development" as exploration, transition from school to work, floundering or trial, stability or establishment, and the years of decline. Super maintains that every person is qualified for a number of different occupations and that the "career pattern"—the occupational level attained and the sequence, frequency, and duration of trial and stable jobs—is determined by the parental socioeconomic level, mental ability, personal characteristics, and the opportunities to which he is exposed. The relative importance or influence of these factors differs with each individual, and the self-concept is of paramount importance in determining vocational choice and satisfaction.

The factors surrounding the choices of occupations he calls the "determinants" of vocational choice. It may seem unfortunate that the term "determinants" is used, for it is likely to imply a belief in determinism—something that is inevitable, something that one is powerless to prevent. As used by Super, the word "determinant" means, first of all, that there is a "relationship between" and that an influence is exerted. While there seems to be a clear relationship between the socioeconomic status of the home and the occupation chosen, we cannot forecast exactly what occupation a boy will enter by knowing the socioeconomic status of his family. Although there is a tendency for a boy to choose an occupation at the same level as that of his father's, no implication is made that it would be best for him to choose such an occupation. In this country the income from an occupation may have more influence on the social status of the individual than the social status of the father had upon the choice of the occupation by the individual.

Super has identified a number of determinants of vocational choice which he believes merit further study and consideration. Three kinds of individual characteristics and experience seem to be important: (1) psychological characteristics, such as intelligence, interests, personality, values, and needs; (2) physical characteristics, such as height, weight, general health, and special physical assets or handicaps; and (3) experiences, such as education, training, work history, and identification or rejection of role models. Three aspects of the individual's personal situation also appear to be significant: (1) family background, including socioeconomic status, reputation in the community, siblings, and interpersonal relationships; (2) family situation, including marital status, dependents, and interpersonal relationships, especially with spouse; and (3) general situation, including occupational and financial situation, personal reputation, geographic residence, race, and religion. Other determinants are found in the individual's environment—the economic, occupational, and technological status of his country—and in such unpredictable factors as illness, accidents, or unanticipated opportunities or liabilities.

The relative importance of different determinants of careers varies from one individual to another, from one occupation to another, and from one period to another. These determinants are instrumental in shaping the individual's self-concept—his understanding of what he is and what he can do. Super's main theoretical contribution lies in his assertion that the act of choosing an occupation constitutes an implementation of the self-concept. As we develop, we get a clearer and clearer picture of ourselves until we say, "This is the kind of person I seem to be"; then the next step is to say, "Therefore, that is the kind of work I might do and enjoy."

Super, with Roe and others, has helped us put our thinking about vocational choice into a framework that permits the testing of hypotheses and the advancement and improvement of basic theory. It is only by the sharpening of theories such as Super's that we can improve the service we offer under the name of vocational guidance.

WORK EXPERIENCE AS A METHOD OF VOCATIONAL GUIDANCE

Work experience is the student's exposure to work in an occupation before he begins a full-time job. Five types of such experience are recognized: (1) Work that is done in some project undertaken for the benefit of the school, usually without pay, but where actual job conditions are maintained as far as possible. Some of these jobs are in connection with work in making or repairing school apparatus, rebinding books, or assisting in the library. Some are not connected with class activities, such as seeding the lawn, planting trees, or laying out an athletic field. (2) Work that is done for the community, performing some public service as a useful citizen, such as mosquito eradication, clearing waste land, or caterpillar control. (3) Job experience, with pay, which is done in connection with the school program, where part of the time is spent in school and part on an actual job. (4) Work experience that is done in connection with a school, where articles are produced in quantity, often for sale. (5) Experience gained in part-time jobs, not connected with the school program, after school or during vacation.

With the growing recognition that the curriculum of the student must include the total activities of his life in school and out of school, these work experiences are considered to be an indispensable part of a well-rounded education. Antioch College, among other institutions, considers actual work experience as an essential part of a liberal education. Some other general values are also recognized, such as cooperation between school and community, recognition of factors in school life other than the purely academic, the retention in school of students who would otherwise drop out, and the financial help to needy students.

In addition, such experiences can be very useful in revealing or developing interests and in disclosing abilities and aptitudes that help in choosing a life work.

For some years many schools have been experimenting with types of cooperative plans by which high-school students in commercial and industrial arts or vocational curriculums could secure practical on-the-job experience while they were still in school. This involves cooperation between school and commercial and industrial establishments so that students may, within the compulsory attendance requirements, be in school part of the time and at work part of the time. The cooperative plan of systematic school-and-work preparation involves learning activities in organized classes in school and business establishments in the community.

This is definitely a guidance project, for its purpose is "to assist the student to prepare for, enter upon, and make progress in an occupation." Although the student may have tentatively chosen his occupation before he signs up for the work, the experience on the job helps him to make a final decision regarding the particular kind of job he desires to have.

Some form of work experience is now in operation involving many different types of occupations. The details of the organization necessarily differ with different occupations and different local conditions.

The types of occupations or jobs listed in the distributive area are found, for example, in various retail and wholesale establishments that sell such merchandise as food, clothing, home furnishings, automobiles, hardware, drugs, dry goods, furniture, jewelry, and farm and garden supplies. Workers in distributive occupations are also in business-service establishments such as banks, real estate offices, insurance companies, savings and loan associations, and dry-cleaning firms. Students may choose a career objective from areas of work such as that of buyer, advertising manager, retail-store owner, interior decorator, jeweler, personnel director, window trimmer, display artist, and wholesale salesman. Persons enrolled in a program of this kind attend classes in school a part of the time and work in a distributive occupation part of the time. The place where a cooperative trainee is employed part time—the laboratory phase of his program—usually is referred to as his "work station."

Features of Good Programs

The effectiveness of the laboratory part of cooperative part-time training depends on intelligent location, selection, establishment, and management of the work station. These procedures are specific responsibilities of school administrators, supervisors and teacher-coordinators of distributive education, counselors, and businessmen.

A good work station is one in which school administrators and employers understand the cooperative part-time plan of training and are wholeheartedly interested in it. They are fully aware of their responsibilities to the program. The school provides good classroom instruction based on job requirements of the students, and the employer provides practical work sufficiently important to require training. Both the employer and the school provide for effective on-the-job supervision of the trainees. Each trainee is evaluated periodically and informed of the progress he is making.

Moreover, the work the trainee performs involves occupational knowledge and skill sufficiently important to justify the extended period of training which he devotes to them. A schedule of working time is specified for each trainee, and he is paid according to a fixed wage scale that usually provides for gradual increases to be granted when merited.

Many things can be done to make the work-experience program a good one. The coordinator of work experience is the key to the success of the program. Authorities have suggested ways in which he can be sure that the work experience has maximum value for the student. The coordinator should visit each trainee regularly to watch him perform his duties on the job. For instance, if a trainee is observed giving a poor sales demonstration, the coordinator should provide additional classroom practice in presenting merchandise. If he sees that the trainee lacks information about the merchandise being sold, he may direct him in a study of merchandise facts. When a trainee first begins his work, he will often feel that he lacks certain skills and knowledge for satisfactory job performance. The coordinator and the trainee should discuss any such deficiencies and determine the instruction needed to improve job efficiency. Persons working with the trainee daily should be able to point out weaknesses in his job performance and suggest further study that the school can provide. If a trainee is working in a selling position, one good technique for checking his job performance is that of making a service shopping report. During a "customer" purchase the trainee is observed and rated on his selling techniques. A detailed account of his actions is then written up by the "customer." The description may later be analyzed for sales weaknesses.

The vocational-minded coordinator will make a point of relating classroom and job instruction to trainee work experiences and will therefore use imagination and originality in selecting appropriate teaching methods and techniques. He will constantly be on the lookout for new instructional materials that will provide opportunity for individual trainees to study specific subjects related to their work activities. Group instruction should be given in the classroom on those subjects helpful to all trainees, such as employment opportunities in the field of distribution, how to apply for and hold a position, and the principles of business ethics. Job-progress reports should be examined and discussed by the coordinator and the trainee, and then classroom instruction should be based on these reports.

The daily assistance the employer gives each trainee should also help meet specific job needs. Both the coordinator and the employer should encourage the trainee to study trade journals, sales manuals, and other such business publications. Both may provide flexibility of on-the-job learning activities by encouraging a trainee to attend employer-employee meetings and such organized training courses as may be available in the business establishment. Style shows, salesmen's displays, visits to market exhibits of new merchandise, and film showings may provide further appropriate learning experiences for individual trainees.

Inasmuch as experiences in a business laboratory are an integral part of the cooperative program, school credit should be given for them just as it is given for laboratory experience connected with other classes. Enrollment in chemistry or in physics almost always includes the laboratory, with no school credit being given for one without the other. Enrollment in the cooperative program includes assignment to work stations as a part of the course, and the school credit allowed is based not on either the classroom instruction or the laboratory work experience but on both together as in chemistry or physics. Therefore only one grade should be given for the combined program of classroom and on-the-job activities.

Value of Work Experience

Good work-experience programs can help develop better cooperative relationships between the school and the community. They can provide benefits for student trainees, for employers, and for the school.

For trainees, they provide business experiences that should aid in further attainment of a career objective, motivate learning activities on the job and in the classroom, and provide specific vocational skills and work habits. For employers, they attract better trainees and encourage them to continue working for the business establishment in which they receive training, help develop more efficient personnel, and afford opportunity for them to contribute to the extension of the community's educational facilities. For the school, they encourage better school-community relations through stimulating businessmen's interests in the school and educators' interests in local business affairs, enrich the curriculum by providing a work-experience laboratory needed in effective preparation for specific occupational goals, contribute more meaning to vocational guidance activities by facilitating the making of occupational choices, help hold students in school until graduation, and extend school laboratory facilities at little added expense. These and other values make the work-experience program an important educational and guidance technique.

Responsibilities of Key People for the
Success of the Program

General responsibility for the quality and effectiveness of work stations in the cooperative program rests on the school superintendent and the principal, but the teacher-coordinator has the direct responsibility in this matter. School counselors, employers of the students, and state representatives of distributive education also have specific duties.

School administrators should understand and appreciate the distinctive features of work stations in the cooperative program and how they should be selected and administered; they should make such schedule and curriculum adjustments as are necessary for including the work-experience laboratory in the total school program. They will need to provide guidance facilities that will aid in enrolling in the training program those students who can profit most from it and see that the effectiveness of work stations is systematically evaluated. Administrators will also need to provide qualified coordinators to supervise the work-experience phase of the program and acquaint teachers and other staff members with work-station standards, objectives, and procedures.

Coordinators should develop high standards for work-station selection, management, and evaluation. They must select and place students in jobs that are related to their career objectives, or aid them in further exploration of vocational opportunities, and assist employers with the development of procedures for supervision of trainees and management of work stations. They will also relate classroom instruction to the trainee's job requirements and occupational objectives and see that the parents of trainees are informed about the cooperative program and that they approve the work-station agreements for their children.

School counselors will need to help explain the characteristics of work stations in the cooperative plan, assist in assigning to work stations those students who have decided on or are seriously considering career objectives in the distributive occupations, discourage any possible notion that the cooperative program is designed especially for students who have failed in other school subjects or programs, and help evaluate student progress on the job in order to determine the effectiveness of counseling activities.

Employers will profit most if they understand the characteristics and management of work stations in the cooperative program and provide on-the-job supervision and instruction that will contribute to student career objectives. They will also need to consult with the coordinator and other representatives of the school on the work progress of trainees.

Representatives of the state department of education should assist local coordinators and school administrators in developing criteria for selecting and administering work stations; they should also help in evaluating and improving standards for work stations and suggest the elimination of those work stations that do not meet high standards.

OTHER VOCATIONAL GUIDANCE RESOURCES

The potential human resources of guidance for any individual are all those persons in and outside the school whose influence might be utilized to help him make decisions and adjustments. The most important of the resources outside the school are the parents, whose influence is bound to be very strong whether it is consciously exerted or not. Others in the family and community are also potentially important. Pastors of churches and other church personnel are also potentially significant, although at present their influence seems quite negligible except with a very few young people. Organizations in the community, especially service clubs such as Rotary and Kiwanis, may be of great value and, in many cities, are very influential. Individuals in the community—physicians, nurses, engineers, lawyers, businessmen—are other sources of valuable help, although seldom utilized. Community ideals and community mores exert powerful influences on young people. Vacation experience in camps, summer jobs, and recreation trips may also be useful.

The School As a Resource

The school itself is by far the greatest potential source of help. Its fundamental purpose is guidance—to give help in learning, in conduct, in the development of habits, skills, and ideals. Every member of the school staff—secretaries, teachers, counselors, nurses, physicians, psychologists, and custodians—all exert powerful influence on the students. The school life, as seen in classes, in athletics, in student government, and in social activities, is potentially a very powerful force.

To make them as valuable as they should be, these forces must be so organized and coordinated as to become a real team utilizing all the knowledge and skills of each member and bringing to bear on each case the combined wisdom of the entire group.

Home, Social, and Play Activities

Another source of guidance is found in the life of the student out of school. Obviously, if we wish to learn all we can about students, we cannot neglect their home life, their social activities, and their play experiences where they may reveal characteristics, abilities, and interests that do not appear in their life in school. Parents can often give helpful information about health, study habits, general traits, and special interests and guide their children's vocational interests. A careful record of the total life of the student, after school hours and on vacations, is also very helpful. Much influence determining the vocational choices of students comes from these sources.

Unity of Efforts

Vocational guidance has been defined as the assistance that is given in connection with "choosing, preparing for, entering upon, and making progress in an occupation." It would be well to stress again the point already made many times, that it is impossible to separate sharply the vocational aspects of guidance from the educational, moral, and cultural aspects. The future occupation often plays a large part in choosing a school or a course. Occupational choices frequently depend upon educational background, and they are often governed by health, social, and cultural problems. The counselor cannot, and should not, try to keep the various aspects of guidance entirely distinct. This would be working directly contrary to that unity of character and personality which is essential. In spite of this unity and the impossibility and undesirability of separating vocational guidance from other kinds or aspects of guidance, it is helpful to consider certain parts of vocational guidance separately from others. Sometimes the vocational aspect stands out so clearly that it dominates everything else, and the civic, moral, cultural aspects shrink into comparative insignificance. Often choice of occupation and getting a job are absolutely necessary and pre-requisite to everything else—good citizenship, culture, and even good character itself. Recognizing the impossibility of complete separation, we have attempted to stress the methods that are commonly used primarily to assist in choice of occupation, in getting a job, and in becoming adjusted to the job.

SUMMARY

One of the major responsibilities of the secondary school and the college is to assist youth in the choice of a life occupation. The occupation chosen should be suited to the abilities, aptitudes, interests, and needs of the individual. It should be one that will enable him to provide adequately for himself and his family and that will assist him in the attainment of a worthy life goal.

Freedom of occupational choice is the right of every individual, but there is much help that can be given without violating that freedom. Ability and aptitude tests, interest inventories, and personality estimates may all be used to advantage. Experiences in and out of school and vacation and after-school jobs are also often useful in vocational guidance.

Roe has studied the interests of people in different types and levels of occupations. It may help to compare the interests of those in occupations with the interests of the student to help him make a vocational choice. Super has found certain elements that seem to act as influences or "determinants" in the choice of occupations.

Of even greater value is Super's conception that readiness to choose an occupation is a gradual process and that the time of "maturation" differs with different individuals. There is danger, therefore, in urging a student to choose an occupation before he is ready to do so.

EXERCISES

1. List the chief determinants that led you to your present occupation. When did you make your major vocational decisions, and what further information about yourself or the occupation would have been helpful to you at that time?

2. Does Roe's or Super's theory seem most helpful to you in explaining your own vocational choice? Why?

3. Interview one student, one employer, and one teacher who has been involved in a work-experience program and learn from them the advantages and disadvantages they see in this technique.

REFERENCES

Baer, Max F., and Edward C. Roeber: *Occupational Information*, 2d ed., Science Research Associates, Inc., Chicago, 1958.

Hoppock, Robert: *Occupational Information*, McGraw-Hill Book Company, Inc., New York, 1957.

Norris, Willa, Franklin R. Zeran, and Raymond N. Hatch: *The Information Service in Guidance*, Rand McNally & Company, Chicago, 1960.

Roe, Anne: *The Psychology of Occupations*, John Wiley & Sons, Inc., New York, 1956.

Super, Donald E.: *The Psychology of Careers: An Introduction to Vocational Development*, Harper & Brothers, New York, 1957.

CHAPTER 10

ORGANIZATION OF GUIDANCE SERVICES IN SCHOOLS

The concept of the place and function of guidance presented in previous chapters makes any adequate description of its organization in a school system very difficult. Guidance organization cannot any longer be described by the use of diagrams that were once the pride and joy of the administrator. Guidance is not something that can be completely separated from the general life of the school by tucking it away in the office of the counselor or the principal. Because it is the duty and the responsibility in some measure of every member of the school staff, it is a function that must be shared by all and should be so understood and administered. The problem of organization is one of coordinating the guidance services of the entire school staff in such a way that the total facilities of the school may be utilized and brought to bear upon the center of our efforts —the problems of each child.

PRINCIPLES OF GUIDANCE ORGANIZATION

The Connecticut State Department of Education has developed a statement regarding the organization of guidance which admirably expresses the necessary interrelationship of guidance with the total school program. This statement, which is used here by special permission of the Commissioner of Education of Connecticut, does much to place guidance in its proper educational perspective.

Purpose and Functions of Guidance

The statement begins by reaffirming the basic purposes and goals of American education.

> Our educational program should provide every youth with knowledge and skills which he needs and can use. It should develop his ability to think independently and constructively. It should enable him to acquire an understanding of himself, of his environment, and of the concepts and principles upon which a satisfactory life in our American democracy is based. It should help him develop desirable social, civic and vocational attitudes. It should provide him with a background which makes it possible for him to earn a living.
>
> Among the conditions necessary for the realization of these goals are the following:
> That teaching be geared to the outcomes sought and to the ability of the student,
> That pupils be helped to cope with those emotional tensions and environmental handicaps which impede learning and inhibit healthy behavior,
> That pupils be given skilled individualized help in understanding themselves and their relationship to their environment, and in making certain types of decisions,
> That special provisions be made for those with serious difficulties which impede learning and adjustment. These provisions should be based upon a careful study and should use special techniques appropriate to the problems involved.

Not content with pointing out the purposes of the total educational enterprise, the writers continue by specifying the special contribution to be made by guidance through the services of the school personnel workers.

> Every member of the educational profession has a responsibility for providing these conditions. (In addition to classroom teachers and administrators, there are many specialists trained to render certain supplementary services. Included are workers in the areas of health, remedial teaching, curriculum, research, instruction of the mentally and physically handicapped, attendance, social work, psychology, and counseling services.) This bulletin will consider the roles of the school social worker, the school psy-

chologist, and the school counselor and the ways in which they facilitate the educational process. They are a part of the team of school personnel workers.

School personnel workers, as members of the school staff, are concerned with helping pupils:

to clarify their interests and attitudes,

to understand their personal motives,

to know their abilities, to formulate goals, to try to realize their potentials and to evaluate their goals realistically,

to have a feeling of worth and a sense of belonging,

to feel that someone is concerned with them as individuals—someone whom they can trust and who can help them,

to develop and realize an adequate and acceptable self-concept,

to understand themselves in relation to their environment,

to see ways in which frustrating and tension-creating situations may be handled,

to understand ways in which adjustment may mean change in self or change in the environment,

to orient to new situations and to understand difficult situations,

to understand and accept the need for limitations on their behavior,

to get on well with others,

to develop plans of action based on a careful analysis of themselves and of the factors influencing their situations,

to discover and engage in activities or programs which will contribute to their educational growth and development.

School personnel workers also approach pupil problems:

by respecting the responsibilities of parents for their children, and by recognizing that parental responsibilities are particularly important in the phases of child development listed above, by working with the family and other persons or groups important in the child's environment,

by referring pupils to those who can render help not available in home or school,

by affecting various changes that improve the environmental situation.

School personnel workers assist the school staff:

by helping to identify pupils who need special attention and by suggesting ways in which teachers can help them,

by furnishing teachers with more comprehensive knowledge about individual pupils and their backgrounds so teachers can work more effectively,

by identifying and clarifying needs of pupils which can be met through the curriculum,

by engaging in research which will help the school perform its functions,

by helping teachers plan activities for evaluating individual pupil progress and for defining learning weaknesses and strengths,

by working individually with pupils identified by teachers as having learning or adjustment problems,

by cooperating in the planning of a total program of testing and evaluation,

by helping teachers keep up to date on developments in special areas of psychology—especially in the areas of learning and adjustment.

Guideposts for Effective Organization

Having examined the major aims of guidance and one of the major roles found in the guidance program, we may now look at some signs of a sound organization of services in a local school system. The previously mentioned Connecticut report lists nine guideposts useful in considering guidance programs.

1. Services should be based on the needs of the pupils and the school system and should be an integral part of the total school program. This requires careful identification of these needs and coordinated cooperation among all school personnel.

2. All special services should be coordinated in a single department.

3. The director has an overall function affecting all pupils. He should be responsible directly to the superintendent or assistant superintendent.

4. The director in all except the very largest system will serve in a supervisory as well as in an administrative role. He should, therefore, have a broad knowledge of the special service fields and education as well as administrative qualifications. In certain instances, the superintendent, or assistant superintendent, will serve in this capacity.

5. A helpful pattern of line and staff relationship should be established.

6. Clear descriptive material on relationships and responsibilities should be developed so that special service workers themselves as well as all school staff members will know what these relationships are.

7. Some definite provision should be made for regular conferences among supervisors and staff to integrate thoroughly the services included in the pupil personnel department.

8. Provision should be made for coordination of this department with all other departments in the school system.

9. Provision should be made for adequate interviewing space in each school building. Central office facilities with sufficient secretarial staff should be made available to handle the stenographic and clerical details incident to the program.

Obviously there may be situations where deviations from these generalities will be both wise and necessary, but in most cases schools will benefit from following these suggestions.

PRACTICES IN GUIDANCE ORGANIZATION

Perhaps the best way to test the adequacy of these principles of guidance organization is to examine the actual functioning of a program, keeping in mind the purposes to be served by guidance. The Gloucester, Massachusetts, schools have developed brief descriptions of their guidance programs at the elementary- and secondary-school levels which indicate how general principles are translated into specific practices.

Typical Elementary-school Guidance Program

The Gloucester program consists in activities which constitute the minimum essentials necessary for the provision of guidance.

I. Maintenance of personal inventory to provide for:
   A. The introduction and use of an adequate cumulative record to be started when the pupil enters school and to continue until the pupil leaves school, with provisions for follow-up studies and placement.
   B. The identification of the pupils who have problems both in and outside the school, such as:

1. Pupils who have specific weaknesses in mastering the basic skills, knowledge, and understanding taught in the elementary grades—educational problems. Identification should be made by the use of achievement tests given to groups and to individuals.
2. Pupils who have difficulty in fitting into a regular school program because of mental ability, high or low. In this group will be found the students needing special class placement because of low mentality, the group of slow learners needing remedial treatment who, in the Gloucester public schools, will constitute the transfer students. Identification will be made by the use of intelligence testing, both group and individual.
3. Pupils who have health conditions not conducive to good school and home adjustment; those needing the care of the oculist, physician, and other medical personnel.
4. Pupils who have problems of social and emotional adjustment needing the attention of a child psychologist, social worker, or a behavior clinic.
5. Pupils who have unusual talents or very intense interests needing special attention by the teacher.

II. Cooperation with other staff members in the development and maintenance of good habits of study.

III. Cooperation with other staff members in the development and maintenance of good habits of school citizenship.

IV. Use of materials in the classroom to show not only how people live but how they make a living.

V. Establishment of a healthful relationship between the parents and the school, in order that there may be mutual understanding of both the home and the school program for the pupil.

VI. Cooperation with pupil's next school by furnishing it with pertinent information about the pupil and by enabling the pupil to gather data about the school to which he expects to go.

VII. Cooperation with the attendance officer in the study of cases of poor school attendance and employment of measures to remedy or prevent absence or tardiness.

While this program is not an elaborate or complex one, it has the advantage of practicality and is solidly based on principles similar to those previously listed.

Typical Secondary-school Guidance Program

The Gloucester secondary-school program follows the traditional approach of defining guidance in terms of the services provided for students.

1. Maintenance of personal inventory.
   a. Cumulative records should be kept and used for each pupil.
   b. Testing program should be developed to include intelligence, achievement, aptitude, and interest tests.
   c. Cumulative records, anecdotal records, teachers' rating scales, and similar material should be used when counseling pupils as to choice of courses, scholastic failures, attendance problems, behavior difficulties, and other evidences of maladjustment, such as personal, social, and physical problems.
2. Cooperation with other staff members in the study of cases of poor attendance and in taking steps to remedy or prevent absence or tardiness.
3. Collection and dissemination of occupational information.
   a. Secure information concerning local occupational requirements and opportunities.
   b. Organize and prepare for presentation the information secured relative to local occupations.
   c. Secure and present a general background of occupational information, including requirements, opportunities, and trends, locally, regionally, and nationally.
   d. Assist in establishing, preferably in the first year of high school, classroom units on occupations.
   e. Assist in correlating occupational information with regular school subjects.
   f. Use printed, illustrated, and visual material in presenting occupational information.
   g. Plan visits to view various types of local and regional employment.
   h. Plan local and regional career conferences.
4. Collection and dissemination of education and training information.

a. Secure, organize, and disseminate information concerning available educational and training opportunities at all levels for all educational and occupational fields.

b. Plan for student visitation to various types of educational institutions and training programs.

c. Arrange for directors of admissions and directors of training programs to meet with interested students at local school.

d. Arrange for counselors to visit colleges, universities, technical schools, and other types of post-secondary institutions.

5. Counseling.

a. Assist pupils in the interpretation of personal data as contained in the cumulative record.

b. Assist the individual in the identification of his major problems, educational, vocational, personal, social, and physical.

c. Assist the individual in the planning of possible solutions to his problems.

d. Help the individual in making a start toward carrying out those plans.

e. Help the individual, when necessary, in the modification of his plans.

6. Placement.

a. Assist pupils in securing part-time jobs and vacation employment according to aptitudes, abilities, and interests.

b. Assist those pupils desirous of seeking permanent employment when leaving school or graduating, taking into consideration aptitudes, abilities, and interests.

7. Follow-up study.

a. Maintain contacts with all school-leavers (graduates and dropouts) for a period of years for the purpose of rendering further aid and assistance.

b. Check individual achievements for the purpose of evaluating and improving the guidance program.

c. Furnish information as a basis for the evaluation and possible revision or enlargement of the educational program in light of school-leavers' experiences.

The Gloucester school system has defined its program for the upper elementary school (grades 7 and 8) and for the vocational school by reference to this same model of services made available to aid in the guidance of students. In each case the same principles of integration, coordination, and systemization are expressed through the guidance practices.

TEAMWORK AS BASIS FOR GUIDANCE ORGANIZATION

The effectiveness of guidance in any school is dependent on a clear understanding by all the school personnel of the purpose of guidance and the guidance function of each member of the staff; it also depends on cooperation among them, that is, teamwork. Teamwork, which is more than mere cooperation, involves conferences among different members of the school staff. In teamwork conferences teachers, counselors, nurses, and specialists in various areas exchange information and understanding about the child which result from their special professional knowledge, skills, points of view, and competencies. In such conferences all available data are pooled, possible causes for the problem are discussed, and group decisions are made regarding the most effective treatment to be employed.

In this approach everyone on the school staff at one time or another is an important member of the team. Moreover, real teamwork results in more than the sum total of all the contributions of its members. It is a situation where the knowledge and skill of each member help every other member of the group to understand the total problem of the child. The result is a real consensus, and it is often different from the concept of the problem held by any one member before the conference. From the various perceptions of the team members comes a synthesis none could have made alone. The working together of the team results in a superior product because of the mutual stimulation occasioned by this joint professional enterprise.

A real team is an organic whole engaged in a common enterprise, each one performing the part of the job assigned to him; but what he does and how he does it must fit into the entire pattern. We might say that it is like a chemical compound, not a mere mechanical mixture. We must keep continually in mind the ultimate purpose of the enterprise and understand not only the job that has to be done but what each of the other jobs is and how they all fit together.

Whenever a case is referred to the team, it is considered by the team as a whole, each person contributing the understanding and wisdom that he has gained from his study and experience in his special field, each respecting the contribution of other members, and, finally, the result being a joint conclusion regarding the problem and the best method to be used in helping the individual referred. It is a shared responsibility, with each member keeping in mind the solution of the problem rather than merely his own point of view. Such cooperation is very difficult to attain, and it should be recognized that it is very difficult or sometimes impossible for some persons to see it; but it should be one of the requirements for membership on such a team.

Example of Teamwork Organization

Teamwork of various kinds is now being used in many schools throughout the country. A very interesting plan was developed in Snyder, Texas, a city of about 18,000 population in a school district of about twice that size.[1] There are six elementary schools, one junior high school, and one senior high school, with a total school enrollment of about 4,000. The personnel staff involved in this project includes the coordinator of pupil personnel services, the curriculum administrator, four visiting teachers, two counselors—one in each of the two high schools—two nurses—one for the elementary school and one for the high school—one speech specialist, and one speech-improvement teacher.

The team approach was developed in each of the eight schools for the purpose of holding case conferences to study children who were having learning or adjustment problems. The general objective of the enterprise was to improve the school experiences of children and by so doing improve their learning and give them greater happiness and satisfaction. The case conferences attempt to arrive at clarification and agreement about goals through the contribution of the special knowledge and skills of each member of the team. The different functions and ways of functioning of members of the team are brought together for a specific, common purpose: the adjustment of the child. This is most effective when each member realizes the special values of the different points of view which the

[1] This cooperative project was developed by Dwane Collins in 1955. He has now developed a similar type of program for college students attending Colorado College.

individual members bring to the team process and its objectives. The team aims at the development of an understanding of roles and procedures by providing a framework in which each member has an opportunity to share in the skills, roles, limitations, and capacities of the other members. This method capitalizes on the strengths inherent in a democratic way of life by arriving at conclusions based on the shared judgments of all the personnel, with due consideration of the feelings of the members of the group.

The team conclusions are related to the basic problem of the child, the best method of helping him solve the problem, and judgments regarding who is best qualified to give the help needed.

Each team member must be professionally competent in his special area. The more specialized they are and the better they are versed, the more potent will be their force. Furthermore, there must be acceptance of the goals agreed upon by all members and a sharing of ideas, concerns, and understandings. Finally, members of the team must fit together at strategic points to achieve the great flexibility which is also desirable.

The team has a definite relationship to the structure of the school. The teacher has the responsibility and the obligation to bring the "case"—the child with his problems—to the attention of the principal of the school, who in turn refers the child to the team. The responsibility for each child is also shared by the nurse, with her special competency in physical health; by the visiting teacher, who is competent in social and emotional problems; and by the counselors, who are specialists in education evaluation and the assessment of ability. The teacher who made the original referral is usually called in when her "case" is discussed.

One value of this type of teamwork is to increase the number of children who can be considered at a given time. Team consideration can be facilitated because the entire team is present; the child's problem can be discussed, and each member can give his own knowledge and opinion to the team instead of requiring the person who has the chief responsibility for the child to go to each specialist separately.

The influence of this experiment has stimulated schools in a number of other states to adopt similar programs of guidance, apparently with outstanding success.

There are many school systems which are using a more

simple form of teamwork. It is not desirable to have the guidance team made up entirely of specialists, such as remedial speech or remedial reading experts, for each is likely to see symptoms of difficulties that relate to his specialty. A teacher—"just a teacher"— is often better able to find the real problem of the child than the specialist, for he sees the child as a whole. Most teamwork approaches, however, make use of committees staffed by personnel who can make special guidance contributions.

It is unfortunate that the librarian is not always appointed to the guidance team, for he is in a very favorable position to observe students in situations quite different from the classroom.

Librarians, in their efforts to serve the entire school, should, through study and consultation, become familiar with the aims and objectives of the guidance program. Understanding of the guidance services offered will enable them to become aware of many areas in which they can make definite contributions. Librarians should keep the guidance staff informed, by notes, telephone calls, periodic bulletins, or personal visits, of available library materials in their field. They should particularly call the attention of staff and students to materials dealing with such matters as counseling and guidance, vocations, colleges, scholarships, testing, psychology, personal and social adjustment, study habits, and significant economic and social conditions. Librarians who discuss the acquisition of materials with counselors will build a better supply of functional items and make the library a more useful source of guidance information. By welcoming and seeking opportunities to work with counselors, they can contribute to a better understanding of mutual problems, keeping in mind that all staff members have a common goal—the good of the students.

Because of the somewhat informal relationships existing in a library, librarians sometimes have occasion to learn of individual problems affecting the happiness, welfare, or educational progress of certain pupils. They may be able to help these pupils seek the aid of their counselors in handling such problems. Individual reading records, which are kept in some school libraries, can be made available to counselors and filed as a part of the student's permanent record.

Publicizing materials that relate to special features of the guidance program can be a real service to counselors. As they place special emphasis on career or college choice, for instance, librarians can direct additional attention to available materials in the library. Perhaps an idea on a bulletin board, a book title in a display, or a film presentation can be just the spark to cause the pupil to seek further knowledge and counseling that may greatly influence his future. Librarians may also be able to help counselors with suggestions for bibliographies or directories of resource people who may supply occupational information.

Librarians often have an opportunity in their work with pupils and teachers to direct attention to materials that aid the guidance program by centering on personal and social problems or on vocations. Book jackets that will stimulate reading in areas of personality development, family relationships, careers, or hobbies may be supplied to classrooms. Librarians should call the attention of teachers to items of this nature and to specific professional materials in order to develop greater awareness of guidance objectives.

Librarians can also assist the counselors in follow-up work with individual pupils. When counselors inform them of pupils with special needs or send pupils to consult them on specific matters, librarians can give individual reading guidance. Reading matter that brings extra understanding of the counselors' suggestions may help in the solving of a problem and, at the same time, lead to a greater appreciation of reading.

It has been seen by examining the potential contribution of one staff member—the librarian—that many resources are available in every school which could enrich the guidance program if they were but properly used.

Students As Resources to the Guidance Team

Although the guidance team is usually considered to be limited to members of the school staff, there are many other sources of help, both in and outside the school, which can be utilized.

One source of great potential value is the student himself. Young people who have been closely associated with one another for several years often know much more about each other than do their parents or their teachers. There are, to be sure, many difficulties in securing such information and in evaluating it. Students are quite properly reluctant to reveal information that has been given in confidence, and this loyalty must be respected. However, when such information is given, it should be utilized.

Parents As Resources to the Guidance Team

The parents have an important part to play in any guidance program that plans to utilize sources of help from outside the school. They not only have a stake in the future of their children but have a responsibility as well. However, few, if any, satisfactory methods have been developed to secure and utilize their help in the guidance program. Many different means of establishing better relations with parents have been tried, and the most promising one seems to be the face-to-face contact between teachers or counselors and parents. The plan of having parents come to the school for consultation seems to be particularly helpful.

Community As a Resource to the Guidance Team

Another source of assistance to the guidance program is the community itself, which also has a stake in the future of the youth. Community members are potentially of very great value not only as sources of information but as sources of direct help to the students. Some highly significant examples of such help have been reported from different parts of the country. Business and professional men are found to be very cooperative in giving information to students and in providing opportunities to secure experience in different types of work. In some cases businessmen have helped to secure scholarships to college or business school for boys and girls who are worthy of help and financially unable to enroll. As all the above shows, parents and other community members must be used as resource people if the guidance program is to be based on teamwork of the most effective kind.

Teamwork between Secondary Schools and Colleges

Another significant development involving a somewhat different type of teamwork is the Michigan State Secondary School–College Agreement Program, which is a direct outgrowth of the Michigan Study of the Secondary School Curriculum. The major objective of this study has been the improvement of secondary education through helping the "communities, the schools, and the people study themselves and to assist them in developing points of view in planning and in utilizing effective, democratic ways of working at the improvement of the community's program of education."[2] The Agreement Program involves cooperation on state, regional, and local levels. Except on the local level it is not directly concerned with assistance given to individual students; it is more concerned with curriculum improvement, tests, records, types of preparation for college, and methods of admission to college. On the local level, however, it definitely includes assistance given to students in all phases of guidance.

Colleges which are members of the program agree to disregard the pattern of subjects pursued in considering for admission the graduates of selected accredited high schools, provided they are recommended by the school from among the more able students in the graduating class. However, this agreement does not imply that students must be admitted to certain college courses or curriculums for which they cannot give evidence of adequate preparation. Secondary schools are urged to make available such basic courses as provide a necessary preparation for entering technical, industrial, or professional curriculums. It is recommended further that colleges provide accelerated programs of preparation for specialized college curriculums for those graduates who are unable to secure such preparatory training in high school.

High schools which are members of the program agree to assume responsibility for initiating and continuing a program involving the building of an adequate personal file about each student, including test data of various kinds, anecdotal records, personality inventories, and achievement samples. The high-school staff assumes responsibility for developing a summary of these personal data for submission to the college and for a basic curriculum study and evaluation of the purposes and program of the secondary school. The high schools also agree to maintain a continuous follow-up of former pupils and a continuous program of information and orientation throughout the high-school course regarding the nature and requirements of certain occupations and specialized college courses. They also agree to devote special emphasis during the senior year to the occupation or college of the pupil's choice.

[2] Leon S. Waskin, "The Michigan Secondary School–College Agreement," *Bulletin of the National Association of Secondary-school Principals,* January, 1949, p. 49.

A joint committee studies applications of new schools, recommends certain of these schools to colleges for inclusion in the agreement, and determines from time to time whether the schools on the list have met the criteria. This joint committee includes three representatives from the Michigan Secondary School Association, four from the Michigan College Association, and one each from the Michigan Department of Public Instruction and the Michigan Education Association.

In its beginning there were only comparatively few schools and colleges operating in this program, but the numbers grew rapidly as the advantages of this type of teamwork became apparent. State, regional, and local conferences were held, and there were exchanges of experiences regarding types of organization and methods used. In individual schools members of the staff were appointed for special work on curriculum organization and guidance methods. In some schools such teachers had "released" time for this work, and some were given extra pay for work out of school hours. Some took courses in nearby colleges dealing with curriculums, testing, and counseling. A digest of reports on the program led the director of the Michigan Study of the Secondary School Curriculum to write as follows:[3]

> These descriptions contain ample evidence that the Secondary School–College Agreement in Michigan has provided the stimulus for a great many promising activities at the local level that, in the aggregate, point toward the general improvement of instruction in secondary schools throughout the state. It is in this facilitation of the development of functional local programs that the principal significance of the Secondary School–College Agreement lies rather than in the fact that it provides an alternate method for securing admission to college. At the same time, any school that assumes seriously its obligations under the Agreement will be in the position of providing each college with far more comprehensive and significant information about each applicant than has been customary in the past. Furthermore, the whole program provides a clear demonstration of the fact that the relinquishing of the untenable assumption that any college or any state educational authority knows exactly what is best for each high school need not result in chaos nor in frustrated, helpless fumbling by the local school. Here is one way of both releasing

[3] *Ibid.*, p. 64.

and harnessing the energies of local communities in a cooperative attack upon the numerous and difficult problems of developing a truly democratic educational program in our American democratic society.

This example of teamwork shows that the principle of cooperation is useful in many ways as a method of improving guidance programs.

HOMEROOM AS BASIS FOR GUIDANCE ORGANIZATION

Homerooms have been widely adopted in the junior and senior high schools. They were originally a device used to overcome the evils of departmentalization in the high school. In the elementary school the pupil had one teacher who taught all subjects and who had the complete responsibility for his attendance, for reports about him to the administration and to parents, and for his general conduct. This teacher was the only person in school who really knew the student and could help him with his problems. In the high school the student had a different teacher for each subject, and there was no one person who knew him or to whom he could go for general help. The situation became much worse when the junior high school came into being and the change to a departmentalized organization came at the seventh instead of the ninth grade. Someone needed to take a definite responsibility for each student—to study him, to learn all about him, and to assist him in his adjustments to school. The homeroom teacher is the only one who has the student every day, whose duty it is to know all about his work, study his characteristics, and exercise a general direction over him, and become his friend, his confidant, and his counselor. The homeroom at its best has become the basis for much of the guidance in some high schools.

Methods of Organizing a Homeroom

Homerooms are organized in different ways. Sometimes a homeroom sponsor has a group for a term or a year only; sometimes he has charge of the same group for the full time of their attendance in the school. The usual plan is to have the students in the homeroom all from the same grade. There may be two advisers for each class—one for boys and one for girls.

Sometimes each homeroom is a segment of the entire school; that is, each class or grade in school is represented in the homeroom. Under this plan in a four-year high school, each homeroom might have twelve freshmen, ten sophomores, eight juniors, and five seniors. Although in some cases this plan has been found to work exceptionally well, it does make the process of group counseling somewhat more difficult because at least some of the problems facing each class may be different. Unfortunately, most homeroom organizations do not provide opportunities to meet the need which gave rise to them. The usual homeroom is a place where, at the beginning of each day, absence and tardiness are checked and notices read. The teachers in charge are responsible for recording grades and sending out reports. To give opportunity for attaining the objectives for which the homeroom is designed, there must be at least one full period a week given to homeroom activities and a period each day longer than ten minutes.

Purposes of the Homeroom

The chief aims of the homeroom as usually given are (1) to develop desirable pupil-teacher relationships, (2) to assist in the guidance of pupils, (3) to develop desirable ideals and habits, both personal and civic, and (4) to expedite the handling of administrative routine.

If the analysis of guidance already given is correct, the first three of these aims are directly concerned with guidance. Desirable pupil-teacher relationships are possibly the most important of all the guidance functions. This relationship is fundamental in the adjustment of the pupil to all phases of school life and in assistance in study. It is also essential in finding many facts about the pupil himself. Such facts could not be discovered in any other way.

The homeroom sponsor has the opportunity of knowing the members of his room more intimately and accurately than the classroom teacher can ever know them, especially if each pupil stays in the same homeroom for at least three years. The relationships thus established are cumulative in their effects and provide the best possible basis for certain forms of assistance. Not only does the homeroom sponsor know each pupil more intimately, but he can be of great assistance to the classroom teacher in many ways. Discouragement and failure of pupils may often be prevented by information regarding home conditions or health such as only the homeroom sponsor may have. Knowledge of outside interests of pupils may often be of great help to the classroom teacher in planning his work and in utilizing special interests. All such information enables the classroom teacher to make the assistance he gives to his pupils more effective. The homeroom sponsor should and usually does have much more intimate knowledge of the entire pupil than anyone else in the school system. He is, therefore, a very important part of the guidance setup; probably no guidance of any kind should be undertaken without his cooperation.

It is not necessary that he actually initiate every guidance activity; in fact, it is probably important that he not do so. Every part of the school system is and should be vitally concerned with assisting the pupil and should be alert to discover problems of students and to initiate guidance procedures; but it is highly probable that more of these problems will come to the attention of the homeroom sponsor than to any other person. But it is also true, however, that the particular type of assistance needed often requires detailed knowledge and technical skill that the sponsor does not have; where this is the case, he should not himself undertake such guidance but should refer the case to the counselor or to some other specialist. In many instances effective help can best be given by the cooperation of the staff, each contributing his part and performing his particular function.

Limitations of the Homeroom

The homeroom has been a very important factor in the development of organized guidance, but as guidance became more clearly defined, the homeroom has been found to be very inadequate to meet all the needs of an effective guidance program. Some of its functions, for example, have been taken over by class organizations and class sponsors which are concerned chiefly with class activities.

One of the deficiencies of the homeroom is the difficulty in finding time for its activities. In many schools the only time available was ten or fifteen minutes at the beginning of the school day which were devoted to checking on attendance and to reading notices of special events. When one full period was allotted for the homeroom every week or so, it was very difficult for the teacher to plan a program that was really profitable.

One of the chief difficulties in considering the homeroom sponsor as the center of guidance work is the impossibility of finding anyone who is expert enough in all phases of guidance to be efficient. If such a person were found, he probably would not be a homeroom sponsor but the director of guidance. As we have already seen, efficient guidance demands experts—experts in collecting information, in teaching, in counseling, and in all other phases of guidance. Students, in some way, must have the benefit of such expert assistance. On the other hand, we cannot look with favor upon the practice of sending the student who needs help to occupational experts, college experts, social experts, or educational experts for counsel and not providing some means of unifying and interpreting the help those experts give. Such more or less unrelated counsel would be confusing in the extreme. Specialists in medicine are very necessary and very helpful, but unless the specialist has had broad training and general experience, he is likely to be one-sided and biased in his diagnosis. The coming of specialists in medicine has brought about and necessitated the specialist in diagnosis. Once the specialist knows the trouble, he can treat the case intelligently and effectively. Specialists in guidance require a diagnostician, someone who knows the student from many points of view and who cannot only diagnose but also unify the treatment. We must in some way provide for unified whole-child counsel. In most cases the homeroom sponsor is not qualified for such a task, but he can be of great assistance to the school counselor in giving an overall view of the pupil.

INITIATING A GUIDANCE PROGRAM

The importance of a right beginning cannot be too strongly emphasized in getting a guidance program off to a good start. Many desirable plans have failed merely because of a poor start. A principal learns of some desirable practice; it has been used very successfully in other schools and should greatly improve the work in his school. He becomes enthusiastic about it; he works out a plan of organization for his school and presents it to his teachers as something that will be initiated at the beginning of the next month. After a time, he finds it is not working well; investigation discloses that some teachers are actively opposing it because they resent innovations or because it is an added burden, "one thing more"; others are in passive opposition or indifferent because they do not understand what it is all about; some, while actively supporting the plan, are doing just the wrong things because they, too, misunderstand. It is difficult, indeed, to start afresh with any hope of success after such an initial failure.

Need for Staff Preparation

The initiation of any new plan, whether it is supervised study, core curriculum, or guidance, requires careful preparation of the staff and should be undertaken only after the changes are understood and generally accepted by teachers. Too often we forget that the basic elements for effective learning are important in the successful introduction of any new method or plan. These elements are (1) an understanding of what is to be done; (2) an acceptance of the plan; and (3) a sense of responsibility for putting it into operation. Unless these three elements are present at least in some degree, the new undertaking will not succeed. This preparation takes time and careful planning—often months or even years. Patience and the willingness to put up with the delays that are inevitable in democratic methods are essential. "Do not be in a hurry; expect initial setbacks. Be patient."

Methods of Initiating the Program

It is not possible to lay down any definite rules for beginning a program of guidance because the method will vary with the conditions in any school or community. A few suggestions only can be given.

It is always well to begin with those guidance needs which are recognized by all teachers. Sometimes it is best not to call them "needs for *guidance*" but "problem cases" that disturb the teacher and interfere with teaching. Recognition by teachers of elements that disturb or distract and make it difficult to achieve the purposes of the school is of fundamental importance and should precede the initiation of the guidance program. A testing program, a study of the causes of failure, a follow-up of pupils who have graduated or who have left school before graduation are among the most helpful methods of developing this recognition of needs and problems. Many schools have found the evaluation studies conducted under the stimulation of the Cooperative Study of Secondary School Standards very effective in revealing pupil needs and problems and in indicating weaknesses in the educational program as organized. When the problems are recognized and the weaknesses revealed, it is usually very easy to begin a study of how the weaknesses can be removed and of what methods can be developed to aid in the solution of the problems. This study will at once show the ineffectiveness of the usual school program and the necessity for giving some special attention to guidance techniques. It will also indicate the wisdom of placing on some one person or committee the responsibility for the development of a plan for the school.

When teachers begin to recognize what the problems really are and realize their own inadequacy to meet them, they will be more ready to accept the help that can be given by someone who is specially trained for the work and who is given time from the teaching schedule to help them. This planning should not be done in such a way as to indicate that the teacher is to be released from all responsibility for guidance or that he can turn over all his problems to the counselor; rather, it should be in such a way that each teacher may be helped to do his part in guidance more effectively. Each teacher's efforts will become more meaningful and effective if done within the framework of a total school guidance program and if coordinated with the guidance efforts of the counselor and of other teachers.

In initiating the program, most schools find it more advisable to select some teacher from the regular staff to direct the program, even though he has not had special guidance training, than to import a specially trained person from outside. The local teacher already knows the school, the staff, the pupils, and the community and can at once adapt his methods to the local conditions. The other teachers know him and, if the groundwork is properly laid, are not so likely to resent the assignment of special duties to one of their own number as to one who comes from outside. In many cases the assumption of guidance responsibilities is a gradual process. The chairman of a special guidance committee carries on his work in addition to a regular teaching schedule and gradually, as the need is felt, is released from part of the teaching load in order to do the extra things necessary. In some schools the chief guidance responsibility is placed on one of the administrators in order to give the authority necessary for carrying out the program.

Of course, it is not always advisable to select one of the regular staff. There may be no qualified or interested person available, or there may be jealousy among the teachers, which would work against the success of the plan. Some well-qualified person, even though he does not know local conditions, may be the most effective person to begin the work. If the need for help has been made apparent, a person better qualified than anyone on the regular staff to give the help will be accepted by the teachers. In order to succeed, such a person must have an unusually understanding and sympathetic nature and must be very tactful in dealing with situations involving long-established customs and special prerogatives. In the initiation of effective guidance programs we need more teachers with a "passion for anonymity" who are interested more in getting things done than in getting credit for doing them.

Every plan for the initiation of a guidance program should include a program of in-service training for every member of the school personnel—principal, counselor, teachers, and clerks. Suggested readings, faculty meetings, college courses, visits to other schools with good guidance programs, the collection of guidance materials of all kinds can all be useful in upgrading the guidance capabilities of the staff.

Examples of Successful Initiation

From the principles for the organization of a guidance program it would seem clear that the task of initiating a program would be no easy matter and would require careful thought and extensive preparation. A number of principals have recognized the need for such careful planning and have inaugurated projects involving several years of preparation before being put into effect.

A junior high school in Wilmington, Delaware, began with an effort to develop the feeling of a need for a program of guidance. The principal asked every teacher in the school to make a case study of one pupil selected from any one of his classes. Few of the teachers had any clear idea of what a case study was or how to go about starting such a study. The principal then had conferences with teachers in which case studies and material for making them were discussed and helpful references given. Help also was given to individual teachers in making such records. Not all teachers were completely successful in their efforts, but each became more conscious of the problems of the pupils and developed a feeling of the need for an organized program to provide for more effective service to children.

This approach to the initiation of a guidance program is a very useful one, for it begins with a realization of the needs and problems of children. Any plan should arise out of the interests and problems of the pupils themselves and provide for in-service education of teachers in guidance. Many projects have been found helpful in the study of guidance needs and the initiation of guidance programs, for example, a study of dropouts, comparison of pupils' grades and their scores on achievement and aptitude tests, a study of tests and test results, a follow-up study of graduates, a survey of the cumulative records and the use made of them, a study of community resources that might be used in guidance, group discussions of guidance needs and practices, visits to other schools and observation of guidance practices, organization of a reading club with discussions of practices and methods described in various books and magazines, and community conferences on problems and guidance methods and conferences with parents regarding problems of pupils.

So long as the purpose is to develop a consciousness of what problems need attention and of the necessity for cooperative effort in solving them, the particular method of beginning the plan is comparatively unimportant. There will be critics of both the need for the program and the methods proposed to initiate it, but discussions among groups of teachers who have the same problems and who have been successful in dealing with them will go far in changing the critical attitudes. This approach will promote growth from within the school and will be far more effective than any plan initiated by the principal alone. Critics are often the most effective agencies for the organization and improvement of guidance practices. There should be no need for emphasizing that leadership of the plan should be by either the principal or a teacher who is recognized to be outstanding in ability and who has the confidence of other teachers.

The organization of guidance within the school differs greatly with the size of the school and with the facilities and personnel available. In large school systems there is usually a guidance or personnel department in the central office which serves to coordinate the work in all the schools of the system. This department largely determines the organization of the guidance activities in each school and provides assistance of various kinds as needed. The guidance department may direct the testing program and provide city-wide interpretation of test results.

In many schools the guidance department consists of a committee that is responsible for the guidance activities in the school. The chairman of this committee is usually the counselor. Help is also available, usually from the central office, in remedial work in reading or speech and in problems of emotional adjustment. In many schools there is also a placement service that helps in problems relating to choice of occupations and securing jobs. Particularly in the large schools a great variety of help may be available, but sometimes these services complicate the guidance program and reduce the intimate personal relationship found in the small school, thus making the problem of really personal guidance more difficult.

Guidance has also reached a stage where there are guidance departments in many county departments of education and in practically all states. These departments are often very helpful in stimulating local schools to inaugurate guidance programs by giving them help in methods of organization and by supplying them with various services. Sometimes they supply trained personnel who periodically go to the school and help the staff and students with their problems and difficulties. In some states even the smallest schools are able to have such help.

The far-reaching plan of the Office of Vocational Rehabilitation, which works in cooperation with the public schools in providing help to schools where there are disabled students, may well become a pattern for cooperation in guidance problems of all kinds. However, one of the problems in connection with help from trained persons who are not school personnel is the difficulty of utilizing services which are available only at irregular times, therefore creating lack of personal contact between the specialist and the student which makes more difficult a real understanding between them. But these trained persons may by their presence in the school do much to upgrade the understanding and skills of the staff by providing in-service education for teachers.

The small schools cannot expect to provide all the facilities that are possible in the large school, but they do make it possible for the staff to have close relationships with students, with each other, and with the parents and the community. In small schools there is usually a guidance committee of teachers appointed by the principal. The chairman is the counselor, if there is one; otherwise he may be a teacher who is especially interested in guidance and who is the kind of person students come to for help with general problems. This committee may organize an adequate program even though highly trained specialists may be lacking.

As a final word on organization it might be well to keep in mind some real dangers in overorganization. The purpose of the organization of guidance is to provide effective guidance for pupils in the school, but for some people there is a fascination in organization for itself. As a consequence, there may be so much time and energy spent on the organization and its maintenance that there is too little time left for the guidance of the pupils. It is important to remember that the simpler the organization, the better. Finally, because the problems of the child are the important consideration, the organization should be fluid enough to care for the new and unforeseen problems as they occur.

SUMMARY

The purpose of the organization of guidance is to increase the effectiveness of the services to all students. Guidance should be under the authority and general supervision of the principal of the school. Guidance organization should be as simple as possible and flexible enough to provide for the changing conditions in the school and the needs of youth. A unified approach to the guidance of the student should be provided to avoid the confusion that often results from conflicting points of view of different members of the staff. Such an approach requires teamwork. The members of the team might well vary from time to time because of the nature of the problems, the characteristics of the student, and the identity of the persons who have had the closest contact with him. Team members must meet together with mutual consideration and respect for one another and for differing points of view. By pooling all the available information and points of view, they may come to a joint opinion regarding the problem, the best methods of giving help, and the member of the group who can best aid the student.

In initiating a program of guidance, it is well to begin very simply and first develop a feeling of need among the school staff for such a service. As this feeling becomes general, the kind of organization that is best suited to the character of the school and the school staff can emerge. No blueprint for organization is possible, but certain guideposts are useful in setting up an effective program.

EXERCISES

1. Outline a guidance program for a coeducational high school of approximately two hundred students. Take into account the types of school personnel to be included and the functions of each, cooperation among school personnel, steps desirable in initiating such a program, and agencies outside the school to be included in the program and the functions of each.

2. Describe the guidance organization in the school in which you are working or any other school familiar to you. Include the guidance duties of the counselor, librarian, and teachers. Tell what provision is made for job placement, counseling, disseminating occupational information, and gathering data about students.

3. What do you perceive as the advantages and disadvantages of having (*a*) full-time, as opposed to part-time, counselors; (*b*) homerooms; (*c*) a job placement service in the school?

REFERENCES

Andrew, Dean C., and Roy D. Willey: *Administration and Organization of the Guidance Program*, Harper & Brothers, New York, 1958.

Barry, Ruth, and Beverly Wolf: *Modern Issues in Guidance: Personnel Work*, Bureau of Publications, Teachers College, Columbia University, New York, 1957.

Hatch, Raymond N., and Buford Stefflre: *Administration of Guidance Services*, Prentice-Hall, Inc., Englewood Cliffs, N.J., 1958.

Roeber, Edward C., Glenn E. Smith, and Clifford E. Erickson: *Organization and Administration of Guidance Services*, McGraw-Hill Book Company, Inc., New York, 1955.

Stoops, Emery (ed.): *Guidance Services: Organization and Administration*, McGraw-Hill Book Company, Inc., New York, 1959.

PART V

GUIDANCE STRATEGIES
AND METHODS

CHAPTER 11

COUNSELING AND
COUNSELING TECHNIQUES

The point of view presented in Chapter 1 indicates that the author does not believe that guidance is merely a specialized, separate function of the school or that it is the special prerogative or responsibility of any one particular member of the school personnel. It is a service that should permeate all the activities of the school, and every member of the school staff from the principal to the custodian must participate if it is to be effective. Nor is there any one technique that is always best. The techniques used by the teacher, the librarian, and the counselor may be very different from those used by the clinical psychologist. It is sometimes true that one technique will be more effective in dealing with one person and another with another person, but the techniques themselves are important only as they produce desirable results. The center of the guidance work is found in the actual help given to the individual, the counseling process itself. The concept of counseling has radically changed in the past twenty-five years and even now is undergoing considerable modification. It is still centered upon the individual, but the ways in which the help is given are being reconsidered and new methods explored. The guidance service of the school will be effective only if we keep constantly in mind the individual student and his need. We must keep an open mind regarding the particular techniques to be used and not use one just because some authority has praised it.

Guidance, like all other services of the school, uses and should use many different techniques suited to the special need, the special situation, and the abilities of the counselor or the teacher. In this respect it is like teaching. Effective teaching is not dependent on any one technique since the one that is most effective for the dull student may not be suited to the bright student.

The effective counselor will study each student, each problem, each situation, and then select from the many techniques available to him the one that, in his judgment, will be the most effective in helping the particular student to solve his particular problem. The value of any technique is determined in large measure by the special skill of the counselor in using it. It is worse than foolish for a counselor not trained in a particular technique, however good it may be, to try to use it just because it is recommended by authorities or because it is fashionable at the time. Techniques, like fads and fashions, often sweep the country and, just as often, fade away into obscurity.

A librarian can be very helpful in the guidance program, but his technique, which should be suited to the kind of help a librarian can give effectively, may be very different from that used by the teacher or the skilled counselor. The teacher, although not trained especially in guidance techniques, is often a key person in discovering the problems and needs of students and, by passing this information on to the counselor or to other teachers, may be of real help to the student. The teacher also constantly gives help to the student but may use a technique very different from that used by the counselor or the librarian.

COUNSELING

One of the standard techniques of guidance is counseling. There does not seem to be any specific definition of counseling which is acceptable to all authorities. A well-organized attempt by a group of clinical psychologists to develop such a definition is described in *Roles and Relationships in Counseling*.[1] The authors make a careful analysis of counseling and developed principles and techniques that, in the judgment of the participants, are important for effective counseling.

[1] Ralph F. Berdie (ed.), *Roles and Relationships in Counseling*, Minnesota Studies in Student Personnel Work, no. 3, University of Minnesota Press, Minneapolis, Minn., 1953.

What Is Counseling?

On the basis of these considerations the following definition was constructed by Gustad:[2]

> Counseling is a learning-orientated process carried on in a simple one-to-one social environment in which the counselor, professionally competent in relevant psychological skills and knowledge, seeks to assist the client by methods appropriate to the latter's needs, and within the context of the total personnel program, to learn more about himself and to accept himself, to learn how to put such understanding into effect in relation to more clearly perceived, realistically defined goals, to the end that the client may become a happier and more productive member of society.

This long, comprehensive definition contains nearly all the factors and principles that are considered desirable for effective counseling, but it is quite unwieldy and somewhat confusing. It makes no provision for the possibility of ineffective or bad counseling. It does not recognize as counseling a situation in which an unscrupulous counselor may, by consultation and discussion, guide a susceptible client to make a decision that would be advantageous to the counselor and harmful to the client.

It would be much more useful to formulate a simple definition that would apply to all counseling, good and bad, and then to list the conditions and principles that are essential for effective and desirable results. The following definition by Bordin[3] is an excellent example, although not entirely complete: "Counseling is the process of aiding an individual to solve his problems through the medium of the interview."

Conditions Essential for Counseling

It is generally accepted that rapport is a necessary precondition for counseling. Rapport between counselor and counselee is thought to be present when the counselee feels the need for help, when he comes to the counselor willingly because he feels that the counselor can help him, and when the counselor is deeply understanding and sympathetic and has only one purpose—to be of assistance to the counselee. There seems to be a difference of opinion

[2] *Ibid.*, p. 17.
[3] *Ibid.*, p. 3.

regarding the place of rapport in counseling. Some authorities feel that rapport is essential for counseling, that is, that it is necessary to establish rapport before counseling can function. If this is true, then the great majority of high-school students, being sent by teacher or principal, cannot have any counseling until rapport is established. Other authorities, with whom the author agrees, believe that establishing rapport is a function of counseling and that therefore the counselor's effort to attain rapport is itself counseling.

Who Should Receive Counseling?

Counseling should not be limited to students who have difficulties and who are conscious of problems; it should be extended to include all pupils as an aid to their optimum development. It should be directed toward the prevention of maladjustments, not merely toward their removal. This brings in another point of view—that in many cases the feeling of need for help is not always necessary. Berdie[4] expresses this as follows: "The important part is the establishment, even in the absence of a pressing problem, of a warm, sound relationship of the pupil with a mature adult, to feel that such a person is genuinely and personally interested in him." Many times the mere feeling that such a person as the counselor is there to help, or even the memory of what a teacher, a father, or a mother stands for, is real counseling help.

Who Should Do Counseling?

This question leads inevitably to the rapidly growing belief that counseling should not be confined to the counselor but should be used, as far as possible, by the entire school staff, especially the teacher. In fact, counseling is basically a teaching technique. Guidance is more and more considered as a *learning* activity by an increasing number of authorities.

It is important to recognize the fact that this close personal relationship between counselor and counselee and between teacher and pupil is not achieved quickly; it may be long in developing and may be present long before the pupil is conscious of the problem. Because he often is not aware of the developing problem, the pupil's feeling that he needs help may often be slow in emerging. If the counselor or teacher sees in advance what the problem of

[4] *Ibid.,* p. 10.

the student will be, he can be of maximum assistance by preparing the student to meet it as it appears.

It should also be kept in mind that all people are not equally able to develop the necessary rapport. The ideal relationship is that of father-son and mother-daughter. This is not to say that the father-son or mother-daughter relationship is always ideal, but it has all the elements that make possible such rapport. Parents are with their children day after day and year after year as they grow up and are in the best position to see and understand problems due to growth and developing maturity.

Counseling is a combination of science and art. It involves an intimate relationship between counselor and client. This relationship depends in large measure on the counselor. He must like people as people and must have the ability to show that he likes them and to act really interested in them. He must also be a person whom people like and in whom they can trust. But this characteristic alone may be a liability, not an asset. Confidence men have it to a high degree. The counselor must also want to help people, not exploit them. He must at the same time be objective in his attitude toward the client and not allow his liking for him to warp his understanding; he must be able to see the client as he is. In deciding who should do counseling, one must keep in mind the above considerations.

Does Counseling Help?

It is apparent that good counseling does not necessarily provide solutions to the problems of the client. The provision of such solutions is not only difficult but often undesirable. The value of counseling cannot be measured by the ability of the counselor to discover what is the best choice of occupations or college for the client or by his ability to influence him to accept this choice. Even if he could do this, there is no statistical procedure that would enable us to find whether the choice made was the best one. Even if the student were successful in the college he chose or in the occupation he entered, there is no way of determining whether he could not have been equally successful if he had made another choice. We cannot relive our lives with all conditions the same. The fundamental purpose of guidance is not merely to bring success to the client but to help him develop the ability to choose wisely. Initial success may lead to satisfaction with lesser goals, and initial failure may stir one to greater effort in attaining more adequate goals.

TYPES OF COUNSELING

Some authorities have attempted to distinguish between such types of counseling as counselor- versus client-centered, directive versus nondirective, controlled versus permissive. The distinction client-centered versus counselor-centered reveals an entire misconception of counseling. All service activities are, by their nature, centered on the person to be helped. All teaching is pupil-centered even when the teacher has fifty pupils in his class. The services of the physician and the nurse are patient-centered. What is really meant by client-centered versus counselor-centered is the relative activity of the counselor and the counselee in the guidance process or in the interview.

Directive versus nondirective indicates also the degree to which the counselor attempts to direct the discussion along the lines that he thinks profitable as compared with encouraging the counselee to determine the direction of the discussion. The nondirective technique is based on the belief that the client has the resources within himself to solve his own problems without direction from others. It is quite probable that teachers and counselors underestimate the resources of young people for making decisions and adjustments, but even a cursory examination of the decisions and behavior of young people would seem to indicate the danger of relying entirely on their ability to choose wisely.

Client-centered Point of View

The nondirective, permissive, client-centered approach is more effective when "emotional" problems are present. It is clear, however, that many problems of students who come to the counselor have few if any such emotional conditions. Many cases merely call for information or some other routine help. Often the student comes with no idea why he is sent and without any desire to come.

Without any intention to detract from the real value of the client-centered technique, it should be pointed out that the "slight suggestion or interpretation" made by a counselor when he is in the "semitrance" of feeling as the counselee feels may be as purely directive as a similar suggestion made by a directive counselor. The value of the suggestion or interpretation in such a case comes from the counselor's wider experience which enables him not only to understand the present feeling of the student but to see more clearly than the student the steps that must be taken to arrive at a suitable solution of the problem.

Directive Point of View

In contrast to the client-centered technique it is often said that the directive counselor is more interested in the problem than he is in the counselee, but this belief is an exaggeration. He is concerned with the student *and* his problem—the two cannot be separated. The directive counselor, however, is apt to be more active, to make use of tests and other records, and to be freer in giving advice and information. It is likely that most school counseling could be classified as directive.

Contrast and Comparison

Although the differences between the client-centered and the directive point of view may be more theoretical than practical, it will be valuable to examine some of the claimed points of opposition.

Differences in Emphasis between
Directive and Client-centered Techniques

Directive	*Client-centered*
Center of Interest	
Counselee with the problem; problem is very important.	The counselee; the problem is incidental.
Need for Assistance	
Counseling is a learning process.	Counselee has within himself the power to solve his own problem. The counselee can see the problem and the solution better than the counselor.
Counselee needs help.	
Counselor can see the problem and the solution better than the counselee.	

Use of Records

Tests, records, past history are very important in finding the origin of the problem.

Past history, tests, and records often interfere with the solution of the problem. Counselor sees the counselee *as he now is.*

Emotional Aspects

Interfere with the solution of the problem. Intellectual element of most importance. Many problems have few if any emotional conditions.

Emotional condition very important as an element in the situation.

Interview

Rapport important, but in many cases not essential.

"Empathy" essential. Counselor must understand the state of mind of the client but not feel as the client feels.

Most counselors are eclectic in their choice of techniques and attempt to use whatever approach seems best suited to the situation. Real help is most often given by teachers and counselors by methods that seem to be more directive than client-centered.

The nondirective technique has, without doubt, made a real contribution to guidance. Viewing the situation in our schools as it is today and as it will in all probability be for many years to come, however, we must realize that, even though this approach may be more effective in certain cases, there is little chance that enough counselors who have the extended training essential to its use will be available.

If an important element in counseling is the intimate relationship between pupil and counselor, it is by no means always essential to have the face-to-face interview. A cheery "hello" and a wave of the hand may do much to continue the needed relationship. A hiking party, a game of tennis may do the same. Time is a very important factor; counseling can take place by telephone or even by correspondence if the necessary rapport has been established. In fact, correspondence may, in some cases, be more effective than face-to-face consultation. It removes inferences drawn from facial expression or inflections of the voice, and the ideas presented are often more carefully thought out than in face-to-face discussion. We should not lose sight of the primary importance of the feeling of relationship between the counselor and the counselee. It is clear that for some time it will be necessary to depend on counselors and teachers who have some knowledge of counseling techniques but who have not had the specialized training essential to the use of the client-centered approach.

GROUP GUIDANCE AND GROUP COUNSELING

Guidance is concerned with help given to individuals. This leads some authorities to conclude that there can be no such thing as group guidance or group counseling. But teaching is also concerned with the individual, and yet we use the term "group testing," meaning testing pupils in groups, but in each case it is the individuals in the group with whom we are concerned. We can, in the same way, speak of group guidance. By this we may mean either one of two things: (1) that group procedures may be used when they are thought to be more effective and economical for helping individual pupils or (2) that group guidance means the guidance of a *group*.

Guidance in Groups

This is the term used by Bennett[5] to indicate the value of group procedures in helping individuals in the solution of their problems. The therapeutic value of group procedures has long been generally accepted. The knowledge that others in the group have the same problems helps the individual to realize that he is not the only person who is faced with this difficulty. The opinion of the group regarding the best method of solving this problem is a powerful influence on the acceptance of the solution by the individual. The results of experiments in the use of group methods indicate that in many cases they are more effective than individual counseling.

Group Counseling

The values of group guidance are generally accepted, but the term "group counseling" is still rejected by many guidance au-

[5] Margaret E. Bennett, *Guidance in Groups*, McGraw-Hill Book Company, Inc., New York, 1955.

thorities. Some believe that group counseling is an "anomaly" and say that "it is as silly to speak of 'group counseling' as 'group courtship.' " Many other clinical psychologists take the same position because they accept the definition of counseling as a "face-to-face," "one-to-one" relationship, as in the interview. Such definitions automatically exclude any notion of the group; but this is merely circular argument and leads nowhere.

Psychologists and sociologists recognize that there is a group "entity"; the group is different from the sum of all the individuals in it. There is a group purpose or objective that is not the same as the objective of any individual in the group. There is a definite group psychology. Mob psychology is not only real but terribly effective for good or evil. Its power is seen not only in men but also in animals. The stampede of horses and cattle and the "death march" of a herd of cattle around the body of a recently killed member are striking examples of mob psychology. Many times the individual in the mob is not even conscious of his existence as an individual—he is just a part of the mob.

In everyday life, in the community, in the home, in the school, problems appear which can be solved more effectively by the group. In the school especially problems of a group often arise, that is, a problem common to the whole group and not merely to any one individual. A group of pupils, perhaps the student council, the members of a class, or an athletic team, may have a problem that affects them as a group. This group comes to the counselor, the faculty sponsor, or the principal not merely to seek approval for some project but to discuss the situation with him and secure his help. In these cases the group is the unit instead of the individual and takes the place of the individual in the counseling process. The group presents its problem to the principal who listens and stimulates discussion. Different members suggest methods that might be helpful in solving it, and a decision is reached. A *group* interview is held because the problem is a group problem and the solution a group solution.

Case Conference Procedures

A technique that combines the techniques of "counseling in groups" and "group counseling" was used by Allen[6] and prac-

---

[6] R. D. Allen, *Case Conference Problems in Group Guidance*, Inor Publishing Company, New York, 1933.

ticed in the public schools of Providence, Rhode Island, more than twenty-five years ago. Although the method has some features that would not be approved today, it still has much to commend it.

The purpose of this method was to provide the counselor with an approach to the discussion of personal and social relationships by means of *group thinking* in order to obviate the need for "preaching." Common problems of young people in the group were presented for study and discussion. After the problem had been stated concretely by way of a case, each pupil reviewed his own experience in a similar situation. Then the leader guided the group away from the more immediate and temporary advantages to be gained and toward more remote and permanent values. Consideration was given to the effect of the proposed line of action upon others and to possible exceptions or other conditions that should be considered in deciding upon a plan of action. Finally, conclusions were summarized in order to see what generalizations could be formulated which would be helpful in other situations. The entire process was really an experience in social thinking.

Allen believed that his method worked best when each case represented a common, usual, or typical situation that concerned most of the group. The case should involve persons and personal or social relations because generalized questions for debate are likely to encourage rambling and aimless discussion. The case should challenge the intelligence of the group by being located "in that doubtful realm where a hair divides the false and true, and where reasonable people may differ in their opinion." A useful case should have a purpose—a definite objective, for the case conference is a method of instruction, not a method of entertainment. A case is good only for the group that it fits and should be stated simply, briefly, and definitely and never be improvised hurriedly or tried without first having been carefully analyzed.

Allen makes several suggestions to ensure the success of his method. The attitude of the conference leader must be different from the typical attitude of the teacher in that the teacher knows the answers to the questions which he asks, and the pupils know that he knows. A good leader never, under any circumstances, enters into the discussion by expressing approval or disapproval of any opinion or attitude or by voicing his own opinions. On the contrary, the leader, without losing control, must be an impartial, open-minded, tactful, tolerant, and courteous presiding officer who must see that all points of view have a hearing, especially the "wrong" attitudes. While care must be taken not to waste school time by aimless discussion, it must always be kept in mind that the conference cannot be hurried without loss of effectiveness since any conference is a leisurely procedure. The counselor need not always follow any particular order of questioning, for in some of the most successful conferences most of the questions have been asked by the pupils. A good conference leader occasionally re-states and summarizes the group thinking at various stages. Some-times conclusions may be noted on the blackboard, sometimes written by a secretary, and sometimes not recorded at all. It is clearly the leader's function to keep the case discussion moving toward a solution and to keep the members informed of the progress of the thinking. Lastly, a conference group should be large enough to represent a diversified range of opinions but not so large as to prevent each member from taking an active part in the discussion.

Allen believes that many important results can be expected from this procedure. One result is that students get the view of the majority on personal and social problems. A pupil is taught to think for himself and to defend his opinions. Everyone is so interested that even shy pupils get excited and talk. The problems are real live topics of today and therefore have meaning for the participants in the case conference. Because the facts sink in deeper when the same things are said by pupils, the conference helps determine the policy of a pupil who is debating the subject within himself. Boys and girls discuss these things privately; why not bring them out into the open for frank debate in a situation where the teacher can learn much about the pupils? When the teacher keeps his views out of the discussion, the pupils give more honest opinions and learn what is best for the group, not merely for the individual. The method keeps pupils to the point by using specific examples of modern problems. It makes them more tolerant of the opinion of others, brings them "out of themselves," and helps them analyze subjects that they might not otherwise think out. It is a good test of one's beliefs to stand up for them in the face of opposition. These and other values convinced Allen that the case conference method was a useful group guidance technique.

Multiple Counseling

Froelich has suggested the term "multiple counseling" to indicate the utilization of group methods in the counseling of individuals. The purpose of such counseling is to assist the individual in the solution of his problems by utilizing the group setting. This is not essentially different from the "case conference problems" of Allen or the "guidance in groups" of Bennett.

There seems to be no logical reason for calling this group method "multiple counseling" just because many (multiple) problems are considered by many (multiple) persons in one group. The chief reason given by Froelich for the term "multiple" is to avoid the criticism centering on the terms "group guidance" and "guidance in groups." It also serves to emphasize the function of the group itself in the guidance of individuals through the utilization of group therapy. A modification of Bennett's "guidance in groups" to "counseling in groups" might well be accepted. This modification recognizes that counseling of individuals may take place in a group setting and that the group can be used effectively both for problems of the individuals in the group and for problems of the group itself. This term, however, can never be accepted by those who still insist that counseling is a one-to-one, counselor-client relationship.

SUMMARY

Counseling is the technique of guidance which attempts to assist the individual to understand himself, his abilities and characteristics, his environment, and his opportunities and prospects for attaining a satisfactory and successful life. This assistance is given not by direct advice or by merely supplying useful information but by personal conferences with trained counselors and by group discussions in which youth who are faced with the same problems participate together.

The purpose of these group conferences is to help each individual to develop the ability to solve his own problems. All counseling is client-centered. To be effective the client himself must take a large and active part in the process. The problem is his, and he must solve it. The counselor should not dominate the process or decide for the client what is the best solution. It is not necessary for the counselor always to know what the best solution is, nor is it essential that the decision made by the client always be the best one; the purpose of counseling is to help the individual grow in his ability to solve his own problems, and mistakes are often helpful in developing this ability.

While the differences between the client-centered and the directive method are great, their purposes are similar. School counseling will probably continue to be largely directive. Time and trained personnel are not sufficiently available to permit the use of other methods.

EXERCISES

1. Study carefully the discussion of counseling in this chapter and those in other textbooks on guidance and personnel work, and come to some conclusion on the fundamental nature of counseling. Can counseling be carried on by correspondence? By telephone? In groups? Give reasons for your belief.

2. What is the place and function of the counselor in the school? Should he teach any classes? Should he be the only one in the school who counsels students? What is his relation to teachers? To the principal? To parents?

3. What is the meaning and function of discipline? What role, if any, does the counselor have in discipline? When a teacher has occasion to send a student to the "office," should he be sent to the principal, the assistant principal, or to the counselor? What types of problems should govern this choice?

REFERENCES

Bennett, Margaret C.: *Guidance in Groups,* McGraw-Hill Book Company, Inc., New York, 1955.

Pepinsky, Harold B., and Pauline Nichols Pepinsky: *Counseling: Theory and Practice,* The Ronald Press Company, New York, 1954.

Robinson, Francis P.: *Principles and Practices in Student Personnel Work,* Harper & Brothers, New York, 1950.

Tolbert, E. L.: *Introduction to Counseling*, McGraw-Hill Book Company, Inc., New York, 1959.

Tyler, Leona E.: *The Work of the Counselor*, Appleton-Century-Crofts, Inc., New York, 1953.

PART VI

NEW AREAS IN GUIDANCE

CHAPTER 12

THE ROLE OF GUIDANCE IN THE DISCOVERY AND UTILIZATION OF HUMAN RESOURCES

One of the striking characteristics of the first half of the twentieth century has been the feverish search for sources of physical energy which can be utilized for the benefit of mankind. Among the motives which have caused this search are the insatiable curiosity of man, which leads him to delve into the mysteries of the universe, and his desire to so change his environment that it will better serve his needs by speeding up production, eliminating waste, prolonging life, and transcending, as far as possible, the limits of time and space. Such sources of physical energy have been found everywhere—on the surface of the earth and in its interior, in the depths of the ocean, in the air above, in the sun, moon, and stars, and in interstellar space. This search has been successful far beyond our wildest imagination, but scientists tell us that we are merely at the threshold of even greater sources of power. Great progress has been made in finding ways of harnessing these powers for our service.

Research such as has been used in these scientific investigations has proved its effectiveness so fully that it is now used in practically all areas of human endeavor. A large number of businesses and industrial enterprises have organized research departments. There are also independent endowed research agencies that offer their services in many different fields. The Federal government has for many years spent millions of dollars every year in research activities. Nearly every governmental department has its research bureau, and these bureaus have amply proved their usefulness.

GUIDANCE AND THE TALENTED

At the same time that we learned more about our physical environment, we learned more about man himself. We learned, for example, that there were great individual differences among us. We realized that some men had unusual and outstanding talents which could be utilized for the benefit of all society. We concluded that the discovery and research activities of man depended upon the prior discovery of talent and that therefore the search for talent must be given a high educational priority.

The Search for Talent

This emphasis upon research and the recognition of the importance of talent have set off the most widespread manhunt in history. Men and women of unusual ability with training in research are in great demand, especially those who have specialized in mathematics, physics, chemistry, and related fields. Scientific and mathematical societies have been organized for the purpose of emphasizing the importance in our economy of training in these areas as a basis for research and encouraging more men and women of high ability to choose occupations in these areas. They are also seeking ways by which the basic training in these areas in secondary schools and colleges may be strengthened and shortened and higher achievement secured. Many high schools are now offering special college courses in mathematics, chemistry, and physics for students of high ability, and colleges are giving advanced credit for those who have taken these courses and admitting them to the advanced courses in college. Thousands of dollars are given each year by industry, private foundations, and the Federal government as subsidies or scholarships to qualified students for undergraduate and graduate work. Research on gifted children has a high priority, and much emphasis is being given to the identification of bright children and the enrichment of their education. This activity has undoubtedly been stimulated by the emphasis on mathematics and the basic sciences in the Soviet Union and by the purported superiority of the Russians in these fields.

It is easy to understand why the emphasis in seeking talent has been on mathematics and science, but it is unfortunate that more attention and effort have not been given to seeking out and stimulating unusual ability in other areas where it is just as necessary, such as in art, music, language, literature, public service, social sciences, and philosophy. We are beginning to recognize the fundamental values of these areas and are taking steps to remedy what many think to be an overemphasis upon mathematics and science. We are not willing to adopt the narrow, intensive method of training used by Russia. It is a growing belief that the engineer, the chemist, the physician is also a citizen and has obligations to society beyond those of his specialty and that the narrowly trained person is, at best, only half a man. Education should be broad enough to make every man an effective citizen and a well-rounded member of society.

The Development of Talent

Guidance has a very important responsibility in this search for new sources of power and for men and women who have special talent. It is concerned not only with helping the individual discover his abilities and powers but with assisting him in their proper development and use for the best advantage to society. Although guidance is centered primarily upon the individual and his developing the ability to find a way of life which is satisfying, it is also concerned with the needs of society. Guidance workers are concerned with giving every student the best possible opportunity to develop whatever talents he has. Both society and the individual benefit most when every child has an education suited to his interests and abilities.

GUIDANCE AND THE PHYSICALLY HANDICAPPED

The need of an individual for guidance depends on his ability to make his choices and to solve his problems without assistance. Some of the chief factors contributing to his lack of ability to make choices are inadequate background and inability to analyze and learn from experience. Inadequate knowledge and unwillingness or lack of courage to take the necessary step may also suggest a need for guidance. Physical, mental, emotional, economic, and social handicaps may also restrict or prevent free decision making regarding an occupation.

A handicapped person may be described as one whose physical, mental, or emotional condition or characteristics or economic and social surroundings make it difficult or even impossible for him to participate in society up to his potential capacity and so to live a normal, useful, and satisfying life. The removal or modification of handicaps may be accomplished by changing the individual or by changing the occupational and sociological conditions so that his effective participation in society may be realized. One of the greatest triumphs of medicine, education, and social science in the past half century has been the progress that has been made in reducing or removing handicaps.

The Office of Vocational Rehabilitation

By far the most comprehensive and well-organized agency for the assistance of the handicapped is the Office of Vocational Rehabilitation in the Department of Health, Education, and Welfare. Its program had its beginnings when President Wilson signed the Vocational Rehabilitation Act for Civilians in 1920. Since that time the Federal government and the states have been partners in conducting a program of services to prepare handicapped men and women for useful work and to assist them in securing jobs.

Each disabled person served by the program receives the combination of the following services which best meets his needs:

1. *Diagnosis and counseling.* Physical examinations are conducted to determine the extent of his disabilities and to establish eligibility for rehabilitation. If he is eligible, counseling is provided to assist in planning a vocational rehabilitation program.

2. *Medical, surgical, psychiatric, and hospital services.* These may be provided if the physical or mental impairment can be substantially corrected or improved and if the applicant is financially in need.

3. *Braces, limbs, hearing aids, or other prosthesis.* These are purchased for him if they are considered necessary to overcome the handicap and if he is in financial need.

4. *Vocational training.* This is arranged for him if he needs

preparation for an occupation at which he can engage within the limitations of his handicaps. Normally, vocational training is provided after the completion of the high-school course and when the individual has demonstrated a need for special training not readily available to him in order to enter employment.

5. *Maintenance and transportation.* This is provided during the training program if it is found necessary to meet the expenses incurred in the training.

6. *Tools, equipment, and occupational licenses.* These are provided if found necessary during the training program or to aid a person in establishing his own business.

7. *Placement on the job.* This is the goal for each person undertaking a vocational rehabilitation program. Every effort is made by the rehabilitation staff and by cooperating agencies to assist in satisfactory placement.

8. *Follow-up on the job.* This is provided for several months to be certain that the placement is satisfactory both to the client and to the employer.

The minimum legal age set by the government for eligibility is sixteen, but the age is lowered in those states where the minimum employment age is lower than sixteen. During a typical recent year over 200,000 disabled people were served, and nearly one-third were rehabilitated. Of these, two-thirds were men, and about half of these were married. Their average schooling was nine years. Three-fourths were unemployed at the time they secured the services. About half were referred by doctors, hospitals, and public welfare agencies.

Values of the Rehabilitation Program

It seems that even from a financial standpoint the rehabilitation program has paid off. The estimated annual earnings of this group the first year after rehabilitation were nearly eight times their earnings the year before rehabilitation. It is estimated that in the three years after rehabilitation, the rehabilitants will have paid back to the government in income taxes much more than the entire program cost. These figures suggest the great increase in available man power which has been brought about by the rehabilitation program. Of much greater basic importance, however, are the values that have come to the rehabilitated person himself. Before rehabilitation he has a sense of economic worthlessness and feels that he is a burden to others, but after rehabilitation he begins again to feel the joy of being a producer, of being independent, of being a help rather than a hindrance. The value to these persons and to society is incalculable.

Cooperation between Schools and Rehabilitation Agencies

One of the most important phases of this program is the cooperation between the Federal government and the states and especially the teamwork which exists in some states between the rehabilitation agencies and the public schools. At present only a few school systems have developed programs that are at all adequate to meet the needs of the older disabled students. Most schools do not have sufficient financial resources or trained personnel for such services, but it is possible for the rehabilitation program to provide help to these pupils when their formal education ends. Schools now generally have educational programs for the handicapped child. These programs—for the mentally retarded, the crippled, or the child with sensory handicaps—are collectively known as "special education." The proper cooperation between special education and rehabilitation will result in more effective educational and guidance programs for the handicapped of all ages.

Some states have already initiated such programs of cooperation between the public schools and the rehabilitation agencies. The general pattern of cooperation is based on the employment by the school of a rehabilitation counselor who is responsible for students who are handicapped and who need the help of rehabilitation agencies.

Teamwork such as this gives promise of the development of adequate services for all kinds of handicaps. It is not too much to hope that soon every child and youth with any kind of handicap will have available in his school sources of help in removing or reducing his handicap. Such an accomplishment would be of far greater significance than all the spaceships or artificial satellites that man can produce.

UNDERACHIEVERS

Closely related to the handicapped are the "underachievers." These are individuals whose achievement is below their proved ability. The present concern is chiefly with children and youth in schools, although some attention is given to college students who are underachievers.

It is estimated that 13 to 15 per cent of students in school or college are underachievers. Special attention is given to underachievers in the upper ability group, but those in the middle group are taken into consideration as well.

Research studies do not as yet determine all the causes of this underachievement. It seems certain, however, that the family is a very important factor. One study found that higher achievement (less underachievement) was related to the following:

1. Homes not broken by death, divorce, and separation
2. Higher educational level of parents
3. Greater agreement on the life values of parents
4. Parents who were concerned about the achievement of their children and who took positive action regarding their progress in school

Other studies seem to indicate that high achievers possess certain personality traits. Among these are the following:

1. They have more positive character traits.
2. They are more reliable and have greater inclination to participate in extracurricular activities.
3. They have greater emotional health, fewer emotional disturbances (in many cases the underachiever had a higher degree of emotional disturbance than the achiever).
4. They are found to have more favorable behavior traits.
5. In many cases bright children, as they grow older, tend to cover up their high ability because they do not want to be called "teachers' pets" or to seem brighter than their friends.
6. Their level of achievement is not temporary but remains fairly consistent.
7. Unlike underachievers, they do not tend to rationalize errors and underachievements in such a way that they do not feel responsible and make no effort to improve.

One study found significant differences between 150 gifted underachievers and 150 achievers. It seems that achievers had more success in the development of work habits, foresight planning, ego strength, and other desirable characteristics. Fifty-one other studies showed that underachievement was associated with the lack of a well-rounded personality. It was also found that such differences became evident early in life and therefore could be foreseen.

General Methods of Assistance

During the years from age five to eleven the school has the best opportunity to give assistance to the underachiever, for this is when evidence of underachievement first appears. Teachers, administrators, counselors, and parents should work together on a cooperative basis to identify the underachiever and to assist him. One of the best services a counselor can give is to have faith and belief in the student and to feel that he can help him.

An imaginative and capable teacher can be of great help in understanding the student and in helping him to realize his situation and to develop the desire to achieve up to his ability.

Studies show clearly the importance of guidance in assisting youth to achieve the level of accomplishment suited to their abilities.

There are, however, some dangers in this process. It is not possible for every individual to attain this goal, nor is it always desirable. One must also consider other facets of his life than achievement in school alone—health, social obligations and development, citizenship, membership in a family, etc. It is by no means unusual for an ambitious student, when the urge is for high achievement, to impair his eyesight and health or to miss the social and cultural values in college life. Some people believe that unusual ability in music, art, literature, inventiveness, etc., is "God-given" and that this gift demands all-out effort to attain its full development.

There is no doubt that in the history of civilization there are many instances where this effort for achievement has been of immeasurable value. But there have been instances where it has been of immeasurable harm. Its value depends upon the nature of the ability. It may be good, or it may be evil. There is also a tendency to forgive the evil conduct of a person who has given something of great value, a sort of bookkeeping of comparing the "good that a man does" with the bad that he does. There are many cases where the great good that is given to the world has far less of an effect than the evil done.

In many cases high achievement in one area makes it impossible to achieve to the highest degree in another. A choice must be made. In the consideration of the achievement level of an individual his entire life must be kept in mind. Chapter 13 deals with this problem in detail.

GUIDANCE AND THE SOCIOLOGICALLY HANDICAPPED

Another very serious vocational handicap is the one that comes, not from the lack of ability to do the work that society demands, but from artificial social and economic barriers. Social prejudices related to race, color, religion, sex, nationality, tradition, previous social and economic position, or language background may interfere with an individual's vocational choice and development.

Practically every fair-sized community in the United States has individuals who have handicaps that are due to some of these sociological factors. Immigrants from other than English-speaking countries encounter handicaps due in part to differences in language and social customs, but in most cases these handicaps disappear rather quickly. In most cases native Americans have gladly made them welcome and have helped them to become adjusted to their new country. American families have even become sponsors for foreign families and assumed the responsibility for securing homes and employment for them. Behavior toward Indians and Negroes, unfortunately, has been in striking contrast to the friendly and helpful attitude toward the immigrants.

Early Attitude toward Indians

Several conditions and circumstances have been important determinants of the place of the Indian in our economy and society. In the first place the American settler or pioneer was a member of an alien group that was invading a land that belonged to the Indians. After many years of warfare the Indians themselves became the alien group and were forced to live under restrictions dictated by the invaders. These events resulted in great economic and social handicaps for the Indians.

A second important factor is that "Indians" are by no means a homogeneous group. It is significant that no satisfactory definition has ever been made of the word "Indian." According to the latest data, there are over 400,000 Indians in the United States, divided into nearly 300 tribes or tribal organizations, and speaking several hundred distinct tribal languages and dialects. Indians differ greatly among themselves in cultural standards, in habitation, in manner of dress, in the production and preparation of foods, in tribal customs, and in physical appearance. Each tribe has its own traditions, its own customs, and its own type of government—some democratic and some largely autocratic. In effect these separate tribes are different nations. These historical facts did much to shape and complicate the attitude of the majority of Americans toward Indians for a long time.

Now, however, the Indians have few legal restrictions or legal handicaps. They are full citizens who can vote and hold, purchase, and sell land. They can go where they wish and attend any school or college in the land if they have the necessary scholastic attainment. Some feel that the Federal government has done too much for the Indians by providing them with food, clothing, shelter, medical services, and schools. This program may have resulted in habits and ways of living unsuited for survival in a highly competitive society.

Present Program for Indians

Recently the Bureau of Indian Affairs adopted a new policy with three basic aims: (1) the creation of conditions under which the Indian may advance his social, economic, and political adjustments to achieve a status comparable to that of his non-Indian neighbors; (2) the encouragement of Indians and Indian tribes to assume an increasing measure of self-sufficiency; and (3) the termination at appropriate times of Federal government supervision and services to Indians. This policy has already begun to show its effects upon Indians in all parts of the country.

There is no doubt of the ability of Indians to take their place beside the other members of our society for, through the help and stimulation of interested men and women, many have received extensive education and have been successful in important places in every phase of the life of the country. Through the success they have made and through their artistic, musical, and literary accomplishments, they have already begun to reap the rewards of integration into the main stream of American culture.

The change in the policy of the Federal government toward

the Indians, that is, no longer considering them as more or less "wards of the government" but fostering complete equality with the non-Indians, though long delayed is admirable in every respect and will be far reaching in its influence. However, there will be many serious difficulties in its fulfillment. To attempt to adopt the new plan immediately would be disastrous for the Indian. The great majority of the Indians who have been on the reservations have had little or no relations with non-Indians in industry, business, or commerce. In some, the long dependence on the government has dulled the desire for independence. There has been little opportunity for them to develop the skills and to learn the techniques necessary to compete on equal terms with their non-Indian neighbors.

The Indians themselves have come to recognize this and are beginning to take a hand in their own future. They are ready to take the initiative in the development of a sense of common citizenship. They are saying, "We want to have and to be better neighbors."

The new plan emphasizes the importance of cooperation in the solution of problems affecting different groups. Differences between groups can never be satisfactorily solved by one of the groups alone. This new viewpoint is the most promising development to date toward ending a relationship that has been unfair and unsatisfactory to all concerned. It is hoped that, in the future, being an Indian will no longer constitute an employment handicap.

Early Attitudes toward Negroes

The history of the Negro in America reveals a very different situation from that of the Indian. Research studies indicate that with equal education and training race differences tend to disappear, but in spite of these findings Negroes often still suffer under the handicap of presumed inferiority.

The Negroes' struggle for equality of opportunity has been going on ever since the Emancipation Proclamation, and considerable progress has been made. Throughout the South the educational facilities for Negroes have steadily improved even though the usual custom is still to have segregated schools. An increasing number of Negroes are taking advanced work in preparation for entrance into professional and technical occupations.

Present Situation of Negroes

The social handicaps are the most difficult to overcome, and progress in this area lags behind educational and economic improvements. Probably one of the most important factors in the improvement of the Negro's position was his participation and contribution in World Wars I and II. In such situations there can be no distinctions based on race. Another factor has been the rapid industrialization of the South, which has greatly reduced the need for unskilled workers and increased the demand for more highly trained ones. Some of these new higher-level jobs have been filled by Negroes, and this has raised their economic and social status. It is hoped that the educational, economic, and social handicaps which curtail the Negro's participation in American life will soon lessen and eventually disappear.

SUMMARY

Democracy, as we understand it in the United States, requires that every individual have the opportunity to secure the education and training suited to his ability and his needs and that the abilities of all be utilized to improve the conditions of living so that everyone may have the opportunity to attain a life that is socially useful and individually satisfying.

These requirements imply that we should seek out individuals who are gifted both in general mental ability and in special types of work and provide facilities for education and training suited to their special talents. Also, we should attempt to remove, as far as possible, the handicaps that prevent individuals from attaining the education and training that will enable them to make their contributions to the general welfare and take their places as productive, independent citizens.

Social handicaps are being reduced by legislation and by cooperative planning. Training for all types of occupations is available in some degree for everyone who wishes it and who is able to qualify for it. The Office of Vocational Rehabilitation has a special responsibility for helping people overcome their employment handicaps. In all programs for finding, training, and utilizing the talents of the gifted and the handicapped, guidance has a very important function to perform.

Sociological barriers to the full utilization of talent must be overcome. The removal of these barriers is dependent upon the good will and the conscience of every citizen.

EXERCISES

1. Some believe that a very important element in the program of the socially handicapped should be the stimulation of the handicapped person or groups to take the initiative themselves in removing the handicap. What evidence do we have that this is being done? Give examples. Do these examples show that this approach has been successful? Give examples.

2. Distinguish between a disability and a handicap. Give examples. Does it ever happen that the "handicap" has acted as a stimulant and enabled the person to reach a higher degree of success than he could have without it?

3. What agencies in your community are concerned with the handicapped? Call or visit one to learn about their policies, support, and procedures.

REFERENCES

Cruickshank, William M.: *Psychology of Exceptional Children and Youth*, Prentice-Hall, Inc., Englewood Cliffs, N.J., 1955.

Ginzberg, Eli, and Associates: *The Negro Potential*, Columbia University Press, New York, 1956.

Lerner, Max: *America as a Civilization*, Simon and Schuster, Inc., New York, 1957.

Passow, A. Harry: *Planning for Talented Youth*, Bureau of Publications, Teachers College, Columbia University, New York, 1955.

Wolfle, Dael: *America's Resources of Specialized Talent*, Harper & Brothers, New York, 1954.

CHAPTER 13

LEISURE-TIME GUIDANCE

One of the most important problems arising out of our complex social, economic, and industrial conditions is the effective use of leisure time. With increased life expectancy, shorter working hours, and more systematic retirement plans the place of leisure in American society has assumed increasing importance. Many feel that the schools, along with other institutions, need to take greater responsibility for preparing students for leisure and giving them guidance in its satisfactory use.

PLACE OF LEISURE IN SOCIETY

Others have pointed to the paradox of considering leisure—a subject associated with reward and relaxation—as a "problem," but a problem it is in the affluent American society of today. The vast majority of mankind would, of course, welcome such a "problem," but this fact does not lessen the dilemma leisure poses for many in this country.

Meaning of Leisure

Although the concept of leisure has varied in some respects from time to time, it has always carried with it the idea of free time, that is, spare time at one's disposal. It is usually interpreted as time not spent on the activities of making a living, keeping alive, or maintaining one's efficiency—eating, sleeping, and the ordinary care of the body. Leisure is synonymous with idleness or with time spent on avocations, hobbies, or recreations. These are merely ways of employing leisure time. It is often difficult to distinguish between one's vocational and avocational activities, but the distinction can be made with sufficient definiteness to give a fairly clear idea of the meaning of leisure.

Variation in Leisure Time

The amount of time for leisure is largely dependent on the time it takes to supply one's physical and social needs. Leisure time may be increased by decreasing needs or by increasing the speed of producing what is needed. Diogenes increased his leisure time by reducing his needs to a bare minimum. We can increase our time for leisure by taking less time for eating, sleeping, and making our toilet. We could also increase our leisure, as some do, by quitting work before the regular time, but this practice usually is not to be commended. We often combine the satisfying of physical needs with social satisfactions, by not gulping down food as fast as we can at meals, by taking time to enjoy beautiful settings and interesting conversation. Although human needs have a way of increasing with increased power to satisfy them, human ingenuity has developed ways of greatly increasing the power to satisfy them. The satisfaction of our needs has been accomplished by increasing man's ability to produce, by increasing the quality and quantity of products of the land, by the discovery of new sources of food, and by the invention of tools and machinery that enable one man to do the work of fifty in gathering and processing food materials.

Early Attitude toward Leisure

There was a time when leisure was considered to be the prerogative of the privileged class. In ancient Athens and Rome and even in America in times of slavery this may have been true. This class, through wealth, power, or tradition, could commandeer the services of a large number of people for the production of sufficient goods of all kinds to enable them to live a life of leisure, free from the necessity of making a living.

It is singular that, in America today, although we have a large group of people who have enough wealth to buy luxuries far beyond the dreams of the richest man in ancient Athens, we have practically no leisure class—at least none that is at all comparable to that of the wealthy citizens of Athens, the powerful barons of feudal times, or the leisured English gentlemen in the time of Locke. Many of our wealthy men are the busiest men we have and have little or no time for leisure. The reason for this anomaly is that we have made a god of work and think chiefly in terms of work, power, and money. This attitude is an outgrowth of our beginnings and of our surroundings. The early New England settlers found life in the new country unexpectedly severe. The soil was poor, the Indians hostile, and the climate cold and bleak. The motto of the Virginia settlers became, "He who does not work shall not eat." "Busyness" and thrift became cardinal virtues with almost religious significance. Some of our church hymns express the same idea:

> Give every flying minute
> Something to keep in store,
> Work for the night is coming
> When man works no more.

These ideals are strongly embedded in the American mind and still color much of our thinking. They have so pervaded society that the idle rich, as well as the idle poor, are considered a menace. The wandering hobo is considered to be little better than a criminal. Many men work hard, taking no time for relaxation, with the avowed purpose of making enough money to retire and enjoy their leisure. When the time for retirement comes, however, they find themselves either so broken in health that they cannot enjoy their free time or unable to enjoy it because they never have learned how.

Present Attitude toward Leisure

Into this atmosphere of struggle and strain, of external striving for wealth and power, of the exaltation of work and efficiency, there have recently come some disturbing elements. First, the conviction has come that, no matter how long and how effectively they work, many men can never, by their own efforts, accumulate enough wealth to live comfortably when retirement comes. Under our present system the distribution of wealth will always be uneven. A living income and a comfortable old age for everyone can be assured only by a social order that plans for them. The present tendency in state and Federal laws seems to indicate that, wisely or unwisely, we are drifting toward a state where this ideal will be realized. Second, production has been so much speeded by labor-saving machinery and improved techniques that enough goods may soon be produced to provide a reasonably high standard of living with a work week of thirty hours or less. Men will no longer need to work long hours for there may not be enough work to keep them busy more than five hours a day. We may have thrust upon us five or six hours a day which cannot be spent in the activities of one's job. The old ideals of work and "busyness" are quite inadequate to deal with such a situation. As a result of these changed economic and social conditions, we are rapidly developing a leisure class, not like the old privileged wealthy class, but a class composed of the entire group of unskilled, semiskilled, and skilled workers who constitute the great majority of the population. We are indeed witnessing the movement of a whole society into a way of life which has hitherto been reserved for a special privileged class.

Whether the same shortening of the hours of labor will apply to professional workers remains to be seen. The problem of leisure time is quite possibly the greatest single problem for education today. Recently Herbert Hoover stated, "This civilization is not going to depend on what we do as we work as much as what we do in our spare time." This situation is both a challenge and an opportunity. As increased leisure becomes available for millions, there will be more time available for individuals to develop their talents to the greatest potential, thereby achieving new dimensions of happiness and satisfaction.

SOCIAL AND PERSONAL FUNCTIONS OF LEISURE

The function of leisure is largely determined by the kind and amount of free time available and the ideals of the time. In different societies leisure assumes different functions—in one it provides an opportunity for conspicuous consumption, in another it enables science and literature to prosper. For different individuals leisure performs different functions also—some benefits are socially and personally desirable, some are not.

Leisure Time As Related to Increased Production

When leisure time is merely a short breathing space between long periods of sustained labor, its function has been to increase production. This is accomplished by giving the worker a rest from time to time—the "coffee break"—so that he can recover from fatigue and accomplish more. Sometimes the employer helps his employees to get comfortable homes and provides better working conditions, rest rooms, or recreation facilities. This practice helps his business, for it creates good will and increases production. The Roman emperors provided holidays for the populace, great gladiatorial combats, thrilling spectacles, and sports of all kinds. These activities helped the common people to be satisfied with their lot and to produce more.

Leisure Time As Related to Increased Consumption

Leisure is also thought of as a means of increasing consumption. The more time an individual has free from work, the greater is his demand for goods that will help him make his leisure more satisfying. This fact is evidenced by the great demand for sporting goods of all kinds. Consumption of this kind also increases production, and so it is good for business. Both these points of view about the function of leisure are founded on a belief in the sacredness of work and the importance of increasing wealth as an end in itself.

Leisure Time As Related to Crime and Delinquency

Crime and delinquency flourish when youth and adults have nothing worthwhile to do, when they have "time on their hands." It has been shown in many cities that, whenever interesting sports and other useful activities are provided, delinquency decreases. Productive people are less likely to engage in crime, but few would subscribe to the notion that we should keep people working simply in an attempt to keep them out of mischief.

Leisure Time As Related to Human Development

The functions of leisure time just mentioned fail to touch the most fundamental and important need of an individual—the need for his development as a human being. This idea is well expressed by James Truslow Adams:[1]

> It is not a dream of motor cars and high wages merely, but a dream of a social order in which each man and each woman shall

[1] James Truslow Adams, *The Epic of America*, Little, Brown & Company, Boston, 1931, p. 404.

be able to attain to the fullest stature of which they are innately capable, and be recognized by others for what they are, regardless of the fortuitous circumstances of birth or position.

Adams also writes:[2]

If we are to regard man merely as a producer and consumer, then the more ruthlessly efficient big business is, the better. Many of the goods consumed doubtless make men healthier, happier, and better even on the basis of a high scale of human values. But if we think of him as a human being primarily, and only incidentally as a consumer, then we have to consider what values are best or most satisfying for him as a human being. We can attempt to regulate business for him not as a consumer but as a man, with many needs and desires with which he has nothing to do as a consumer. Our point of view will shift from efficiency and statistics to human nature.

If we are to meet the problem presented by our enforced leisure, if we are to set up the machinery by which to realize the "dream of America" described by Adams, we must put more emphasis upon the development of the individual himself.

TYPES OF LEISURE-TIME ACTIVITIES

The choice of a leisure-time activity should be suited to the needs of the individual, and the basis for choice may well vary with the individual. In most cases, however, it should be sufficiently different from the activities in the regular occupation to afford recreation and real enjoyment. The required skills should be within the participant's capabilities. Before taking up a leisure-time activity, we may want to ask ourselves some questions: "Do I have time for it? Can I afford it? Will it meet my social needs?"

There is a great variety of leisure-time activities and a great overlapping in meaning and purpose. Each activity has within itself possibilities of different values or objectives. The value of an activity depends largely on the individual who participates in it. For this reason it is impossible to make any completely satisfactory classification of leisure activities.

[2] *Ibid.*, p. 408.

Activities Related to Further Education and Training

Many thousands of youths and adults are using their leisure time to prepare themselves for college, for better positions in business and industry, and for different types of work. Evening schools, correspondence schools, and radio and television courses are utilized for these purposes.

General Cultural, Aesthetic, and Appreciative Activities

These activities broaden our outlook and vision, and increase our appreciation of music, art, literature, and all that is high and noble. They help us keep in touch with the world and maintain and deepen our intellectual, moral, and spiritual nature. They involve cessation of haste and strenuous struggle and require us to take time to stretch, to think, to enjoy, to appreciate. Thoreau had this purpose in mind when he wrote, "I went to the woods because I wished to live deliberately, to front only the essential facts of life, and see if I could not learn what it had to teach, and not, when I came to die, discover that I had not lived." Davies also felt the same longing as he wrote:[3]

> What is this life, if, full of care,
> We have no time to stand and stare.
> No time to stand, beneath the boughs
> And stare as long as sheep and cows.
> No time to stand, when woods we pass
> Where squirrels hide their nuts in grass.
> No time to see in broad daylight,
> Streams full of stars, like skies at night.
> No time to turn at Beauty's glance
> And watch her feet, how they can dance.
> No time to wait till her mouth can
> Enrich the smile her eyes began.
> A poor life this, if, full of care,
> We have no time to stand and stare.

One of the most profitable and satisfying ways of spending leisure time is in quiet meditation. Some of the most valuable con-

[3] W. H. Davies, "Leisure," from *Selected Poems*, Alfred A. Knopf, Inc., New York, 1922. (*Used by permission of the publishers.*)

tributions to literature, philosophy, religion, and science have resulted from this practice. What would our world be today without dreamers? When we think of activity, we too often think of activity of the body only, forgetting that thinking and feeling are also activities.

Creative Activities

These activities are those where one does not sit passively and enjoy the creation of others but participates in the creation. The field of such activities is very wide and offers opportunity for everyone. Under this category would come the composition of music, painting, sculpturing, dressmaking, cooking, working in wood, metal, or other material, writing, and any other activity in which one is not merely a spectator but actually produces something. Such activities give us satisfaction and a feeling of accomplishment.

Recreation

As usually understood, recreation may include practically all types of leisure-time activities, especially amateur sports and games —anything done just for fun. However, its original meaning has great significance. "Recreation" has the meaning indicated in "re-creation." It means to revive, to refresh, to renew. It presupposes that the individual once had something that he valued and has now lost it or is in danger of losing it because of exhaustion, ill health, neglect, or some other cause; through recreation he wants to get it back. "Re-creation" includes the need for rest or for types of exercise which will renew one's strength. It also includes renewal of happiness, faith, courage, trust in people; the meaning of life, of sorrow, of sickness, of death. It thus includes every type of human activity which helps in the renewal of human values.

A common type of recreation is a hobby. A hobby may be described as a nonvocational activity that involves more than a mere passing interest and one to which one turns persistently when opportunity permits. Hobbies are recognized as being among the most valuable of the leisure-time activities. Some authorities say that every person should have some sort of hobby, but this certainly is an exaggeration because not infrequently a number of varied activities is more valuable to a particular individual. Hobbies may have a great prognostic value for the choice of an occupation.

Escape

Escape activities are those engaged in as a release from the daily round of labor or from situations that are unpleasant or disturbing. They are calculated to make one forget unhappiness, at least temporarily. They must, therefore, be absorbing activities and as different as possible from the experience that caused the unpleasant emotions. A large number of people employ their spare time in activities that are entirely of this kind. They read detective stories, romantic novels, the sports page, the comics. They go to second-rate movies that appeal entirely to the eye and ear or spend their time before the television set where conversation is taboo. They attend football, baseball, and hockey games that grip their attention and stir the emotions to a point of forgetfulness; they play bridge, tennis, golf and play as strenuously as they work. When they travel, in order to get the most for their money they join a planned tour which leaves them no time to themselves. On shipboard the steward thoughtfully plans their every minute in deck sports, dances, special parties, or bridge. At times we all need such forms of relaxation, but far too often they are the only ones in which we engage. Anyone who looks upon the usual vacation activities of the tourist may well say, "At work man is sublime; at leisure he is ridiculous."

Service Activities

These are the activities that are done to help others. They may take the form of a personal service to a member of the family or a friend or services to various groups and clubs. Many service activities may also become creative ones. Women who volunteer to help in hospitals and men who work with youth groups are performing service activities. Leisure time spent in such activities may give the feeling of satisfaction which comes from being engaged in a socially valuable task.

Competitive Activities

These are the activities in which one person or group seeks to surpass another person or group in the exercise of certain skills. Indoor and outdoor games and sports of all kinds come under this heading. These activities are among the most popular ways of spending leisure time and may have very great value for the participants. Some critics say, with a fair amount of truth, that with the great popularity of professional sports we are afflicted with "spectatoritis" and do not engage enough in sports directly. There are, however, some real recreational values in being a spectator with a large social group witnessing the same exercises and cheering for "our side."

RESPONSIBILITY OF THE SCHOOL
FOR LEISURE-TIME ACTIVITIES

The curriculum of the school, as defined here, consists in the regular school subjects—English, mathematics, social studies, science, etc.—that are organized and administered by the school faculty and the student activity program that is largely organized by the students themselves. Although leisure-time activities may not be a definite part of the curriculum, the school has a very important influence upon the use of leisure by the students.

Class Instruction and Leisure Time

Through the curriculum are developed the fundamental skills in reading, writing, art, music, home economics, and industrial arts which are essential to effective participation in many of the leisure-time activities. We must rely on class instruction to develop an interest in such activities and a desire to participate in them. There needs to be a somewhat radical change in the attitudes of some superintendents, principals, and teachers before the school can become really effective in its contribution to the leisure-time activities of the students. Even more important is the change that needs to take place in the patrons of the school. The taxpaying public and school boards must be persuaded that activities preparing students for the wise use of leisure are not "fads and frills" to be eliminated when the financial situation becomes acute. More time and attention have to be given to the school's responsibility for assisting the students to develop the skills for effective leisure-time activities and for making wise choices among such activities.

The intelligent choice and wise planning of leisure-time activities are dependent upon knowledge of the different types involved, skill in their use, and real interest and desire to participate in them. Since this is the case, the curriculum of the elementary and secondary school has an important function in leisure-time guidance. Courses in civics, history, general science, English, and geography are now being organized in such a way as to help the pupil learn the facts of modern social, civic, and economic life which are important for him and to develop in him interests and attitudes that will function in his life both in the school and outside it in work and in leisure.

Student Activities and Leisure Time

Although closely related to the organized classes, the various forms of student clubs and activities and the general school life contribute much toward preparing for wise choice of leisure-time activities. Student participation in the government of the school affords splendid opportunity for acquiring facts about forms of government and for developing right attitudes toward service activities, especially those related to citizenship. The best preparation for civic responsibility in later life is participation in the duties connected with the social group with which one is now connected. For the student, the most important group is the school. If students feel that the responsibility for the government of the school rests partly upon them, they will assume a very different attitude toward the life of the school and toward discipline. One of the reasons why so-called "student" government is not more helpful in civic guidance is that it is often student government in name only. Policies are really decided by the principal, and the officers of the organization are mere puppets moving at his behest. To be effective, real responsibility should be placed upon the officers of the student body. The government of the school should be a cooperative matter, with definite responsibility being delegated to the students for some matters. Problems that arise in connection with the government of the school afford excellent material for group discussions, assembly talks, homeroom conferences, and individual conferences between students and principal or teacher.

The student activities program and the general school life are important factors in the acquisition of facts, in the development of skills and attitudes that are useful in adjustment to others, and in general social relationships. Such attainments are vital in appreciation and service activities. Most of one's life is concerned directly with other people, and individual success and happiness are dependent in large measure upon the way in which one gets along with others. Individuals differ by nature very greatly in their power to adapt themselves to social situations; for some, it is very easy; for others, it is extremely difficult; for all, it is largely a matter of training. Everyone needs guidance in social adjustments no matter what sort of home he may come from or how well he may be endowed by nature.

Social Skills and Leisure Time

The necessity for definite assistance in manners and social skills is well stated by Edgar A. Guest:[4]

Why is it some people are liked and others greatly disliked? It is not altogether a question of honesty and fair dealing. Apparently it has nothing to do with respectability, for many respectable people are not popular. It seems to me to be wholly a matter of manners. . . .

Analyzing the various people who seem always to annoy me and "get on my nerves" is not difficult. Some of them are boastful. . . .

There are others who are flagrantly selfish in little things. They are openly bad mannered. . . .

Another type I don't like is simply malicious. Persons of this class have bitter tongues and cruel minds. Their jests always carry a sting. . . .

The two-faced man or woman is difficult to endure. This type leaves a trail of broken confidences behind it. . . .

Churlish people are unpopular everywhere. So are people filthy both of person and of speech. . . .

The art of making friends lies in knowing how to avoid these dangers. It seems to me that he who would properly equip his boy or girl for life in this world should begin early with the teaching of manners. . . .

The man who has many friends has been a friend to many. He has understood the needs of many. He has known, without being told, that other people like to have attention shown to them,

[4] Edgar A. Guest, "The Art of Making Friends," *American Magazine,* vol. 106, pp. 7–9, 141–143, November, 1928.

and he has shown that attention graciously and gracefully. He has slighted no man needlessly. He has walked the earth with all men as one of them. He has understood the need of all for laughter. The fellowship of joy and grief has been an open book to him. The chances are he has suffered sorrow, and he knows how deeply it cuts, and he remembers when another is in trouble.

Manners, then, are of very great importance, and manners can be learned. In our cosmopolitan high schools, students need special help because there are many social customs of which they are entirely ignorant. Since their homes do not give help, someone else must. Help is given in classes set apart for this special purpose, by the definite provision for social occasions in the school, by parliamentary activities in student assemblies, and in club and class meetings and private conferences. Some schools utilize the entire school life for purposes of social guidance. Formal and informal teas are given to accustom students to such occasions and to train them in conduct proper to the occasion. Parents' receptions are organized with the help of students. Formal and informal dances and parties are employed where invitations are issued and letters of acceptance or regret are sent. These activities are all organized and administered with the definite purpose of giving students the most practical help and training in methods of social conduct and forms of social usage. Such matters are often considered in home-room discussions. Several very helpful manuals on manners have been written and are now being used in the schools.

Student clubs often serve to develop or to deepen interest in desirable activities that develop into hobbies or avocations in later life and function as leisure-time activities, cultural and appreciative, creative, and service.

Sports and Leisure Time

The physical education program is directed partly toward the development of skills in certain games, group and individual, and partly toward the development of an interest and desire to continue such participation after one's school life is over. If this work is to become really effective, studies should be conducted which will show the effect that certain forms of recreation have upon the physical and mental life of the participants and the forms that are best suited to meet the needs of different types of people. We need to examine our school program of athletics and student clubs to determine which ones will be helpful in after-school life. We already know, for example, that the great majority of people, after they leave school, will not play football, baseball, hockey, or basketball. They are far more likely to play golf, tennis, or volley-ball, or to swim, go hiking, or dance. Group play is valuable in many ways and should not be neglected, but directors of physical education are coming to feel that such games should not crowd out forms of recreation in which most people will engage after they leave school. Definite provision should be made in school for the development of an interest in these forms of sport which have carry-over value in later life.

SUMMARY

Leisure time is usually understood to mean time that is not needed for making a living or for activities concerned with eating, sleeping, and care of the body. Leisure is not the same as idleness, for idleness is only one way of employing leisure time. Throughout human history, the effective use of leisure time has been a serious problem, and the greater the amount of "time on our hands," the greater the problem becomes. Whenever people have no worthwhile ways of using leisure time, leisure becomes a menace to the idle adults or young people.

The problem is not merely that of keeping busy but of finding activities that will promote the welfare and satisfaction of the individual and be socially valuable. The use of leisure time is extremely varied in purpose and activity. It may be used to increase effectiveness on the daily job, to promote the comfort or convenience of home or community life, to develop some value that the job does not supply—aesthetic, spiritual, creative—or to recreate some value that has been lost.

There are many different ways of achieving these values, depending upon the particular abilities of the individual and his social surroundings. The secondary school has a definite function to perform in developing useful leisure-time activities and in supplying guidance in its wise employment.

EXERCISES

1. Select three to five general criteria that would be useful in the choice of leisure-time activities. State the occupations in which you expect to be engaged for several years at least. On the basis of the criteria you have selected, state several types of leisure-time activities that would be useful and desirable to you.

2. Try to discover the leisure-time activities of three prominent persons now living.

3. What responsibility should the schools assume for guidance and training in leisure-time activities? Describe what one school is doing to prepare its students to use effectively the leisure they will have as adults.

REFERENCES

Donahue, Wilma, et al. (eds.): *Free Time: Challenge to Later Maturity*, University of Michigan Press, Ann Arbor, Mich., 1958.

Larrabee, Eric, and Rolf Meyerson (eds.): *Mass Leisure*, Free Press, Glencoe, Ill., 1960.

Menninger, William C.: *Enjoying Leisure Time*, Science Research Associates, Inc., Chicago, 1950.

Overstreet, Harry A.: *A Guide to Civilized Leisure*, W. W. Norton & Company, Inc., New York, 1934.

Trow, William Clarke: *Recreation and Leisure*, McGraw-Hill Book Company, Inc., New York, 1951.

CHAPTER 14

GUIDANCE TOWARD LIFE GOALS

The wise choice of an occupation is of extreme importance. It should be one that is suited to the abilities of the individual and that will enable him to fulfill his basic needs, to develop his "self-image." The wise choice of leisure-time activities is also important not only to refresh and revive mind and body but also to minister to the aesthetic and spiritual side of life. But neither one nor both together are sufficient to give the highest meaning to life. An effective and satisfying life is not one that is made up of separate, unrelated parts; it is not like a patchwork quilt in which pieces of cloth of different materials, colors, shapes, and sizes are included without a discernible pattern; it is not merely a series of somewhat unrelated thoughts, feelings, and acts that are made in response to surrounding stimuli. Life is more than the sum of all its parts. Some unifying principle is needed which will bind together all the aspects and activities of one's life into one consistent whole. This is found in the concept of the life goal. This being the case, the choice of a life goal is, perhaps, the most important choice in one's life. The process of selecting a suitable life goal is one of the most essential and complex experiences in the area of guidance.

THE MEANING AND IMPLICATION OF LIFE GOALS

A goal is a dynamic concept. It is not merely an end to be reached so that some activity can cease. It is not an ideal which is to be worshiped but which will remain beyond one's reach. A goal involves something that the individual believes is valuable and a compulsion or effort to attain it. It is "a-something-of-value-that-I-am-trying-to-attain."

A life goal is one that permeates all the aspects of one's life at any given time. To attain it may involve all the areas in one's life. It may be reached in a short time or never. The important element is the effort to attain, not the attainment. A life goal is based upon and determined by a set of values that govern, bind together, and give meaning to all the activities of a person's life. It provides a center for the gradual integration of all the physical, intellectual, and emotional factors in life.

A valid life goal must take into consideration the worth of the individual himself and his obligation to society. Such a goal is a rejection of the idea that a man's job is the most important thing in his life and that all his activities should be centered around it. A job is not an end in itself but merely a means to a larger and more important goal. This point of view, while generally accepted as an ideal, is often forgotten in practice. There is danger that the occupation will become an end in itself and that the really important end will be neglected. This does not mean that a job is not important or that one should do less than his best in work but, rather, that there should be a deeper meaning in life— an objective or goal that may serve to unify, integrate, and dignify all the activities of the individual. Any other position is likely to result in a lopsided, misshapen personality and general unhappiness.

The implication of this position is that the life of an individual should be considered as an organic whole, not as a mixture of more or less unrelated and often conflicting elements. Therefore, in considering the usefulness, effectiveness, or desirability of any job or any aspect of life, the entire pattern of life should be taken into account, not merely one segment of it. One should take into consideration how a given job will contribute to the attainment of one's life goal. While there are other elements of value that must be considered—working conditions, wages, chances for advancement, etc.—the life goal itself is the crucial element that ties together and serves to complement and give meaning to the job as a part of the life of the individual.

For many people vocational activities occupy a large part of life—in time, energy, and interest—and they often bring real satisfaction and joy to the worker; but they are not the whole of life, although they may furnish the chief avenue through which the life goal may be attained. Other aspects of life must also be considered, however: home life and recreational and civic activities. Many occupations are of such a nature that they cannot serve as the chief expression of the life goal. A man's central purpose or goal in some cases may be best seen in his home, his civic activities, or his church instead of in his occupation. In order to find whether his various activities are congruent with his real life goal, we must ask this question: Is the same central goal or purpose shown in all these activities? Guidance that relates only to the choice of an occupation can never be completely effective or satisfactory because it includes only one segment of life. Even joy in the activities of an occupation cannot be an entirely satisfactory element by itself because it furnishes no central, guiding principle for the selection of other activities that are nonoccupational.

There is, for most persons, no one best, predetermined avenue through which the life goal may be realized. Any one of a number of different avenues may be equally effective and satisfactory in getting an individual to his goal. The particular avenue that we take is influenced by many different elements in our environment.

One does not always need to change jobs in order to make his occupation more useful in achieving his goal. In most occupations there is some opportunity for a personal adjustment that may make it possible to use the job in such a way that it will be more helpful in the attainment of the life goal. Life is full of illustrations of men and women who have so interpreted their jobs and so governed their activities as to make them avenues through which they have attained their life goal. The lives of individuals we know—carpenters, plumbers, nurses, lawyers—constantly remind us that any job that is not in itself antisocial may be used in such a way as to contribute to human welfare when making such a contribution is the worker's life goal.

Examples of Life Goals

There are as many life goals possible as there are value systems and different social contexts in which the values can find expression. Some may devote themselves to working for the equality of opportunity for all Americans. Some may think that the highest goal is the achievement of peace and good will among nations. "To make two blades of grass grow where only one grew before" may be a life goal. Others wish to emulate Schweitzer, Gandhi, or Lincoln. These and other purposes can give meaning to life and help the individual make choices of all kinds as they are related to this goal.

Difficulty of Choosing Life Goals

It is often very difficult to select a life goal that is suited to the abilities, needs, and interests of the individual and that has a reasonable promise of attainment. After the choice is made, it is sometimes difficult or impossible to reach the goal. Both choice and attainment often require assistance from others. The process of so clarifying our values that we know what we stand for is a lifelong task. Many live confused, shallow lives unable to differentiate the important from the trivial. While we should not expect most students to have clear and expressible life goals, we should assume some responsibility for helping them to learn the dimensions of this human problem and to have some acquaintance with the major tools useful in its solution.

Influences in Choosing Life Goals

A life goal is not a gift from the gods. It is not inherited but learned. Parents, teachers, and associates may do much to shape an individual's life goal as may his general social environment with its war, famine, disease, estrangement of parents, or death of close friends. A person develops his life goal slowly, often unconsciously, and may revise it from time to time. Sometimes a religious conversion or a personal tragedy may cause sudden dramatic changes. Although it is usually not fully developed until maturity and sometimes not even then, the important elements begin to appear in adolescence. It is clear, then, that the period represented by the secondary school and college is of maximum importance in the development of a life philosophy—in the formation of a life goal. The guidance needed for this phase of development lends itself especially well to group discussion, supplemented from time to time by individual counseling. Here, again, is where teachers can be of great help, especially teachers of English, history, science, music, and art. The lives of men and women who have made contributions in these fields can be studied and emphasis given to their special gifts, their purposes, and their motives.

The school will influence the life goals of its students whether it wishes to or not. The only question which remains is whether the influence is to be unconscious, disorganized, and negative or whether it will be conscious, systematic, and positive.

MAJOR LIFE GOALS

While, as has been explained, there may be many life goals, we may group them into three major categories—self-realization, service, and satisfaction. This grouping does not suggest that other possible life goals might not be of comparable merit and importance, but rather that these three divisions lend themselves to illustration and comparison and therefore seem most useful for our present explanatory purposes.

Self-concept As Guide to Life Goal

The importance of a life goal is forcibly demonstrated in the findings of Roe and Super in their investigations of the factors that are associated with the choice of an occupation. Among these factors is the "self-image," or the "self-concept." The self-concept may be described roughly as the elaboration of such statements as, "I am this sort of a person. These are my strengths and my weaknesses. These are the things I like to do." Although a self-concept is far from being a life goal, it is a very important factor in the choice of a life goal. Self-realization is becoming what one wants to be, and what one wants to be should take into consideration what one is—the present self-concept. A life goal, however, is far broader and more comprehensive than the image of what one is now. The selection of an impelling life goal often serves to eliminate weaknesses and to utilize strengths not apparent to the individual; in short, it provides motivation. In the two-way classification of occupations described by Roe, it can easily be seen how a clear life goal might help in the realistic choice of one of the occupational groups, but it would be of even greater significance in the choice of a level of work. The relationship of the self-concept to the life goal is an instrumental one because, while the life goal should underlie and be basic to any valid occupational choice, the self-concept governs the selection of the best avenue or channel for attaining it.

There is real danger that the use of the self-concept may be restricted to the selection of an occupation. To be of maximum value it should include a clarification of factors and traits which may not be closely related to what is called "success on the job" but which are definitely essential to a successful life. Guidance should help an individual relate his self-concept to his goals in such a way that he achieves "peace of mind" or "serenity of spirit." One of the best statements of this relationship was given by Paul: "I have learned in whatever state I am therein to be content." It is important to note that Paul did not say "*therewith*" to be content. Progress never results from contentment *with* one's state; discontent with one's state is an essential factor in progress. Paul was content in shipwreck, in prison, in hunger, and in thirst. Peace of mind, contentment, serenity in the midst of danger, of failure, of difficulties clear the mind of the fear and discouragement that interfere with sound judgment and valid decisions. Such peace of mind comes only from the understanding and acceptance of the fundamental values of life. Finally, there is some danger that the life goal itself may become an idol for worship, and, instead of losing himself in the service itself, the individual may become so enamored of the high value of the activity and of his own importance that he will neglect his work.

Service As a Life Goal

Because a life goal brings together all the forces of the individual upon a single objective, it exerts a tremendous influence on the accomplishment of the objective chosen. The result may be useful or disastrous to the individual himself or to society. History is full of examples of both.

Without question the life goal that has had the greatest influence for good is that of service to others. Service is the keystone on which any stable and enduring government is built. In human history civilization after civilization has fallen because it has placed the selfish interest of the rulers above service to its people. Nearly every world religion is based on the concept of a supreme being and the obligation to serve one another. Service is the core of

Jewish and Christian ethics. Democratic government, too, is founded on service. Sometimes the ideal of service has been too restricted to a particular country.

Certain occupations, such as medicine, nursing, law, teaching, social work, and the ministry, are based directly upon service to others. And all have been of great benefit to society.

There are many organizations like Rotary, Kiwanis, Lions, and Optimists which are distinctly service agencies devoted to high standards of professional, business, and civic life, to good citizenship, and to mutual assistance to fellow members. Many of these service clubs have direct connections with young people in school and college. Fraternal societies such as Masons, Elks, Odd Fellows are also organizations based on service, as are others related to church denominations. It can be seen that service is a powerful and widespread life goal and a useful force in our society.

Satisfaction As a Life Goal

Satisfaction is a state of mind or an emotion that normally results from the successful attempt to reach a goal or satisfy a felt need. It is an essential element in a successful life and an invaluable asset in learning. It is imperative for every individual to have satisfaction somewhere in his life. Satisfaction may also come from the effort to attain the goal even when the goal is not reached or the need satisfied. The very difficulty of attaining the goal becomes a challenge which may have value. As James said, "Keep the quality of effort alive within you by doing some gratuitous exercises every day."

Satisfaction in itself, however, cannot be a safe guide to the choice of an occupation or any other goal. Unfortunately satisfaction may also come from the effort to attain a harmful or undesirable goal. Theft, rape, murder, oppression, cruelty give satisfaction to some people. It is the goal that is important, not the satisfaction in achieving it. But within the group of useful and desirable occupations that are suited to the needs and abilities of the individual, the possible satisfactions are very important in determining choice. Some occupations give opportunity for pride and satisfaction in the quality of the product and by the contribution that the worker makes to it. In some others, however, the worker never sees the finished product but merely feeds an automatic machine that makes only a small part of it. In such situations whatever satisfaction the worker gets is from the wages received and, possibly, from his friendly relations with other workers.

The present tendency is to increase the proportion of occupations that involve complicated machinery. Thus the professions now give the greatest opportunity for satisfaction in work. As already pointed out, although satisfaction alone is not a safe guide for the choice of an occupation, it may be a real help in such a choice. The types of activity which give satisfaction vary with different individuals. Some get their satisfaction in the production of articles made out of cloth, wood, metal, or plastic. Others get satisfaction from gardening, horticulture, farming, or forestry; and others, from working with people in such occupations as teaching, nursing, medicine, the law, and social work. The hope of satisfaction may serve as a guide in choosing an occupation by permitting a comparison of the activities that give the individual satisfaction with those that are involved in various occupations.

In some cases it may not be necessary or possible to choose an occupation that satisfies. The important objective, however, is to find satisfaction somewhere in one's life—in the job, the home, civic life, the church, or recreation. The ideal life is one in which each element supplements and enhances the value of the total in the attainment of a satisfactory life goal.

The selection of a life goal is often very difficult for youth. It is hard to choose one which is suited to the abilities, needs, and interests of the individual and which has a reasonable promise of attainment. Youth's limited experience does not provide sufficient background for a wise choice. Parents, teachers, and counselors can help by suggesting types of life goals for consideration.

COOPERATION BETWEEN THE PUBLIC SCHOOL
AND THE CHURCH IN THE GUIDANCE OF YOUTH

The principle of the separation of state and church is well established in this country. The public school, as an instrument of the state, is obligated to accept this. This principle, however, does not imply that there should be no cooperation between public schools and churches. In fact, it is essential that some sort of concord be provided if the best interests of the state and the church, as well as those of youth, are to be promoted. This need for co-operation is greatest in the guidance program which is designed to assist youth in the choice of a life goal and in the selection of occupational and other activities through which the goal may be attained.

If the church worker is to be of maximum assistance, he must understand the school life of the youth. He must know how the student is progressing in his schoolwork, how he behaves, what special interests he has developed, what points of strength and weakness are evident, and how he is liked by his teachers and his fellow students. This information, which is known by his teachers and his counselor, is usually available in the school records. Some of these records are confidential and cannot be given to out-of-school persons, but there is much valuable information that could be made available to the church worker.

Schools Help Develop Life Goals

Although the schoolteacher and the counselor are barred from exerting any influence regarding the religious beliefs and activities of the youth, the very knowledge that the youth is active in the church may help them to understand his attitudes and conduct. It might aid the counselor in his attempt to give guidance toward life goals.

Especially in assistance in the selection of a life goal are the church and the school on common ground. In this country the basic ideals of character and conduct—honesty, integrity, obedi-ence to authority, sincerity, industry, loyalty, and service to others—are evidences of good citizenship and are essential elements in Christian living. The special contribution of the church is to provide the religious incentive in the selection of a life goal and in the effort to attain the goal selected. Cooperation between school and church is often very difficult to develop, and great care must be taken that neither the public school nor the church assume the special rights and privileges of the other.

For many years there has been very effective cooperation between church and state in many areas of life. The church and church workers are basically committed to service of all kinds. In peace, in the ravages of war or epidemics, in destructive storms, in dealing with crime and delinquency, church workers of all denominations cooperate willingly to help those in need, with no consideration of their religious position. Cooperation between church and state is taken for granted. It seems strange that co-operation between church workers and the school for equally important ends should be considered undesirable.

Church Responsibility for Guidance: An Example

There have been, for many years, sporadic attempts at cooperation between churches and public schools, but they have been largely based on the initiative of individual schoolteachers, counselors, pastors, or church youth leaders. In the past few years, however, there have been some significant and interesting endeavors at more systematic cooperation. One of these attempts, initiated by the Department of Christian Vocations, the Board of Education, the Presbyterian Church in the U.S., in Richmond, Virginia, aims at providing vocational counseling in cooperation with public schools.[1]

The name "Christian Vocations" might well lead one to think that this program was concerned primarily with the recruitment of young people for the ministry, missionary work, or other types of church work, but such is not the case. Without neglecting these vocations, the counselors include consideration of all kinds of honorable occupations, for they believe that any occupation can be a Christian vocation, since the goal of all occupations is service. Therefore, in counseling relating to choice of an occupation, they emphasize the opportunity for Christian service in all occupations. They also consider the usual elements such as kind of work, surroundings, ability needed, and chances for advancement. The reception given to this approach has been very encouraging. In 1956 there were more than a thousand churches participating actively at various stages of the program's development. Seven colleges were cooperating by providing counseling centers for instruction in the use of counseling techniques and by giving and interpreting tests of various kinds. In each church the pastor and the director of Christian education give the actual counseling service. Helpful "counseling kits" are sent to each "vocational aide" of the church after he has been trained in their use. Local churches are urged to

[1] Erwin Haskell Schell, *New Strength for New Leadership*, Harper & Brothers, New York, 1942.

participate by (1) helping youth to acquire a Christian philosophy of life work; (2) assisting youth to plan intelligently for career decisions; (3) referring its youth to Presbyterian guidance centers, if available; (4) informing its youth about community guidance resources and how to use them; (5) encouraging its youth to follow up this guidance by community help; and (6) working to get its Presbyterian Synod to establish and support a Presbyterian guidance center.

Stimulated by the success of this project, the Presbyterian Church in the U.S.A. has inaugurated a similar porject. A well-trained and experienced guidance specialist was appointed as general director of the project, and conferences were organized in which careful study was made of the responsibility of the church in the guidance of youth; methods of cooperation between the church and the public school were also discussed. The difficulties and dangers of such cooperation were clearly recognized, and plans were discussed for pilot projects in selected areas. Reports from these projects indicate definitely that such cooperation is not only possible but accepted eagerly by the school, the churches, and the community.

The basic purpose of the project is to help every youth to find a vocation which is right for him and through which he can express the values of a Christian vocation. In the course of working toward this goal, it is assumed that certain youth will accept church vocations. In fulfilling this purpose discussions among representatives from the churches, the schools, and the community centered on three questions. (1) What are the guidance needs of the young people of this community? (2) What is being done to meet these needs? (3) What yet needs to be done? Agreement was reached that both the church and the school have responsibilities in the area of vocational guidance.

The initial focus was on the relationship between the church and the public school and the points on which they might be able to serve one another. Up to the present time there seems to have been little difficulty in securing cooperation between them. Pastors and directors of young people in the churches do not think of themselves as trained counselors. They restrict their function for the most part to helping organize the program and making available information which will aid students in learning more about the vocations in which they are interested. The church worker does not exert pressure on the youth to become a minister but helps him choose an occupation that is suited to his ability and needs.

Church Responsibility for Guidance: A Second Example

The following statement from the Winter, 1957, issue of the *Catholic Counselor* indicates the interest of the Roman Catholic Church in guidance for youth and the recognition of the importance of life goals that are centered upon and motivated by a religious belief that demands a life of service to others:

> The Catholic can impress upon the profession the need for helping individuals solve their problems, in terms of physical, mental, and spiritual phases, if the person is to live a full life and be able to give his utmost to job, family, and community. Here emphasis on the importance of the individual and his freedom to make choices can help to explain good guidance practices, as well as the Catholic viewpoint.

It is, of course, recognized that public schools cannot be concerned directly with choices related to church affiliations or religious beliefs. However, because both church and school share in a concern for the welfare of youth, there are many opportunities for them to cooperate in the field of guidance.

SUMMARY

A life goal is not a gift from the gods; it is not inherited, although it is often strongly influenced, for good or bad, as pointed out previously, by parents, teachers, or by famine, disease, death of close friends. It develops slowly, often unconsciously, and it may be revised. It usually is not fully developed until maturity and sometimes not even then, but in adolescence the important elements begin to appear. Thus the period represented by the secondary school and college is of maximum importance in the development of a life philosophy. Guidance toward life goals lends itself especially well to group discussion, which may be supplemented from time to time by individual counseling. Here, again, is where teachers can be of great help.

In assisting a student in the selection of an occupation, we should help him to look beyond the occupation itself and to consider what sort of a person he wants to be. He needs to think of an occupation in terms of whether it will be helpful in satisfying his basic needs and enable him to move toward his ideal self. He must consider what sort of a life he wants to live. We should help him in defining his life goal. After this is done, he is ready to consider how the occupation under consideration will fulfill his needs.

Because a life goal has such great potential power for good or evil, it is also very important that it be one that is useful and constructive rather than one that is selfish, harmful, and destructive. One of the most powerful and constructive goals is that of service to others. This ideal has always been especially attractive to youth and should be stressed.

Both the school and the church have responsibilities in helping youth clarify their values and select occupations congruent with them. Many churches recognize their responsibility in this area and are actively working out ways to cooperate with the school in furthering the guidance of young people. Such cooperation, of course, needs to be done without violation of the American principle of separation of church and state.

EXERCISES

1. What do you see as the school's responsibility for guidance toward life goals? Are there differences between the proper roles of public and private schools in this matter?

2. Tell what churches in your community are doing to give guidance toward life goals. Discuss the meaning and techniques of pastoral counseling.

3. Select three public personalities whose reputations would be known to your classmates and decide what you think are their major life goals. Be prepared to elaborate and defend your decisions.

REFERENCES

Farwell, Gail, and Herman J. Peters: *Guidance Readings for Counselors*, Rand McNally & Company, Chicago, 1960.

Hall, Robert King, and J. A. Lauwerys (eds.): *The Yearbook of Edu-*

cation, 1955: Guidance and Counseling, Harcourt, Brace & World, Inc., New York, 1955.

Jones, Arthur J., and Harold C. Hand: "Guidance and Purposive Living," chap. 1 in *Guidance in Educational Institutions,* Thirty-seventh Yearbook, National Society for the Study of Education, part 1, Public School Publishing Company, Bloomington, Ill., 1938.

McDaniel, H. B., et al. (eds.): *Readings in Guidance,* Henry Holt and Company, Inc., New York, 1959.

Miller, Carroll: *Foundations of Guidance,* Harper & Brothers, New York, 1961.

PART VII

GUIDANCE TODAY

CHAPTER 15

PRESENT STATUS AND EVALUATION
OF GUIDANCE

Organized guidance began in the early years of this century. The first definition of vocational guidance, made in 1919, stated the following: "The purpose of vocational guidance is to assist persons to choose, prepare for, enter upon, and make progress in an occupation." A variation on this definition made some time later is now considered standard: "Vocational guidance is assistance given to individuals in choosing, preparing for, entering upon, and making progress in an occupation."

PRESENT STATUS OF THE PROFESSION
OF COUNSELING IN SCHOOLS

It was inevitable that the effort to help youth in problems relating to occupations would reveal problems that were not strictly occupational but had to be solved before a wise choice of occupations could be made. Among these are personal, social, and religious relationships that are essential to the attainment of a satisfactory and useful life and, therefore, important in the selection of an occupation. Although no accepted definition of this broader concept of guidance has been adopted, a good one might well be the following: "Guidance is the assistance given to individuals in the development of the ability to solve the problems and make the adjustments essential to a satisfactory and useful life."

This definition adds two elements to guidance. First, it is not

271

restricted to occupational problems but embraces all types of problems in life. Second, it adds a developmental purpose of helping the individual to grow in the ability to solve his own problems and to make his own adjustments. The emphasis is now placed on the role of the client, not the counselor, in the solution of the problem. This goal is far more important and much more difficult to achieve.

Estimated Need for Counselors

The need for more guidance services for youth and for requirements for certification is stated in the twelve proposals of the White House Conference on Education in April, 1960:

That guidance and counseling programs be strengthened, expanded, and coordinated at all levels; and that the role of the guidance and counseling program be clearly defined.

That guidance and counseling begin in the elementary school with educational and vocational planning based on early, continuous, and expanded testing and diagnostic appraisal of each child, in order to identify abilities, weaknesses and problems, mental, physical, and emotional.

That every secondary school have sufficient trained professional counselors to deal with adolescent problems; that each adolescent be counseled throughout the secondary years by the same staff adviser, acceptable to him; that school planning for adolescents be based on awareness of individual differences in skills and capacities; that community counseling services be made more widely available to youth and their parents; and that coordination between school and community services be emphasized.

That school resources for identification and guidance of the gifted, limited, and otherwise exceptional child, as well as for the average and normal youth, be expanded and improved.

That vocational counseling and guidance programs be provided with adequate financial support from Federal, State, and local sources; that school personnel, boards, and parents interpret to taxpayers the need for increased and improved guidance services; and that these services cooperate closely with Government, employment services, industries, labor unions, armed services, trade and service organizations, higher educational institutions, and other community groups.

GUIDANCE PERSONNEL

That the qualified professional staff (of every school system) include educational and vocational guidance counselors, job placement counselors, physical health personnel, psychologists to assist in diagnosis and continued study of the children, and school social workers or visiting teachers to assist in the treatment of children with special problems.

That the ratio of students to elementary school counselors be 600 to 1.

That the number of students per counselor in secondary schools be decreased from the present ratio of 625 to 1, to 250 to 1.

That more adequate psychological and psychiatric services be provided for all school-age youth in a ratio of 1 specialist to 2,000 pupils.

That all States require the certification of guidance counselors and other specialized personnel.

That the qualifications for certification be continually reviewed and strengthened, in accordance with the latest research findings in the field; and that they recognize and give credit to appropriate training and work experience in lieu of classroom teaching.

That the training of guidance and counseling personnel for elementary and secondary schools, colleges, and community and professional agencies be intensified and improved to meet the demand; and that Federal funds for the education of school counselors be given only to institutions with professionally approved counselor education programs.

These goals point up the great need for expansion of school guidance programs and the training and hiring of more school counselors. According to the U.S. Office of Education, there were fewer than 16,000 full-time counselors in public secondary schools in 1958–1959. In this same year there were over 10,000,000 students. To provide for a ratio of 1 counselor to 500 students, there would need to be nearly 5,000 additional counselors; if the ratio of 1 to 300 is taken, the deficit becomes 18,000; and if the ratio of 1 to 250 is adopted, as recommended by the White House Conference on Education, the deficit would be a staggering 25,000. Furthermore, many of the present counselors do not have an approved counseling certificate. Even with the probable increase in certified counselors it will be many years before there will be an adequate number of counselors, especially when we take into consideration the great increase in the number of secondary-school students from year to year.

Certification of Counselors

In 1962, thirty-four states required school counselors to have special certification, and in four states certification was optional. In some of the remaining twelve states, plans were being made to introduce certification.

The requirements for certification vary in the different states. Those in two typical states—North Carolina and Arkansas—serve to illustrate the usual ones.

North Carolina

1. Hold or be qualified to hold a Class A teacher's certificate
2. Have at least three years of successful teaching experience
3. Have the time equivalent of at least one year of occupational experience in one or more wage-earning jobs other than teaching or counseling
4. Hold a master's degree in the professional field of guidance which includes:
   a. A minimum of eighteen semester hours of professional courses distributed among the following areas:
      1. Principles of guidance (may be taken at the undergraduate level)
      2. Analysis of the individual
      3. Counseling techniques
      4. Occupational and educational information
      5. Administrative relationships of the guidance program
      6. Supervised practicum
   b. Twelve hours of work distributed among related courses in the areas of education, economics, psychology, and sociology

Arkansas

1. Two years of teaching experience in public schools
2. One year of work experience other than teaching
3. A six-year secondary-school certificate, plus fifteen semes-

ter hours of guidance work, nine semester hours of which shall be
at the graduate level, in residence

4. A minimum in each of the following areas:

	Semester hours
a. Principles and practices of the guidance program	2
b. Analysis of the individual	2
c. Occupational and educational information	2
d. Counseling techniques	2
e. Administrative relationships	2

5. A maximum in each of the following areas is accepted as
electives:

	Semester hours
a. Practice and internship	2
b. History and principles of vocational education	3
c. Psychology of motivation	3
d. Psychology of personality	3
e. Labor problems	3
f. Statistics	3

General courses in psychology, educational psychology, sociology, economics, educational administration, educational supervision are not accepted. Educational tests and measurements and
educational statistics are accepted only if taken on the graduate
level.

All states in which certificates are mandatory require the counselor to have a teaching certificate, teaching experience, and a bach-
elor's degree. There is also a tendency to demand experience in an
occupation other than teaching. The specialized training usually
requires a master's degree or its equivalent in guidance.

Duties and Responsibilities of Counselors

The duties and responsibilities of counselors should, of course,
determine in large measure what their preparation should be. Several states have specified the counselor's duties, and it can be seen

that there is general agreement regarding the proper work of the counselor.

Ohio

1. Assisting students with curricular, extracurricular personal-social adjustment, occupational adjustment, placement and related problems

2. Working with teachers in studying the students, planning and conducting group guidance activities, utilizing community resources, and participating in in-service teacher education activities

3. Working with the administrative staff in problems involving planning, developing, and conducting orientation programs, instructional grouping; public relations, research, and curriculum study

4. Working with lay groups and individuals in coordinating school and community resources and activities which contribute to improved pupil personnel services

California

Pupil counseling means those functions inherent in a guidance program over and above those advisory duties and functions customarily performed by a teacher. A person holding a position in this field has as his major responsibility the rendering of specialized services:

1. In pupil guidance

2. As consultant to teachers and other members of the school staff on problems of guidance

3. As consultant to parents in the interpretation of the school in relation to the child

4. In a liaison relationship between the school, the community, and community agencies

Georgia

A counselor is a member of the high-school staff who is primarily responsible for assisting the individual student in recognizing, thinking through, and solving his educational, vocational, and personal problems.

New Hampshire

A counselor assists students in the solution of their problems as the major part of his professional assignment. His counseling duties shall be devoted to work with individuals largely within the school day.

In actual practice the duties of a school counselor tend to be a function of the beliefs of the administrator, the expectations of the community, and his own perceived strengths. There is, however, a sufficiently large core of activities expected of him to serve as a guide to his preparation.

Training of Counselors

Much attention has been given to university counselor preparation programs. Polmantier and Schmidt[1] studied fifty-four state universities to determine the number which offer work in the areas usually required for counselor certification. Their findings are shown in the following table:

Name of course area	Number of universities	Per cent of universities
Basic course in guidance	54	100
Methods and techniques of counseling	50	93
Occupational and educational information	47	87
Supervised practice and internship	39	72
Tests and measurements	36	67
Understanding the individual	34	63
Organization and administration of guidance	32	59
Seminar, special problems in guidance	26	48
Miscellaneous courses in guidance	26	48
Mental hygiene, personality, and adjustment	23	43
Group procedures in guidance	21	39
Statistics	17	32
Elementary-school guidance	10	19

Dugan[2] calls attention to what he considers weaknesses in the

[1] Paul C. Polmantier and Lyle Schmidt, "Areas of Preparation for School Guidance Workers," *The Personnel and Guidance Journal*, vol. 39, pp. 45–46, September, 1960.

[2] Willis E. Dugan, "The Impact of NDEA upon Counselor Preparation," *The Personnel and Guidance Journal*, vol. 39, pp. 37–40, September, 1960.

present program of counselor training and certification. Because a large number of counselors are recruited from teaching, counselor preparation should be focused on closing the very significant gap in the professional education of teachers. This gap is chiefly in the lack of psychological foundations which are necessary for a real understanding of human behavior. Dugan believes that too much emphasis is placed on the "how" and not enough on the "why." Most programs give considerable attention to philosophy and principles of guidance, educational and occupational information, appraisal techniques, and introduction to counseling but give very little to the important areas of personality theory and development, statistics and methods of research, group procedures in guidance, and supervised counseling experience.

Dugan advocates experimentation and development of new approaches in counselor preparation, development of plans for professionally supervised counseling experience, and increased attention to selective admissions and continuing review of candidates for counselor preparation. Certainly all would agree that we still have much to learn about the best methods of preparing people to assume the complex and changing role of the school counselor.

Professional Activities of School Counselors

We can see another aspect of the present status of school counseling by looking at the professional activities of counselors, especially as shown in their organizations and publications.

The major national association dealing with guidance is the American Personnel and Guidance Association, which has six specialized divisions: American College Personnel Association, Association of Counselor Educators and Supervisors, National Vocational Guidance Association, Student Personnel Association for Teacher Education, American School Counselors Association, and Division of Rehabilitation Counseling.

The American Personnel and Guidance Association operates as a coordinator and integrator of the six organizations, each of which has branches that operate as local associations. The membership in these organizations is not restricted to the United States. The American Personnel and Guidance Association participates in White House conferences and has close relationships with the National Education Association, the U.S. Office of Education, the

U.S. Department of Labor, the American Council on Education, and other associations related to education and guidance. The growth of membership in these guidance organizations tells us much about the present status of guidance.

The American Personnel and Guidance Association publishes *The Personnel and Guidance Journal*, and each of its six divisions also publishes a professional journal; for example, the journal of the American School Counselors Association is the *School Counselor*. These periodicals, along with the *Journal of Counseling Psychology*, constitute the main source of professional literature for counselors. The wide coverage of topics and the increasing circulation of these journals are indications that the profession of counseling is growing.

THE NATIONAL DEFENSE EDUCATION ACT AS AN INSTRUMENT FOR IMPROVING GUIDANCE PROGRAMS

The Federal government has always been deeply concerned with the education and welfare of youth. Among the many acts of the government dealing with youth is the National Defense Education Act (NDEA), which was enacted on September 4, 1958. This act was the result of the concern of Congress for the country's youth in the belief that the security of the nation requires the fullest development of the mental resources and technical skills of its young men and women.

Objectives of the Act

The center and core of the act is Title V, Guidance, Counseling, and Testing. The basic objectives of Title V are (1) the identification and interpretation of each student's abilities and aptitudes early in his secondary-school career; (2) the encouragement of students in the development of educational and career plans appropriate to each student's abilities, aptitudes, and skills; (3) the provision of assistance to the student in the selection of courses of study appropriate to his educational and career plans; (4) the development of understanding of educational and career opportunities by the student and his parents; and (5) the encouragement of students to select and persist in educational programs appropriate to their abilities and aptitudes. These purposes are the central objectives of any guidance program, and Congress wrote the act in a way that would stimulate school districts to improve their programs.

Provisions of the Act

Title V-A provided the expenditure of $60,000,000 during a period of four years to help the states establish and maintain vital programs of guidance, counseling, and testing. Except for the first year, the states were required to match the Federal grants on a dollar-for-dollar basis.

The purpose of the testing program is to identify those students with outstanding aptitudes and abilities in both private and public high schools. The test results will then help qualified counselors advise all high-school students on the courses and occupational objectives best suited to their individual needs. Counselors are to encourage outstanding students to complete high school and go on to college.

By enabling states to provide these guidance services, Congress hopes to reduce the wastage of talent which threatens to undermine America's position of leadership in the free world.

Title V-B provides college training opportunities to encourage teachers to qualify as school counselors.

Impact of the Act

Nationwide statistics indicate that high-school guidance programs have been greatly improved since Congress passed the National Defense Education Act. Guidance, counseling, and testing services are now available to thousands of boys and girls previously isolated from such help.

After the act had been in effect less than two years, the states employed 172 professional guidance personnel. Before NDEA, the number was 99. Ninety per cent of the states have indicated their intention of adding even more guidance personnel to their staffs. The number of counselors has increased, and counselor qualification requirements have been raised in at least twenty-two states, indicating a general tendency to upgrade professional standards. More than two million aptitude and achievement tests were administered with NDEA funds to public and nonpublic secondary-school students in the first year of the act.

Each state is required to set up a plan for the utilization of the provisions of the act, and these projects have to be approved by the U.S. Office of Education. The state plan is divided into three major areas of professional activity: state supervision and related services, the state program of testing, and the provisions of guidance services in local secondary schools. During the second year of this program about 85 per cent of the money went to the improvement of guidance at the local level, 8 per cent to testing, and 7 per cent to the state supervisory activities.

Influence on Total Guidance Program

The final evaluation of a program of state supervision or even the provision for the proper identification of talents in youth is dependent upon the effectiveness of the services at the local level. States still vary in the qualifications of counselors and in the counselor-student ratio (ratios range from 1 to 450 to 1 to 1,200), but there is almost universal agreement upon the activities which constitute a program of guidance services. The services described in the regulations of NDEA, Title V, are commonly accepted functions of guidance services in local secondary schools:

> Guidance and counseling programs in public secondary schools under the plan shall serve both to advise students regarding courses of study best suited to their ability, aptitudes, and skills, and to encourage students with outstanding aptitudes and ability to complete their secondary school education, take the necessary courses for admission to institutions of higher education, and enter such institutions. These programs shall provide assistance to students by assessing abilities, aptitudes, interests, and educational needs; developing understandings of educational and career opportunities and requirements; and helping them make the best possible use of these opportunities through the formulation and achievement of realistic goals. Such programs may be carried out by the following activities when directed to the foregoing purposes:
>
> (a) Collecting, organizing, and interpreting such information as may be appropriate to the understanding of the student's abilities, aptitudes, interests, and other personal assets and liabilities related to educational and career planning and progress.
>
> (b) Making available to the student and his parents such edu-

cational and career information as may be essential for
them to understand the various educational and career
opportunities and requirements related to the choice of
an educational program and a career.

(c) Providing individual counseling (1) to help the student
and his parents develop a better understanding of the student's educational and occupational strengths and weaknesses; (2) to help the student and his parents relate his
abilities and aptitudes to educational and career opportunities and requirements; (3) to help the student, with the
assistance of his parents, make appropriate educational
plans, including the choice of courses in the secondary
school and the choice of an institution of higher education; (4) to stimulate desires in the student to utilize his
abilities in attaining appropriate educational and career
goals; and (5) to provide for the student such assistance
as may be needed for the development of his aptitudes and
the full utilization of his abilities.

(d) Providing services to encourage and assist students in making educational transitions, such as placement in educational
institutions beyond the high school.

(e) Providing such group activities as may be necessary to
orient students to the (1) high school program; (2) educational opportunities beyond the high school; and (3)
career opportunities and requirements.

(f) Providing to teachers and school administrators such information about individual students or groups of students
as may be necessary to enable them to plan curricular and
instructional programs appropriate to the educational needs
of the student body and to the manpower needs of the
State and the Nation.

(g) Collecting and analyzing such information as may be
needed to evaluate the guidance and counseling program
and to provide such guidance information as may be available and needed to evaluate the school's program in terms
of the educational needs of the students and of the State
and the Nation.

It is clear that the major goal of this act was to improve guidance programs in their totality, and in all states evidence of its success is to be seen in changed guidance procedures and provisions.

Influence in Decreasing the Shortage of Counselors

While precise figures are hard to obtain, it seems evident that the act has made a start at closing the counselor gap. Some schools which formerly could not afford to hire counselors are now able to do so. Material and equipment needed for a guidance program are available through provisions of the act. Hundreds of poorly trained counselors have received stipends while getting additional education under the provisions of Title V-B. Under these same provisions hundreds of teachers have received counselor education and assumed jobs as counselors. Many more trained counselors are still required, but the NDEA has reduced the need somewhat.

EVALUATION OF GUIDANCE

Evaluation is the process of finding the value of something. In evaluating a function like guidance, we attempt to find out to what degree the objective of the service has been attained. The objective of guidance is to assist individuals to develop the ability to be self-sufficient, to solve their own problems, and to make their adjustments. The following discussion will be divided into three parts: (1) Evidences that are now often used to indicate the attainment of this goal; (2) methods used in evaluation; and (3) outline for a plan of evaluation in a school.

Evidences of Success

Many evidences of success in improving guidance have been described in the preceding pages. An increasing number of people are actively engaged in guidance, as can be seen by the membership in guidance associations, the success of journals devoted to guidance, and the attendance at annual conventions of guidance associations. The efforts to improve the training and requirements of guidance workers indicate improved guidance programs. More proof is seen in the efforts to increase the effectiveness of guidance instruments and techniques of counseling and in the reduction in the ratio of students to counselors. These and other examples of improvement permit us to have some optimism about the future of this movement.

Methods of Evaluation

One approach to the evaluation of guidance is that used by the American Board on Professional Standards in Vocational Counseling. This organization has set up criteria for the approval of all agencies operating in the field of guidance. These criteria include professional and educational standards for the director of the agency and his staff, particularly as measured by membership in professional associations. Negative criteria include insistence that the agency have policies against serving its clients mainly or entirely by correspondence, assuming that adequate counseling can be completed in one interview, having a set number of interviews for every client, or basing counseling entirely on tests. Counselors in the agency must be prepared to use such tests as may be necessary, and the agency itself must have a program for professional development. The staff must be relatively stable, and systematic records of clients must be maintained. Any publicity must be dignified and in accordance with professional rather than commercial standards. If fees are charged, they must be in proportion to the service rendered; no fees may be given to others for referring clients or accepted for recommending that clients go to schools or other agencies. These standards, when applied by objective professional observers, guide the evaluation process and provide criteria by which success in establishing and maintaining a guidance agency may be judged.

The most frequent form of evaluation of guidance services consists in applying external criteria to the existing situation to determine whether the present program meets the standards that have been designated by experts as the mark of a satisfactory program. This application of external criteria may be made by the school staff, by outside experts, or by a combination of the two. This type of evaluation requires a survey of the present situation and provides direction for changes and improvements.

This method is not unlike that of the American Board on Professional Standards in Vocational Counseling except that the criteria deemed relevant are applied to a school rather than to an agency. Typical of these sets of external criteria are those developed by the

Illinois Secondary School Curriculum Program[3] and the U.S. Office of Education.[4] (The list of the latter is in the process of being updated and changed.) Such criteria typically ask for judgments about the personnel involved, the physical facilities used, and the functioning of the several guidance services.

Outline of Steps in Evaluation

The process of evaluation is the attempt to find the worth or value of any enterprise. The evaluation of the school guidance program is the attempt to find its value to the students. While evaluation is primarily concerned with the individual student, it also takes into account the school and society at large.

To evaluate a program of guidance we must take the following steps:

1. Clarify the objectives of the program. Are they valid, clearly stated, understood, and accepted by the guidance personnel, and are they attainable by the students concerned?

2. Consider the guidance personnel. Are they concerned with the guidance program; are they sufficient in number, adequate in training and personality to carry out the program? To what extent, if any, are classroom teachers included in the guidance program?

3. Consider the facilities. Are the facilities and time available for guidance work sufficient for an effective program?

4. Examine the available data about students to determine if they include tests and measurements, estimates and information by teachers, and information from outside the school supplied by family, employers, and others in the community.

5. Examine the records to determine if they are adequate, well kept, and available to all guidance personnel.

6. Consider the extent of cooperation with employers and college personnel. What opportunities are there for students to have conferences and personal contact with employers and college rep-

[3] Harry D. Lovelass, "How to Conduct the Study of Guidance Services of the School," Illinois Secondary School Curriculum Program, Circular Series A, no. 51, Bulletin 6, Superintendent of Public Instruction, Springfield, Ill., May, 1949, p. 263.

[4] Arthur L. Benson (ed.), *Criteria for Evaluating Guidance Programs in Secondary Schools, Form B*, Miscellaneous 3317, Federal Security Agency, Office of Education, Division of Vocational Education, Occupational Information and Guidance Service, Washington 25, 1949, 33 pp.

resentatives for help in the selection of occupations and the choice of college?

7. The last step is to make judgments about the attainment of the objectives of guidance. Among the most common elements given by authorities for determining the success of a guidance program are the reduction in disciplinary cases in school, decrease in failures by individual students, better social adjustment, success in college or university, success in business and industry, salary, and job satisfaction.

By following these seven steps, we may arrive at a reasonable estimate of the extent to which the guidance program is achieving its objectives.

A LOOK AHEAD: THE FUTURE OF GUIDANCE[5]

The past decade has witnessed some very important changes in the concept of guidance and in many of its techniques. The next decades will continue to change our world, our schools, and our guidance programs. What the morrow will bring we can but speculate, yet certain trends seem evident and certain changes predictable.

Social Changes Which Will Influence Guidance Programs

During the next decade our population will expand at an unprecedented rate. We will see a large increase in the age groups that are not economically self-supporting (the young and the old) and therefore a relative decrease of those of the middle-age group. There will be a continuation of the movement of Negroes into urban centers. Young workers will flood the labor market. Women workers will constitute more than one-third of the labor force in 1970. Most of these women will be married, and many will have children. School counselors therefore must take a girl's occupational planning as seriously as marriage. There will be a rapid increase in professional and technical workers and a decrease in farm workers. Automation will change the nature of and preparation for some occupations and reduce or even supplant many present jobs. The family will continue to become less authoritarian. Marriage and

[5] The material in this section is taken largely from C. Gilbert Wrenn's *The Counselor in a Changing World.*

birth rates as well as divorce rates seem to follow levels of prosperity, and the discipline of economics will be of more and more concern to the school counselor who is trying to understand his world and make occupational predictions. Finally, the relation of our nation and our culture to other nations is of supreme importance to youth today, and the school counselor cannot be ignorant of international trends and developments.

Changing Perceptions Which Will Influence Guidance Practices

To be effective, the counselor must keep in touch with the frontiers of the science of human behavior. Among these are such divergent approaches as those expressed in psychoanalytic concepts and those of behaviorism. The neo-Freudian approach with its emphasis on the social as well as the biological elements may be particularly important to the future of guidance. The phenomenological explanation of behavior has already profoundly changed counseling techniques and may well influence guidance practices in still other ways.

Recent studies show that our older ideas of intelligence and aptitudes were far too simple. Our understanding of "talent" now goes far beyond performance in academic tasks, and we realize that the creative student is not necessarily the same as the talented student. Predictive appraisal by tests alone has been found to be far from sufficient, and new evaluative techniques must emerge.

Changes in Schools Which Will Influence Guidance

One of the important problems of the counselor is the relative attention he should give to developmental needs and how much to the crisis needs. In the future it is likely that he will spend more time on the psychological development of students and less on emotional first aid. The creative ability of students must receive as much attention as their handicaps. The counselor must be concerned both with intellectual development and vocational preparation and with a balance between socialization and individuality. Schools will be more concerned with helping students to solve problems with maximum competence and personal security, to grow in skill in evaluating evidence, and to develop their capacity for being mentally and culturally creative.

Proposed Changes in Guidance Practices

At the present time elementary-school counselors are more likely to be assigned full-time guidance duties than are secondary-school counselors. These full-time counselors spend from one-fourth to one-third of their time in counseling individual students. Elementary-school counselors spend more time consulting with parents or teachers, and secondary-school counselors spend more in group work with students. An overwhelming number of high-school counselors emphasize individual counseling with students, while elementary-school counselors see the clinical emphasis with children as being less important than working with teachers and parents and coordinating the counseling facilities in school and community.

In the future the confusing term "guidance services" should be abandoned and "pupil personnel services" used to designate the activities performed by a team of workers—school counselor, school psychologist, school social worker, school health officer, and school attendance worker. The counselor member of this team will (1) counsel a wide range of students using both individual and group approaches, (2) consult with parents and teachers as they have need for better understanding of individual pupils, (3) assume responsibility for continuing the study of the changing characteristics of the student population and interpreting this information to administrative and teaching staff for use in curriculum planning and in the development of administrative structure and regulations, and (4) serve as liaison among the various student personnel specialists and as coordinator of counseling resources within the school and community.

As is true of the members of many professions, the counselor will be both a generalist and a specialist—a generalist in the sense of knowing school resources thoroughly and being available to the total range of students and staff and a specialist in his specific knowledge of student behavior and in his understanding of the dynamics of human behavior generally.

At the elementary-school level there must also be a strong emphasis upon the early identification of both pupil talents and origins of nonsocial behavior. Elementary-school counselors must be particularly competent in diagnosis and in an understanding of play therapy, reading problems, and work with parents. Elementary-school and junior-high-school counselors are also responsible for the vocational counseling of students who may leave school at the end of the eighth or ninth grade.

Proposed Changes in the Education of Counselors

Soon we must decide such major issues in the education of counselors as the amount and the kind of psychological preparation needed, the amount of attention given to an understanding of the changing nature of cultures, the means by which an understanding of school purposes and procedures is reached, and the development of research competencies together with counseling sensitivities.

The education of counselors must begin in the undergraduate program for no graduate program alone can provide the necessary cultural underpinning for the development of an educated as opposed to a "trained" counselor. It is proposed that the undergraduate program of some students be freed from the necessity of meeting the requirements of a teaching certificate as a prerequisite to the securing of teaching experience before becoming a counselor. The pattern might be (1) teaching experience of from one to four years, followed by graduate study and supervised counseling experience; (2) two years of graduate study directly following undergraduate work, one year of graduate work to be in full-time supervised internship, followed by one or two years in a paid position as a "junior counselor"; or (3) undergraduate education followed by several years' experience in any one of many life experiences which contribute to one's knowledge of human behavior and societal functioning, to be followed in turn by graduate study and supervised counseling experience in a school setting.

The following emphases in counselor education have been proposed:

1. A minimal two-year graduate program for school counselors which would include one major core in psychology, emphasizing developmental and child psychology, personality growth and dynamics, and group psychology, and a second major core in the study of societal forces and culture changes involving the graduate areas of sociology, anthropology, economics, and international relations. This would also involve supervised experience in both

individual counseling and planned group situations to the extent
of not less than one-fourth of the total graduate program and provision for the essential applied or technique courses in counseling,
measurement, educational and occupational information, etc., to the
extent of not more than one-fourth of the total graduate program.
There should also be training in elementary research methods,
including an introductory understanding of electronic computer
programming and the outcomes to be expected from computer
use; an understanding of the basic educational philosophies and
school curriculum patterns; and an introduction to the problems of
ethical relationships and legal responsibilities in counseling.

2. The graduate faculty in this field should give attention to
the need for the graduate student in counselor education to understand himself through some form of personal counseling.

3. There need to be professional associations in pupil personnel
work to develop appropriate criteria of proficiency in counseling
and to work with graduate schools on selection procedures.

4. The state departments of education, in close collaboration
with graduate schools, should modify state counselor certification
requisites in order to require a block of graduate work in the social
sciences and in the humanities and supervised experience as part of
the graduate school program and to liberalize the experience requirements of state certification to permit the acceptance of various
kinds of experience other than that of teaching, provided there
is an adequate block of time as a supervised intern in a school situation.

Changes such as these may profoundly alter the training and
duties of the school counselor over the next few years.[6]

A Message from the Author of "The Counselor in a Changing World" to School Counselors Now on the Job

Consider professional updating as a continuous process lest
you become fixated at one level of understanding and practice
while the world of psychological and sociological thought and
practice moves on and leaves you behind. Include in your continuing professional education graduate courses and public lectures in

[6] C. Gilbert Wrenn, *The Counselor in a Changing World*, The Commission on Guidance in American Schools, American Personnel and Guidance Association, 1961, p. 185.

the social and behavioral sciences. Travel widely as a planned part of your attempt to understand other cultures and peoples. Study your own interviewing *habits and attitudes,* and secure professional assistance in this process whenever possible. Attempt to understand yourselves better through counseling or other professional help. Give thoughtful attention to your purposes and goals as counselors. One crucial decision regarding counseling goals must be made by every school counselor: Are you a specialist for a few who are in trouble, or are you a specialist for many with normal growth problems? Engage in self-study and in discussion with others to clarify your own deeply held convictions and ethical concepts so that greater personal insights and better counseling relationships will result. Develop a program for living in a personally satisfying manner. You need concerts, reading, travel, stimulating companionship, and a reservoir of deep emotional and spiritual experiences upon which to draw if you are to become, or to remain, a person who is interesting to students and to colleagues.

SUMMARY

This chapter has been chiefly concerned with the attempts to increase the effectiveness of guidance practices. The present status of guidance indicates a great need for more and better-trained counselors. Certification, which has been extended to practically all states, needs revision and enforcement. Clarification of the duties and responsibilities of school counselors must be made so that revision of training programs for them can proceed intelligently. The growth of professional associations and the expansion of professional journals combine to suggest that counseling is changing from a pedagogical side line to a defensible and respectable profession.

The National Defense Education Act has probably done more to improve school guidance programs than has any other one governmental action. Programs have been strengthened and expanded, tests have been made available, and counselors have been trained. A turning point in the history of guidance is the NDEA—for it recognizes that guidance is the gyroscope controlling education and that the nation's defense requires good schools.

Finally, as we evaluate guidance, we must look not only at

what has been but at what will be. Here we see a vision of social changes which will put new students in new schools with goals, techniques, and procedures suited for a country and a time we can but dimly foresee.

EXERCISES

1. Read one issue of any of the journals listed in this chapter and be prepared to discuss the usefulness of the articles for your present job.

2. Talk to a student, a teacher, and an administrator at the same school and learn their ideas of the strong and weak points of the guidance program.

3. Name five of the most important developments in the field of guidance which have taken place during the past thirty years. Describe each and give reasons for the selections. Name five more that are likely to be made in the near future. Give your reasons for the selection.

REFERENCES

Brewer, John M.: *History of Vocational Guidance*, The Macmillan Company, New York, 1942.

Farwell, Gail F., and Herman J. Peters: *Guidance Readings for Counselors*, Rand McNally & Company, Chicago, 1960.

Miller, Carroll: *Foundations of Guidance*, Harper & Brothers, New York, 1961.

Wrenn, C. Gilbert: *The Counselor in a Changing World*, The Commission on Guidance in American Schools, American Personnel and Guidance Association, Washington, 1961.

Yearbook Committee, Melvine Drahein Hardee (ed.): "Personnel Services in Education," Fifty-eighth Yearbook, National Society for the Study of Education, University of Chicago Press, Chicago, 1959.

INDEX